"For over a decade, Roxana has kept Los Angeles fed long before the sun even thinks about rising, letting whole grains anchor her craft and our palates. This book is a tribute to the joyful, quiet legacy she's built on the streets of Hollywood, inviting LA, and now the rest of the world, to become Morning Bakers."
—Paola Velez, author of *Bodega Bakes*

"With a clear, concise, and confident point of view, Roxana Jullapat has once again invited us inside her unique mind. Her work shows deep respect and reverence for local whole grains, seasonal fruits, and vegetables. Taking inspiration directly from her ingredients, she teaches us how to expand our repertoire to create pastries with both depth and character. 100% whole grain croissants that will stand proud on any Parisian bakery counter, yes please!"
—Kim Boyce, author of *Good to the Grain*

MORNING BAKER

MORNING BAKER

Recipes and Rituals for Breakfast and Beyond

Roxana Jullapat

with ARI SMOLIN

PHOTOGRAPHY BY KRISTIN TEIG

W. W. Norton & Company

Independent Publishers Since 1923

To all the Morning Bakers,
who rise before the world stirs,
guided by rhythm, skill, and care.
May your work never go unnoticed.
And may the first warm bite always go to you.

CONTENTS

Introduction — 9
Baking with Whole-Grain Flour — 14
About Weights and Measures — 16

CHAPTER 1
Muffins — 23

CHAPTER 2
Biscuits and Scones — 49

CHAPTER 3
Pancakes and Friends — 79

CHAPTER 4
Doughnuts and Fritters — 117

CHAPTER 5
Whole-Grain Croissants — 139

CHAPTER 6
Whole-Grain Breads — 187

CHAPTER 7
Anytime Whole-Grain Bakes — 277

My Favorite Flours — 313
Sources — 322
Acknowledgments — 325
Index — 327

INTRODUCTION

A year after opening our bakery, Friends & Family, I hesitated to write "Baker" beside "Occupation" on my customs form during an international flight. It felt like a bragging right I hadn't yet earned. Fast-forward one decade and I call myself nothing but a Baker. A Morning Baker to be exact, one of many who wake up hours before sunrise to bake bread and pastries. On my drive in to work, I pass two local hospitals and one fire station. I like to greet them as I roll by, proud to share the graveyard shift with folks whose jobs are far more important than mine. Heading to work during these quiet, dark hours, it's impossible not to feel part of something larger than myself.

According to the US Bureau of Labor Statistics, us late-night and early-morning laborers make up 3 percent of the workforce. We provide essential and often critical services: healthcare, transportation, manufacturing, emergency response, and, here in Los Angeles, TV and film production. Graveyard shifts allow businesses to maximize resources and increase productivity, but also meet industry-specific demands. And in the bakery business, the demand for fresh-baked goods with your morning coffee requires us to be up and running before 97 percent of the general public.

When we opened in 2017, I knew I would have to train myself to go to bed early in order to wake up in the middle of the night for a full day of work. It took about six months to fully feel like myself in the new role. Nowadays, I have it down to a science. The recipe for success starts the night before. For me, that looks like eating dinner a couple of hours before going to bed, avoiding heavy and spicy meals, and never imbibing on school nights. At 6 p.m., I put on pj's, even if it's still light out, and grab a book or catch up on my favorite show before falling asleep. Upon rising, I do a ten-minute meditation, feed my cat, get ready, and I'm out the door.

I happen to live very close to the bakery; it takes me less than ten minutes to get there.

Many in my crew also live in the neighborhood. A short journey is key when you're commuting in the middle of the night. I arrive first, then the bakers begin rolling in. Our front door stays locked for safety, so we have a secret knock of sorts. It never gets old—hearing the knock and opening the door to one smiling baker after another, joining me fresh and ready to get down to business at 3 a.m. (and even earlier on the weekends!).

The first thing we do is start the coffee. Once we're fully caffeinated, the morning unfolds smoothly with well-established rituals. Every now and again, I might exchange a text message with a fellow baker down the street, in another city, or even in another country. Perhaps about a recipe, a hard-to-find ingredient, or a piece of equipment in disrepair. Every time, I'm filled with a warm sense of kinship. We, the weirdos who wake up super early to do this fulfilling work, get to chat about faulty ovens or ask to borrow butter while the rest of the world is still sleeping.

From the time I attended culinary school at the turn of the century (yes, I graduated in December 1999) to today, I've witnessed a reassuring rise in our regard for local bakeries and the folks that make them possible. Where you once saw an impersonal, factory-style workforce that used bakery jobs as a stepping stone, you now see ambitious and skilled artisans with a deep appreciation for their craft, eager to push the envelope to reach new heights of baking excellence.

The morning baker's process is unique in the culinary industry. It's fair to say that the work is introspective by nature, and the vibe of a bakeshop is, by definition, welcoming. Most of the recipes are completed over the course of a few days. This requires planning and foresight, adding a level of predictability and normalcy. The ability to forecast brings Zen energy to the workday, keeping chaos at bay. This isn't to say that there aren't stressful moments—after all, maintenance and repairs remain 2 percent of our monthly budget. But it's nothing compared to the hectic nights I experienced as a pastry chef.

Dessert service in a restaurant is a different beast. Your work rhythm is proportional to the number of guests booked at any given time. It's imperative to work as fast as you can while staying focused on the details. These days, kitchen decorum is more polished than ever, but I'm old enough to remember a time when your shortcomings were pointed out in demeaning and humiliating ways when you were at your busiest. In spite of the high-pressure environment, this was a job I loved and was very good at, but deep down, I knew I would have to find a change of scenery. The bakery life isn't without challenges, but even when things unfurl in hapless ways, I am grounded in baking's steady rituals.

The tasks assigned to an individual baker in one day can seem monumental. But in tackling them, you begin to feel like a superhero. For example, take making croissant dough. One baker will scale and mix sixteen portions of dough, each weighing 3 kilos. The dough will be laminated into croissants the next day, and each will yield about thirty croissants. This is the inception of 500 beloved bakery items. The sense of

accomplishment from being part of this chain of events is life affirming.

Due to the scale of the recipes, not many things can be made from start to finish by a single baker; therefore, you rely on your teammates to get things done. Also, the breadth of products is often so wide that it's impossible for one person to excel at everything. Knowing that others will be better than you at some tasks while you will be stronger at others makes working in a bakery a humbling and convivial

experience. You learn to appreciate each fellow baker for their individual strengths, knowing that your own work is counted upon. Unlike restaurants, bakeries don't revolve around a central chef in whites, so the responsibilities and the accolades fall on the entire team.

It's a common misconception that only certain personality types thrive in a bakery. After all these years running Friends & Family, I can debunk this myth. Some come here in pursuit of what they want to do with their lives; others stay because they finally found it. Some will hold yearslong tenures, while others stay a few months. From the most high-strung perfectionist to the most easygoing, laid-back individual, if you can adjust to our unconventional schedule, you can succeed as a baker. In my experience, the best crews are a combination of people from all walks of life. Among our staff we've had multilingual college graduates, farmers, aspiring actors, parents of young children, graphic artists, film workers in between jobs, and even a former Department of Defense staffer with security clearance status, all working alongside self-taught and formally trained bakers.

Is a morning baker fundamentally different from other bakers? Yes and no. At the end of the day, we're all doing different versions of the same job. But where we distinguish ourselves is in the fact that the busiest, most intense part of our day takes place in the middle of the night. You have to come in ready to hit the ground running, which requires intense planning and organization ahead of time so that in the heat of the bake, it's all carpe diem.

How could you not be proud? By noon, you've scratched a dozen projects off a list—projects that require your best effort and produce beautiful, delicious things because the ingredients you put in them were carefully sought and thoughtfully handled.

Some of my closest friends are also professional bakers, and we constantly exchange tricks of the trade and general kitchen wisdom. The conversation is enriched by engaging with others who bake for fun, too. The home baking community is a meaningful part of our collective. In fact, I have recruited many eager home bakers over the years and trained them to work in professional kitchens. The transition is almost always smooth. Just like the pros, home bakers can be organized and creative, and they know how to follow a recipe. They're willing to try new things, seek good ingredients, and adjust their lifestyles to make more room for baking.

My goal in this cookbook is to provide you with the same tool kit I offer to those who come apprentice at Friends & Family. The scope of the work may be different—you'll be making batches of tens, not hundreds, and managing all the components yourself rather than sharing tasks with coworkers—but the same rules and best practices apply. Throughout these pages, I've distilled my morning rituals and routines to arm you with the recipes, techniques, and insights I've learned while baking long before the sun is up, so you can be a morning baker in your own kitchen, at whatever hour you please.

BAKING WITH WHOLE-GRAIN FLOUR

At grain-centric bakeries like Friends & Family, bakers gain a unique understanding of the role flour plays in our day to day. Transforming flour that has been milled from a wide range of sustainable grains into breads and pastries frames our perception of grain as a finite agricultural product, one that represents the time, manner, and region in which it was cultivated. Just like farming, our work is tied to the rhythms of the morning, and after seeing and comparing flours from different producers, we've come to value their work as much as the contribution of every actor in the grain supply chain.

As in my previous cookbook, *Mother Grains: Recipes for the Grain Revolution*, baking with whole grains continues to be the guiding principle of my recipes. This new compendium carries on, expanding and enriching our collective understanding of these ingredients in creative and delicious ways.

Sometime after finishing *Mother Grains* and before deciding to write this second book, I started to look at my whole-grain habit as a spiritual practice and an ethical choice. I use these words—spiritual and ethical—with pause, never seeking to exclude or preach to anyone making different choices to feed themselves or their communities. But as a baker with the knowledge to make an informed selection, as well as access to these ingredients, it would be neglectful not to lean on whole grains without reservation.

To this day, baking with whole grains is the prevailing mission at Friends & Family. Year after year, we've increased the quantity of whole-grain flours in our recipes, adjusting to the technical, financial, and marketing challenges that evolution presents. You'll find the same principles at play here. Many of the following recipes are made exclusively with whole-grain flour, while others include refined all-purpose flour or bread flour to ensure the recipe's success. Grain accessibility ranges from state to state, and store to store. With that in mind, I've tailored each recipe to use common domestic grains with substitution potential. In the My Favorite Flours section (page 313), you will find a nationwide directory to help you find the whole-grain flours used throughout the book. Many of them can also be found in your local grocery store. Always consider that the whole-grain flour landscape is ever changing, and, in time, you might discover new sources on your own.

ABOUT REFINED ALL-PURPOSE AND BREAD FLOURS

The main difference between refined flours, such as store-bought all-purpose or bread flour, and whole-wheat flours is the presence of bran. This is why you can't always swap one for the other and expect the same results. Bran in whole-grain flour acts like a sponge, making it absorb liquids at a higher rate than refined flours. With this in mind, use *refined* all-purpose or bread flour whenever you see "all-purpose flour" or "bread flour" in the ingredient list. This is not to be confused with "whole-grain all-purpose flour," which refers to flour made from wheat varieties that are generally mild-tasting and considered "soft" or low in gluten, such as Sonora, Frederick, or Sirvinta (see My Favorite Flours, page 313).

You can also use flours produced by more boutique, independent mills labeled "all-purpose whole-grain flour." This flour isn't necessarily variety-specific because the miller doesn't always use the same wheat to produce it, or because it might be a blend of a few different varieties. In this instance, we trust the miller's assessment that this flour is indeed appropriate for all-purpose cooking and baking.

To add to the confusion, your artisan miller might label hard wheat flour "bread flour" to indicate that it's high in gluten and appropriate to make bread with. Be aware that this is whole-grain bread flour, a great flour to be sure, but not the refined bread flour the recipe might be calling for.

When in doubt, read through the recipe headnotes, which will go over the choice of flour(s).

ABOUT WEIGHTS AND MEASURES

The recipes in this book include weight measurements in grams and volume measurements in milliliters, cups, and tablespoons whenever the amount exceeds ¼ cup. While you may use whichever you feel more comfortable with, I strongly encourage using weight measurements for their high level of accuracy. If you don't already own one, purchase a reliable digital scale for your home kitchen. My preferred brands are Taylor, Escali, and OXO. They are inexpensive and durable. It is equally important to have a trusty set of measuring spoons for ingredients that have a big impact on a recipe in small amounts, such as instant yeast, baking powder, baking soda, spices, and, naturally, salt. Once you've become proficient at weighing on a scale, you'll see yourself using your measuring cups less and less, but it's certainly good to have a set.

Pay special attention to salt, a key ingredient that can alter a recipe dramatically and is almost always listed in teaspoon/tablespoon amounts. When adding kosher salt, keep in mind that grain size varies across brands. I always recommend Diamond Crystal, which tends to have a larger granule size and can weigh less per volume than other brands, such as Morton's. Opt for fine sea salt in bread making—it dissolves quickly and can be easily incorporated into the dough.

To measure liquid ingredients, I recommend a liquid measuring cup—those are the ones that look like a pitcher. If you're looking to upgrade, go for a beaker, a 16-ounce capacity cup designed specifically to measure liquids with multiple equivalences that are very easy to read.

Most of the recipes we've developed at Friends & Family call for metric weights, but as American bakers, we are fluent in both systems. In *Morning Baker*, I've chosen to use the metric system (grams and milliliters) instead of the imperial system (ounces and fluid ounces) to make the recipes more versatile and scalable in case you want to halve or double a recipe. The more standardized metric system also makes the recipes more universal, since the majority of cooks and bakers around the world already use it.

Notice that in many instances the weight amounts have been rounded up or down (by less than 10 grams) to call for amounts that most home digital scales can register. Rest assured that every recipe has been tested a minimum of three times to verify that the indicated measurements are accurate.

YOUR CUP IS NOT MY CUP

Here's a fun experiment: Ask two bakers to fill a 1-cup measuring cup with flour. Weigh on a scale and compare the two. Don't be shocked if the amounts differ, sometimes by 20 grams or more. How you fill your cup will greatly determine how packed your cup will be. When it comes to filling technique, there are two main camps: the dipping method and the spooning method. I belong to the dipping camp, which involves dipping the cup into the flour, pulling it out when it's full, tapping on the side with an offset spatula (or the back of a knife), and leveling the top by sweeping with the edge of the same offset spatula. Spooners prefer spooning the flour into the cup and then leveling the top. The latter method tends to make lighter cups.

Using the dipping method, my average cup of all-purpose flour weighs 140 grams. With spooning, my average goes down to 125 grams. This diversity in cup measures affects all ingredients, not only flour, and it can explain why a recipe that works for you doesn't necessarily work for another baker. This is the reason I strongly recommend using a scale and weight measurements over volume. The weights in this book are an average of my weighing practices. And yes, whenever you see 1 cup of all-purpose flour in this cookbook, rest assured that I mean 140 grams.

Given the artisanal nature of whole-grain flour, cups tend to vary even more. But after many years of working with them, I find that 1 cup of finely ground whole wheat flour, regardless of the variety, weighs 130 grams on average.

ABOUT RECIPE TESTING

At the time of this writing, all flours used for recipe testing were available to consumers in the continental US by at least one purveyor. Because wheat and rye tend to vary the most across brands, recipes using them were tested with at least two varieties. Throughout the book, I will indicate if a certain variety is crucial to the recipe's success. Most recipes can be made with the variety of your choice. It's not necessary to be variety-specific with other ingredients, like cornmeal, buckwheat flour, and rolled oats—they're more forgiving and less variable between brands. Keep in mind that in the evolving artisan grain industry, old varieties fall out of favor as newer ones are introduced. Get to know your favorite flours, but make room for discovering new ones.

SETTING UP THE PASTRY CASE

It's 6:30 a.m. The last pastries came out of the oven a few minutes ago. Morning bakers are putting on their finishing touches . . . brushing a fruity danish with glaze, dusting laminated pastries with confectioners' sugar, and grating Parmesan over savory chaussons. Soon, all pastries will be consolidated on one rolling cart, ready for the case. The early sunlight is brightening the dining room. It's time to get in the zone. Let's open this nifty app and play some music. Playlist choice is of utmost importance here: nothing too sleepy, nothing too raucous, and, under no circumstances, any top 40.

I polish the quartz pastry case with a soft rag, wipe off a smudge on the glass, and start arranging a stack of wooden boards and ceramic platters at the very front. Larger bowls, stands, and pedestals follow. I cut parchment paper into perfect squares and use them to line the dishes. I prefer the tan-colored kraft type over paper doilies that make everything look cheap. Cake stands, risers, and even upside-down dishes help create height, but they can also wreak havoc if you don't place them strategically. Multiple levels make the most beautiful pastry cases, but remember, it's not Legoland. Use height wisely, making sure the taller serving dishes are placed toward the back where they don't block anything shorter. The material of our serving pieces is also integral to our aesthetic. Wood, earthenware, and wicker remind me of the ingredients we put in our recipes. In a way, they are an extension of the pastries they display.

Next, we let the pastries do the talking, using their colors and diversity to draw you in. I try to follow a pattern, placing specific pastries in the same general area every day to make it easier for the counter staff to maneuver. Quiches, breakfast galettes, ham and cheese croissants, biscuits, and other savory pastries are the first thing customers will see. As you move along, the assortment gets sweeter, ending with a high tower of Sonora wheat croissants. New items that I want people to try should go in the front, while bestsellers that don't need much of a push can go in the back. I show them off by piling high or fanning away, keeping in mind that pastries can be fragile and won't always do what I want them to. I might have to try a few options to determine which serving dish works best for each one. A wooden board might be best for slightly juxtaposed flaky heart-shaped tarts, but chunky cookies might want to lie one on top of the other on a small plate. One of the first questions a new baker asks when they first set up the case is how many pieces go on each plate. The heck do I know?! As many as possible. There's power in numbers, and a basket overflowing with morning buns will tell the story of who we are and what we do more eloquently that any minimally plated pastry ever could.

The importance of proper labeling cannot be understated. I get a kick out of coming up with catchy names—dilly, poppy, fairy, puff—that sound as delicious as the pastries look and loosely suggest what's in them. The names are an endless source of entertainment for both customers and staff. And believe me when I tell you that hearing a grown man order a chocodoodle and a bitchy bun to go with his latte will make your day.

There are also other practical considerations, such as monitoring that refrigerated items aren't displayed for too long at room temperature, choosing garnishes that hold well without wilting or becoming dull after a few hours, and making sure whole cakes and tarts are sliced and ready to be served. Throughout the morning, a baker will come back to refill, fluff, and clean, but at this point, we like to leave the case locked and loaded for the morning rush.

This art installation takes me about an hour to construct. I give myself plenty of

time and space. It's not something I can do in a jiffy. Once finished, I stand right in front and take it all in. Last chance to move things around if they seem out of place. These golden, caramelized, glossy, sugary, and scrumptious creations are

looking back at me reassuringly. They are a daily reminder that there's nothing else I would rather do. By this time, the baristas are here. They start brewing a fresh pot. My job here is done. I'm gonna grab a cup.

The full pastry case at Friends & Family on a winter morning.

CHAPTER 1

MUFFINS

FROM TOP TO BOTTOM, LEFT TO RIGHT:
Berry Oat Muffins (page 30), Banana-Date Muffins (page 35), Chocolate Morning Muffins (page 43), Glazed Lemon Muffins (page 41), Buckwheat Joy Muffins (page 46), Sweet Potato Muffins (page 37), New-School Whole-Grain Muffins (page 26), Apricot Butterscotch Muffins (page 32), Einkorn Carrot Muffins (page 28).

Recipes

- New-School Whole-Grain Muffins 26
- Einkorn Carrot Muffins with Cream Cheese Glaze 28
- Berry Oat Muffins 30
- Apricot Butterscotch Muffins 32
- Banana-Date Muffins 35
- Sweet Potato Muffins with Pecan Streusel 37
- Glazed Lemon, Poppy Seed, and Olive Oil Muffins 41
- Chocolate Morning Muffins 43
- Buckwheat Joy Muffins 46

Once, when I was young, my dad asked me what kind of cake I wanted for an upcoming birthday. "Muffins!" I replied gleefully. Taken aback, he refuted: "But Roxana Marie, muffins are not cake." I've been a muffin lover and connoisseur for as long as I can remember. The quintessential American morning pastry, as recognizable as it is overlooked, can be a source of daily delight when prepared thoughtfully. Muffins belong to the quick bread family, alongside other mainstays like biscuits, scones, soda bread, banana bread, and cornbread. What these baked goods have in common is that they're leavened with baking powder or baking soda instead of yeast, making them faster to prepare. In my estimation, muffin recipes should be achievable in a reasonable amount of time, ideally one hour or less. They should be easy to execute with a couple of ingredients on hand, and even fewer pieces of equipment. I also think they should be somewhat nutritious. Sure, they're sweet treats, but wholesome ingredients like whole grains, fruits, seeds, nuts, and healthy fats add nutritional value and variety in flavor and texture. Despite their resemblance to a cupcake, my dad was right: Muffins are not cake.

The approach I use most to mix muffins is called, unsurprisingly, the muffin method (also known as the quick bread method or two-bowl method). The creaming method used for cake making, in which butter and sugar are beaten together, is also popular, but I'm always happier with the muffin method's results. It involves combining dry ingredients in one bowl, and eggs, liquid, and fat in another. The wet ingredients are whisked by hand, then added to the dries. Simply put, it's a reliable method because it's hard to overwork the batter. To leaven the muffins, I count on the aforementioned artificial leaveners, as opposed to building volume by aerating the butter or eggs. Baking powder makes the muffins peak, while baking soda makes the muffins expand. My choice of liquid is almost always buttermilk. Its tart flavor balances the sweeter elements in the bowl, and its lactic acid reacts with the leaveners, creating the carbon dioxide that prompts the batter to expand and rise. As far as fat, my preference is vegetable oil over butter. Oil is better at coating the proteins in the flour and preventing gluten formation (too much gluten formation equals dry, tough muffins). Plus, oil is a nonsaturated fat, and I'm trying to bake healthier muffins.

Next, a word about muffin tins. The most universal tins have 12 cavities, each holding about ⅓ cup of batter, and are usually made out of aluminum, aluminized steel, high-carbon steel, cast iron, or silicone. My preferred type are coated aluminized steel, which are a tad pricier and require a little more care, but are widely available. Coated tins don't need to be lined with paper cups. You may choose to do so for aesthetic reasons, but it won't be necessary to prevent the muffins from getting stuck. A popular muffin mold used in professional bakeries is the jumbo muffin tin. It typically has 6 cavities that hold ½ cup batter. If you're baking muffins of this size, keep in mind that baking times will be different. Another piece of equipment I find useful is a cookie or batter scoop, which can be found in many cooking supply stores; they make filling the cavities a breeze. Finally, here's some advice from the many muffin makers who bake them every day at Friends & Family: It's easier to unmold the muffins while they're slightly warm, 15 to 20 minutes after coming out of the oven, or as soon as they're cool enough to handle.

Now, let's talk about oven temperature. The muffin textures in this chapter range from soft to pleasantly dense. Lighter batters make tender muffins, while grain-rich batters make muffins with more heft. Generally, muffins should be baked at a higher temperature because they're small and in the oven for a short period of time. A brief stint at 375°F (190°C) on the middle rack is enough to achieve a tall, perfectly browned muffin that remains moist inside. This is true for the Einkorn Carrot Muffins (page 28), Apricot Butterscotch Muffins (page 32), Banana-Date Muffins (page 35), Sweet Potato Muffins (page 37), Glazed Lemon Muffins (page 41), and Buckwheat Joy Muffins (page 46). For my more action-packed muffins, like the New-School Whole-Grain Muffins (page 26), Berry Oat Muffins (page 30), and Chocolate Morning Muffins (page 43), I prefer 350°F (175°C) to ensure that the grainy morsels bake properly while preserving the muffin's moisture.

Last but not least: finishing touches. Many of the muffins in this chapter are sprinkled with sugar, oats, or streusel; brushed, dipped, or bathed in luscious glaze; or studded with fruits, chocolate, and seeds. And I absolutely love what these creative flourishes do to my muffins. However, know that this is a matter of preference. You can ignore the adornments altogether or even mix and match them. It's far more important that you bake a muffin you love.

Muffins are legendary for freezing well. Wrap them tightly in plastic wrap and freeze for up to 2 months—though chances are you'll eat them sooner. I recommend leaving the muffins unadorned if you're going to freeze them, then adding your finishing touches once they thaw out. You don't have to refresh the muffins in the oven, but if you'd like to warm and soften them a bit, 5 minutes in a 350°F (175°C) oven will suffice.

NEW-SCHOOL WHOLE-GRAIN MUFFINS

MAKES 10 MUFFINS

EQUIPMENT: muffin tin

1 cup (100 g) old-fashioned rolled oats

¼ cup (40 g) coarse yellow cornmeal

1½ cups (360 ml) buttermilk

½ cup (65 g) whole-grain all-purpose or hard red wheat flour, such as Sonora or Red Fife

⅓ cup (35 g) flax meal

2 teaspoons baking powder

½ teaspoon baking soda

¾ teaspoon kosher salt

2 tablespoons unsweetened shredded coconut

2 teaspoons chia seeds

½ cup (80 g) dried fruit, such as dried currants, golden raisins, or chopped dried apricots

⅓ cup (65 g) turbinado sugar, such as Sugar in the Raw, plus extra for sprinkling

1 large egg

Finely grated zest of 1 orange

¼ cup (50 g) coconut oil, melted and cooled slightly

These muffins are my take on the bran muffins of the '80s. In this recipe, the combination of rolled oats, cornmeal, seeds, and robust hard wheat means the muffins will stay fresh for days. Unlike the original, these are made with bran-rich whole-grain flour, instead of the kind of extracted bran you find at the grocery store. Any whole-grain wheat flour will perform well here, but it's an ideal opportunity for heavy hitters—the redder and more intense, the better (see My Favorite Flours, page 313). I do recommend soaking the oats and cornmeal in buttermilk to hydrate them, but you can slash this step in a pinch. The grains will be a bit toothy but not unpleasantly so. I love adding flax meal and chia seeds for their binding abilities and orange zest, shredded coconut, and dried fruit for layered texture and flavor. Which dried fruit is up to you; classic golden raisins or dried black currants are great. I also love chopped apricots, which pair well with coconut. To finish, a simple sprinkle of turbinado sugar adds sparkle and crunch. They're tastier and less dense than the bran muffins of my youth and, thanks to minimal sugar and a good helping of coconut oil, probably much healthier.

Because they keep and travel well, the muffins are a great choice for bringing on outdoor activities. They can be made the night before, and the recipe doubles easily if you'd like to stash some in the freezer for later.

1. Place the oats and cornmeal in a nonreactive container, pour in 1 cup (240 ml) of the buttermilk, cover with a lid, and refrigerate for 2 hours or overnight.

2. Place an oven rack in the middle position and preheat the oven to 350°F (175°C).

3. Combine the flour, flax meal, baking powder, baking soda, salt, coconut, chia seeds, and dried fruit in a mixing bowl. Using your hands, make a well in the center of the dry ingredients. In a separate bowl, whisk together the soaked oats and cornmeal, turbinado sugar, egg, orange zest, and remaining ½ cup (120 ml) buttermilk. Pour the liquid mixture into the well in the dry ingredients and whisk slowly from the center out to draw the dry ingredients into the liquids. Then whisk vigorously to ensure the batter is well combined. Add the coconut oil and whisk to combine.

4. Coat a muffin tin lightly with nonstick spray.

5. Evenly distribute the muffin batter, filling each cup almost to the top. Top each muffin with a sprinkle of turbinado sugar. Bake for 15 minutes. Then rotate the tin and bake for 15 minutes more, or until the muffins are golden around the edges and a skewer inserted in the center of a muffin comes out clean.

6. Let the muffins sit until cool enough to handle. Carefully release the muffins from the tin, running an offset spatula or a paring knife along the edges if necessary. Serve at room temperature. The muffins will keep in an airtight container at room temperature for up to 2 days.

EINKORN CARROT MUFFINS WITH CREAM CHEESE GLAZE

MAKES 9 MUFFINS

EQUIPMENT: muffin tin

FOR THE MUFFIN BATTER
1¼ cups (155 g) whole-grain einkorn flour
1 teaspoon baking powder
½ teaspoon baking soda
¼ teaspoon kosher salt
½ teaspoon ground cinnamon
½ teaspoon ground ginger
½ cup packed (110 g) dark brown sugar
¼ cup plus 2 tablespoons (90 ml) vegetable oil
2 tablespoons orange juice
½ cup (120 ml) buttermilk
2 large eggs
1 cup (112 g/4 ounces) shredded carrot (1 medium carrot)

FOR THE CREAM CHEESE GLAZE
½ cup (112 g/4 ounces) cream cheese, at room temperature
1 cup (115 g) confectioners' sugar, sifted
1 teaspoon lemon juice
1 tablespoon whole milk
2 tablespoons finely chopped pistachios

When baking with produce, I want the fruit or veggie in question to be the star of the show—an ethos wholly on display with these carrot cake–inspired muffins. Alongside supporting players like toasty einkorn and warm spices, they taste distinctly of earthy-sweet carrot. The muffins are excellent plain, but if you have the time, opt for the simple cream cheese glaze and a sprinkle of chopped pistachios. The recipe makes more glaze than you need—don't let it go to waste. Refrigerate or freeze it to use later.

If you've never baked with einkorn flour, you're in for a pleasant surprise. As the oldest documented member of the wheat family, it is considered the mother of all wheats. Einkorn is fairly common these days, but depending on your location, some shopping around may be necessary to wind up with a bag in your pantry (see My Favorite Flours, page 313). Einkorn is so versatile, it can be used like the commonplace all-purpose flour you find at the supermarket, but because it costs significantly more, I save it for special recipes in which I can taste and appreciate it. Combined with all the makings of a carrot cake, assertive einkorn takes a step back, providing a honey-wheat background for carrots and cinnamon to do their thing. And while I would never want to deter anyone from einkorn, if you can't get your hands on it, it's easily replaced with another whole-grain wheat.

1. Place an oven rack in the middle position and preheat the oven to 375°F (190°C).

2. Sift the einkorn flour, baking powder, baking soda, salt, cinnamon, and ginger into a mixing bowl. Using your hands, make a well in the center of the dry ingredients. In a separate bowl, whisk the brown sugar with the oil, orange juice, buttermilk, and eggs. Pour the liquid mixture into the well in the dry ingredients and whisk slowly from the center out to draw the dry ingredients into the liquids. Then whisk vigorously to ensure the batter is well combined. Fold in the shredded carrot using a silicone spatula.

3. Coat a muffin tin lightly with nonstick spray.

4. Evenly distribute the muffin batter, filling each cup almost to the top. Bake for 10 minutes. Then rotate the tin and bake for 8 to 10 minutes more, until the muffins turn light brown and a skewer inserted in the center of a muffin comes out clean.

5. While the muffins are baking, make the glaze. In a small bowl, mash the cream cheese against the sides of the bowl with the back of a wooden spoon to soften. Add the confectioners' sugar and mix until it forms a creamy and smooth paste.

6. Whisk in the lemon juice and milk, making sure to work out any lumps. The glaze should be thick. If you prefer a lighter glaze, add an additional tablespoon of milk. Put the glaze in a small, deep bowl, where you can comfortably dip the tops of the muffins.

7. Let the muffins sit until cool enough to handle. Carefully release the muffins from the tin, running an offset spatula or a paring knife along the edges if necessary, and transfer to a cooling rack.

8. Place the rack with the muffins over a rimmed baking sheet. Glaze the muffins one at a time while they're still warm by dipping them top down into the glaze, then place them back on the rack to let the excess glaze drip onto the baking sheet underneath. The warmth of the muffins will melt the glaze a bit, making it easier to work with. If your glaze is too stiff, you can heat it over a warm bath until softened or in the microwave for a few seconds. Garnish with the chopped pistachios. Serve at room temperature. The muffins will keep in an airtight container at room temperature for up to 2 days.

BERRY OAT MUFFINS

MAKES 12 MUFFINS

EQUIPMENT: muffin tin

1½ cups (150 g) old-fashioned rolled oats, plus extra to garnish (optional)

1 cup (240 ml) buttermilk

½ cup (65 g) all-purpose or hard red wheat whole-grain flour, such as Sonora or Red Fife

1 teaspoon baking powder

½ teaspoon baking soda

½ teaspoon kosher salt

½ cup packed (110 g) dark brown sugar

½ cup (120 ml) unsweetened Applesauce (recipe follows) or store-bought

2 large eggs

⅓ cup (80 ml) vegetable oil

1 teaspoon vanilla extract

¾ cup (100 g) frozen blueberries or other berries of your choice

This was the last recipe I added to the cookbook. After reading the finished manuscript, I realized we didn't include a blueberry muffin. A muffin chapter without a blueberry muffin? Not on my watch. My go-to spelt and blueberry muffin ran in *Mother Grains*, and I doubted I could match it, but after tinkering in the kitchen, this muffin was born. You could consider it the whole-grainier relative of my tried-and-true blueberry muffin, but do use any berry you like.

Made with more oats than flour, these berry-packed muffins remind me of overnight oats, but baked into a handheld treat. I use old-fashioned rolled oats, which are thicker and more wholesome than quick or instant oats. Plan on soaking the oats in buttermilk overnight or for a couple of hours beforehand. Skipping this step will cause the muffins to be too wet, since the oats won't have enough time to absorb the liquid. You still need a little flour so that the batter holds together. I normally use an all-purpose wheat, like Sonora, but a robust red will work well, too. Usually I opt for fresh fruit whenever possible, but muffins are an exception—frozen berries won't bleed too much into the batter as you stir and mix them, as long as you do so at the very last minute.

These muffins are loaded with many tenderizing ingredients: hydrated oats, applesauce, oil, brown sugar, and, of course, berries. Not surprisingly, they stay moist—almost juicy—for a few days. They also refrigerate and freeze well if you'd like to make a batch to last the whole week. For a rustic finish, save a few oats and sprinkle them onto the muffin tops before baking.

1. Place the oats in a nonreactive container, pour in the buttermilk, cover with a lid, and refrigerate for 2 hours or overnight.

2. Place an oven rack in the middle position and preheat the oven to 350°F (175°C).

3. Combine the flour, baking powder, baking soda, and salt in a mixing bowl. Using your hands, make a well in the center of the dry ingredients. In a separate bowl, whisk together the soaked oats with the brown sugar, applesauce, eggs, oil, and vanilla. Pour the liquid mixture into the well in the dry ingredients and whisk slowly from the center out to draw the dry ingredients into the liquids. Then whisk vigorously to ensure the batter is well combined. Fold in the blueberries.

4. Coat a muffin tin lightly with nonstick spray.

5. Evenly distribute the muffin batter, filling each cup almost to the top. If you'd like, top each muffin with a sprinkle of additional oats. Bake for 12 minutes. Then rotate the tin and bake for 12 minutes more, or until the muffins are golden and a skewer inserted in the center of a muffin comes out clean.

6. Let the muffins sit until cool enough to handle. Carefully release the muffins from the tin, running an offset spatula or a paring knife along the edges if necessary. Serve at room temperature. The muffins will keep in an airtight container at room temperature for up to 2 days.

APPLESAUCE

MAKES 1 TO 1½ CUPS (240 TO 360 ML)

Homemade applesauce has a pure fruit flavor and smooth texture rarely replicated in store-bought options. It's also quick and easy to make. I use homemade applesauce in a number of baked goods and as a topping for oatmeal and yogurt. Opt for tart apple varieties that aren't too firm, like Granny Smith, Gala, or McIntosh. Leave it unsweetened for maximum versatility, or add sugar to taste.

3 small apples, peeled, cored, and cut into ½-inch (1.25 cm) cubes
½ cup (120 ml) water
1 cinnamon stick
Sugar to taste (optional)

Put the apple pieces in a small saucepan and add the water and cinnamon stick. Cover and cook over low heat for 15 minutes, or until the apples are fork-tender. Remove the cinnamon stick and puree the apple mixture in a blender or food processor while still warm. If desired, sweeten with sugar to taste. Use the applesauce right away, or store in the refrigerator for up to 1 week or in the freezer for up to 6 months.

APRICOT BUTTERSCOTCH MUFFINS

MAKES 12 MUFFINS

EQUIPMENT: muffin tin

FOR THE MUFFIN BATTER
2 to 3 medium ripe apricots, pitted
1¼ cups (165 g) whole-grain spelt flour
½ teaspoon baking soda
1 teaspoon baking powder
1 teaspoon ground ginger
¼ teaspoon kosher salt
⅔ cup packed (150 g) dark brown sugar
⅓ cup (80 ml) vegetable oil
2 large eggs
¾ cup (180 ml) buttermilk
5 dried apricots, diced (optional)

FOR THE BUTTERSCOTCH GLAZE
¼ cup (55 g/½ stick/2 ounces) unsalted butter
¼ cup (60 ml) heavy cream
½ cup packed (110 g) dark brown sugar
Pinch of kosher salt

These muffins are coated with an apricot–brown sugar glaze after baking—a technique inspired by British sticky toffee pudding. When I was a pastry chef, sticky pudding always scored high points, easily becoming a dessert menu's bestseller. To make things more Californian, I would incorporate seasonal fruits, from apricots (as I do here) to persimmons and quinces. It was only a matter of time before I tried transforming that reliable bake into a muffin.

The butterscotch glaze keeps the muffins moist and brings a satisfying ooey-gooey factor. You may think that anything topped with brown sugar caramel shouldn't be enjoyed for breakfast, but these aren't as sweet as the name might suggest. The floral tartness of the apricots shines through in both the batter and the butterscotch glaze. The ginger and buttermilk balance the molasses-y brown sugar, while the optional dried apricots boost the muffins' fruitiness. For a lighter version, you could skip the glaze—the muffins are complete all on their own.

Spelt is one of the most popular ancient grains out there (see My Favorite Flours, page 313). I almost always buy spelt flour from my local miller, Grist & Toll, but Bob's Red Mill, Central Milling, and independent mills across the country offer spelt flour and berries in grocery stores, farmers' markets, and online. Just like einkorn, spelt flour can be used in lieu of regular all-purpose flour in a one-to-one ratio.

1. Place an oven rack in the middle position and preheat the oven to 375°F (190°C).

2. Puree the apricots in the food processor until smooth. You should end up with about ½ cup (120 ml) of apricot puree.

3. Sift the flour, baking soda, baking powder, ginger, and salt into a mixing bowl. Using your hands, make a well in the center of the dry ingredients. In a separate bowl, whisk together the brown sugar, oil, eggs, buttermilk, and half the apricot puree. Pour the liquid mixture into the well in the dry ingredients and whisk slowly from the center out to draw the dry ingredients into the liquids. Then whisk vigorously to ensure the batter is well combined. Add the dried apricots, if using, and stir to combine.

4. Coat a muffin tin lightly with nonstick spray.

5. Evenly distribute the muffin batter, filling each cup almost to the top. Bake for 10 minutes. Then rotate the tin and bake for 10 minutes more, or until the muffins turn golden brown and a skewer inserted in the center of a muffin comes out clean.

6. While the muffins are baking, make the butterscotch glaze. Melt the butter in a small saucepan over medium heat. Add the cream, brown sugar, and salt and bring to a boil while stirring. Reduce the heat and let the glaze simmer for 1 minute. Add the remaining apricot puree and reduce for another 2 minutes. Remove the pan from the heat but hold it in a warm spot.

7. Let the muffins sit until cool enough to handle. Carefully release the muffins from the tin, running an offset spatula or a paring knife along the edges if necessary, and transfer to a cooling rack. Spoon the warm butterscotch glaze generously over each muffin while they're still warm. Let them sit for a few minutes, then serve. The butterscotch glaze ensures that the muffins will stay moist in an airtight container in the refrigerator for up to 3 days. Let them come to room temperature before enjoying, or reheat in the oven for a few minutes and serve warm.

BANANA-DATE MUFFINS

MAKES 12 MUFFINS

EQUIPMENT: muffin tin

13 raw walnut halves
1¼ cups (165 g) whole-grain hard red wheat flour, such as Turkey Red or Red Fife
1 teaspoon baking powder
¾ teaspoon baking soda
½ teaspoon kosher salt
⅔ cup packed (150 g) dark brown sugar
1 large egg
1 large egg yolk
¾ cup (180 ml) buttermilk
⅓ cup (80 ml) vegetable oil
1 cup (215 g) mashed ripe banana (about 2 medium bananas)
5 Medjool dates, pitted and cut into ¼-inch (6 mm) pieces

How many banana breads can a baker come up with? Just when you think you've tried everything, you dream up a new tweak, and boom, there's another version. Take this as my permission to make these muffins your own, subbing any other dried fruit for the dates or your go-to nut or even chocolate chips for the walnuts.

The nuttiness of hard red wheat is a great match for bananas. For these muffins, I use Red Fife (see My Favorite Flours, page 313), a common variety in my region. They can also be made with Turkey Red, a similar hard red wheat found in the Midwest. The key is to use a dark, assertive variety that can match bananas' intensity. Red wheats are the most represented variety in the whole-grain industry. The whole wheat flour available in supermarkets is made with them, and local grain hubs typically have more red wheats than white ones. This probably is because their flavor evokes what we all think of as whole wheat—earthy, nutty, warm, and bold.

Here, I bolster the red-wheat batter with Medjool dates, toasted walnuts, and tenderizing buttermilk. This muffin is all about big flavors and textures. It's not the most elegant muffin, but it's certainly one of the most satisfying. Picky eaters won't find them challenging, and more adventurous ones will appreciate the details. They come together quickly and keep for a few days.

The result is a hearty, nutrient-dense muffin, great for packing on hikes and bike rides, or having as a quick on-the-go breakfast during a busy workweek. They're also an excellent pick-me-up with dark coffee in the middle of the afternoon. As with many banana breads, the muffins taste even better a day after baking.

1. Place an oven rack in the middle position and preheat the oven to 350°F (175°C).

2. Scatter the walnuts on a rimmed baking sheet and toast in the oven for 8 to 10 minutes, until a nut cut in half is golden inside. Let cool completely.

continues

3. Increase the oven temperature to 375°F (190°C).

4. Sift the flour, baking powder, baking soda, and salt into a mixing bowl. Using your hands, make a well in the center of the dry ingredients. In a separate bowl, whisk together the brown sugar, egg, egg yolk, buttermilk, oil, and mashed banana. Pour the liquid mixture into the well in the dry ingredients and whisk slowly from the center out to draw the dry ingredients into the liquids. Then whisk vigorously to ensure the batter is well combined. Add the dates and stir to combine.

5. Coat a muffin tin lightly with nonstick spray.

6. Evenly distribute the muffin batter, filling each cup almost to the top. Top each muffin with a walnut half. Bake for 12 minutes. Then rotate the tin and bake for 10 to 12 minutes more, or until the muffins turn golden brown and a skewer inserted in the center of a muffin comes out clean.

7. Let the muffins sit until cool enough to handle. Carefully release the muffins from the tin, running an offset spatula or a paring knife along the edges if necessary. Serve at room temperature. The muffins will keep in an airtight container at room temperature for up to 2 days.

SWEET POTATO MUFFINS WITH PECAN STREUSEL

MAKES 12 MUFFINS

EQUIPMENT: muffin tin

FOR THE PECAN STREUSEL

10 pecan halves
3 tablespoons whole-grain hard red wheat flour, such as Turkey Red or Red Fife
2 tablespoons granulated sugar
2 tablespoons packed dark brown sugar
¼ teaspoon kosher salt
Pinch of ground cinnamon
2 tablespoons cold unsalted butter, cut into ½-inch (1.25 cm) cubes

FOR THE MUFFIN BATTER

1 large sweet potato (195 to 225 g/7 to 8 ounces), peeled and cut into 2-inch (5 cm) chunks
1¼ cups (165 g) whole-grain all-purpose or hard red wheat flour, such as Sonora or Red Fife
1 teaspoon baking powder
¾ teaspoon baking soda
½ teaspoon kosher salt
⅔ cup packed (150 g) dark brown sugar
1 large egg
1 large egg yolk
¾ cup (180 ml) buttermilk
⅓ cup (80 ml) vegetable oil
⅓ cup (50 g) golden raisins (optional)

As these muffins bake, the aroma conjures a crisp fall morning, crinkly leaf-lined sidewalks and all. The contrast of crunchy streusel and moist, tender muffin is classic for a reason, and I adore the added toastiness whole grains bring to the bash.

Any whole wheat flour will work, but I urge you to use a red wheat (see My Favorite Flours, page 313). When choosing a flour variety, I follow the advice of California-based miller and grain advocate Nan Kohler and use the logic of food and wine pairings. Just like you'd marry hearty meats with bold red wines, warm fall flavors meld with darker, nuttier red wheats. Combined with mashed sweet potato, toasted nuts, and a touch of spice, a feisty red wheat can find its groove dancing to a more mellow tune.

I love baking with sweet potatoes as a pumpkin alternative. The latter already gets plenty of play in the fall. Plus, sweet potato prep is quick and easy. Since they're smaller, you can just boil as many as needed. For this recipe, you can mash them in advance and keep them in the fridge for about 3 days or in the freezer for up to a month.

1. Place an oven rack in the middle position and preheat the oven to 350°F (175°C).

2. Scatter the pecans on a rimmed baking sheet and toast in the oven for 8 to 10 minutes, until a nut cut in half is golden inside. Let the pecans cool. Chop the toasted pecans into pieces.

continues

3. Increase the oven temperature to 375°F (190°C).

4. For the streusel, combine the flour, sugars, salt, and cinnamon in a mixing bowl. Add the butter cubes and toss to combine. Quickly cut the butter cubes in with your fingertips until the mixture resembles a coarse meal with pieces the size of peas. Add the chopped pecans and toss to combine. Refrigerate the streusel until ready to use.

5. Put the sweet potato in a small saucepan and cover with water. Boil for 25 to 30 minutes, until very tender when poked with a fork. Drain, transfer to a bowl, and mash with the back of a fork while the potato is still warm. Let the mash cool completely before using. You can make the mash up to 3 days ahead and store in an airtight container in the refrigerator.

6. Sift the flour, baking powder, baking soda, and salt into a medium bowl. Using your hands, make a well in the center of the dry ingredients. In a separate bowl, whisk together the brown sugar, egg, egg yolk, buttermilk, oil, and ¾ cup (180 ml) of the sweet potato mash. Pour the liquid mixture into the well in the dry ingredients and whisk slowly from the center out to draw the dry ingredients into the liquids. Then whisk vigorously to ensure the batter is well combined. Stir in the golden raisins, if using.

7. Coat a muffin tin lightly with nonstick spray.

8. Evenly distribute the muffin batter, filling each cup almost to the top. Top each muffin with a spoonful of streusel. Bake for 12 minutes. Then rotate the tin and bake for 12 minutes more, or until the muffins turn golden brown and a skewer inserted in the center of a muffin comes out clean.

9. Let the muffins sit until cool enough to handle. Carefully release the muffins from the tin, running an offset spatula or a paring knife along the edges if necessary. Serve at room temperature. The muffins will keep in an airtight container at room temperature for up to 2 days.

GLAZED LEMON, POPPY SEED, AND OLIVE OIL MUFFINS

MAKES 12 MUFFINS

EQUIPMENT: muffin tin

FOR THE MUFFIN BATTER
1¼ cups (165 g) whole-grain all-purpose wheat flour, such as Sonora or Frederick
1 cup (140 g) whole-grain durum wheat flour
2 teaspoons baking powder
½ teaspoon kosher salt
1 tablespoon poppy seeds, plus extra for sprinkling
1 cup (200 g) granulated sugar
¾ cup (180 ml) olive oil
2 large eggs
Finely grated zest and juice of 1 lemon
¾ cup (180 ml) whole milk

FOR THE GLAZE
1¼ cups (145 g) confectioners' sugar, sifted
3 tablespoons lemon juice
3 tablespoons olive oil

Soon after finishing the first draft of this cookbook, I baked all the muffins in this chapter, packed them tightly, and shipped them to my editor in New York. It was a great exercise, seeing them all side by side and comparing their individual contributions to the book. These shiny lemon muffins were my favorites of the bunch. They looked so unassuming among their crumble-topped, berry-filled, and chocolate-packed siblings, but it was because of their simplicity that they stood out. If your morning starts with a cup of black tea or Earl Grey, this recipe is for you. I could eat these any time of day, but they're a particularly special treat with a cuppa in the early morning.

It's common for us Californian bakers to include olive oil in our creations. Considering how many olive farms are just a stone's throw from a citrus orchard, we often marry the two ingredients. The pairing is so evocative of Mediterranean baking that my mind naturally gravitated toward durum flour—a common grain in that region. Think of it as semolina's whole-grain sibling. Though not readily available in supermarkets, you can source durum flour online from Camas Country Mill, Central Milling, or Janie's Mill (see My Favorite Flours, page 313). While not overbearing, the oil's flavor is fairly present. Select something you wouldn't mind dipping bread into or using in salad dressing.

A few poppy seeds woven into the batter remind us that this is a muffin after all. Go the extra mile and dip the tops in the olive oil–lemon glaze, which further emphasizes the happy marriage of these ingredients, or serve them bare for a more rustic (and less sweet) look. Intensely lemony and perfumed with fruity olive oil—who knew a muffin could be so elegant yet so happy and bright?

continues

1. Place an oven rack in the middle position and preheat the oven to 375°F (190°C).

2. Sift the flours, baking powder, salt, and poppy seeds into a mixing bowl. Using your hands, make a well in the center of the dry ingredients. In a separate bowl, whisk together the granulated sugar, oil, eggs, lemon zest and juice, and milk. Pour the liquid mixture into the well in the dry ingredients and whisk slowly from the center out to draw the dry ingredients into the liquids. Then whisk vigorously to ensure the batter is well combined.

3. Coat a muffin tin lightly with nonstick spray.

4. Evenly distribute the muffin batter, filling each cup almost to the top. Bake for 10 minutes. Then rotate the tin and bake for 8 minutes more, or until the muffins turn light golden brown and a skewer inserted in the center of a muffin comes out clean.

5. While the muffins are baking, make the glaze. Whisk the confectioners' sugar, lemon juice, and oil in a mixing bowl until smooth. Put the glaze in a small, deep bowl, where you can comfortably dip the tops of the muffins.

6. Let the muffins sit until cool enough to handle. Carefully release the muffins from the tin, running an offset spatula or a paring knife along the edges if necessary, and transfer to a cooling rack.

7. Place the rack with the muffins over a rimmed baking sheet. Glaze the muffins one at a time while they're still a bit warm by dipping them top down into the glaze, then place them back on the rack to let the excess glaze drip onto the baking sheet underneath. Wait 5 minutes, then dip the tops again. The double dunk will ensure well-coated muffins. Alternatively, you can leave the muffins on the cooling rack and spoon the glaze over their tops. If you'd like, sprinkle with a few poppy seeds. Let the glaze set completely. Serve at room temperature. The muffins will keep in an airtight container at room temperature for 2 to 3 days.

CHOCOLATE MORNING MUFFINS

MAKES 12 MUFFINS

EQUIPMENT: muffin tin

- ⅔ cup (160 ml) boiling water
- ⅓ cup (40 g) Dutch-processed cocoa powder
- ½ cup (60 g) whole-grain or dark rye flour
- ½ cup (65 g) whole-grain all-purpose wheat flour, such as Sonora or Frederick
- 1½ teaspoons baking soda
- 1 teaspoon baking powder
- ½ teaspoon kosher salt
- ½ cup (90 g) bittersweet (65–80%) chocolate chips, plus ½ cup (90 g) extra to garnish (optional)
- ¼ cup plus 2 tablespoons (90 ml) vegetable oil
- ⅓ cup (80 g) Greek yogurt or skyr
- 2 large eggs
- 1 teaspoon vanilla extract
- ¾ cup (150 g) sugar

I love when people are down with chocolate for breakfast. It's a defiant move that contradicts our puritan prejudice against indulgence early in the morning. And one must wonder, is chocolate all that bad? I've hung out with enough marathoners to know that the answer is no. After all, cacao is a powerful superfood that pairs naturally with both coffee and tea. The trick lies in combining it with other nutrient-dense ingredients. Case in point: these muffins. With Dutch-processed cocoa, dark chocolate, yogurt, and rye flour, they're intensely chocolaty but not overly sweet.

I toss in a handful of chocolate chips, but feel free to omit them—the muffins will be just as delicious. Never skip the step of dissolving the cocoa powder in boiling water prior to adding it to the batter, which is also known as "blooming." Blooming is the best way to thoroughly dissolve the powder and further enhance its chocolaty flavor. Make sure to use a tangy, full-fat yogurt such as Greek yogurt or skyr—it will react with the cocoa powder to create an assertive yet balanced muffin that remains moist long after baking.

Rye's woody, earthy flavor pairs beautifully with chocolate's bold intensity, making it the obvious flour choice here. Check out My Favorite Flours (page 313) for my recommended rye flour sources.

This recipe results in a moist, rich muffin that stays soft for a couple of days. I like to pop one in the oven or microwave to turn it soft and gooey.

1. Place an oven rack in the middle position and preheat the oven to 350°F (175°C).

2. Combine the boiling water with the cocoa powder, whisking vigorously until smooth. Set aside to cool completely.

continues

3. Sift the flours, baking soda, baking powder, and salt into a mixing bowl. Using your hands, make a well in the center of the dry ingredients.

4. Put the chocolate chips and oil in a medium heatproof bowl. Fill a medium pot a quarter of the way with water and place over low heat. When the water is barely simmering, fit the bowl on top, making sure the bottom of the bowl doesn't touch the simmering water. Stir occasionally with a heat-resistant spatula until the chocolate is completely melted.

5. Remove the bowl from the heat. Whisk in the cooled cocoa mixture, yogurt, eggs, vanilla, and sugar until fully incorporated. Pour the liquid ingredients into the well in the dry ingredients and whisk slowly from the center out to draw the dry ingredients into the liquids. Then whisk vigorously to ensure the batter is well combined. Fold in the additional chocolate chips, if using.

6. Coat a muffin tin lightly with nonstick spray.

7. Evenly distribute the muffin batter, filling each cup almost to the top. Bake for 10 minutes. Then rotate the tin and bake for 10 to 12 minutes more, until a skewer inserted in the center of a muffin comes out clean.

8. Let the muffins sit until cool enough to handle. Carefully release the muffins from the tin, running an offset spatula or a paring knife along the edges if necessary. Serve at room temperature. The muffins will keep in an airtight container at room temperature for up to 2 days.

BUCKWHEAT JOY MUFFINS

MAKES 12 MUFFINS

EQUIPMENT: muffin tin

¾ cup (100 g) whole-grain all-purpose or hard red wheat flour, such as Sonora or Red Fife

¾ cup (110 g) whole-grain buckwheat flour

1 teaspoon baking powder

½ teaspoon baking soda

¼ teaspoon kosher salt

½ cup (100 g) turbinado sugar, such as Sugar in the Raw

¼ cup (60 ml) vegetable oil

1 large egg

1 cup (240 ml) unsweetened Applesauce (page 31) or store-bought

½ cup (120 ml) whole milk

¼ cup (60 ml) buckwheat honey, plus extra for brushing the muffin tops

1 firm apple, peeled, cored, and cut into ½-inch (1.25 cm) dice

I call these buckwheat joy muffins because, well, buckwheat always brings me joy. For a buck lover like me, it's hard to accept that buckwheat is a polarizing ingredient, and that many find its flavor too strong. To gently convert them into enthusiasts, I soften buckwheat's in-your-face personality with mellow ingredients. Enter applesauce and apple morsels. The applesauce lightly sweetens, while the morsels bring out buckwheat's fruity qualities. After all, buckwheat is more fruit than grain. It comes from a leafy flowering bush, not a grass, and is related to rhubarb and sorrel.

The scent of freshly milled buckwheat flour is a magical thing: damp soil and wild greens and flowers with hints of toasted nuts and dark chocolate. Whenever possible, purchase freshly ground buckwheat (see My Favorite Flours, page 313) from specialty mills like Grist & Toll and Anson Mills. Popular suppliers such as Bob's Red Mill and Central Milling are also consistent and reliable.

Buckwheat honey—made by bees that collect nectar from buckwheat flowers—is equally assertive. It's a dark amber color and boasts a warm, robust flavor comparable to molasses. Look for it in well-stocked grocery stores or farmers' market stalls. Brushing the warm muffins with buckwheat honey allows its flavor and fragrance to shine (you can skip this step for a less sweet iteration). Be sure to varnish the muffins while they're still a bit warm so that the honey will run thinner as it melts slightly and you will end up brushing on just enough.

Pay attention when you're scooping the batter to ensure that each muffin ends up with a similar amount of diced apple. When I make these in the early fall I nerd out, selecting a beautiful heirloom apple variety. They keep well for a few days, so a batch will last for a few breakfasts.

1. Place an oven rack in the middle position and preheat the oven to 375°F (190°C).

2. Sift the flours, baking powder, baking soda, and salt into a mixing bowl. Using your hands, make a well in the center of the dry ingredients. In a separate bowl, whisk together the sugar, oil, egg, applesauce, milk, and honey. Pour the liquid mixture into the well in the dry ingredients and whisk slowly from the center out to draw the dry ingredients into the liquids. Then whisk vigorously to ensure the batter is well combined. Fold in the diced apple.

3. Coat a muffin tin lightly with nonstick spray.

4. Evenly distribute the muffin batter, filling each cup almost to the top. Bake for 12 minutes. Then rotate the tin and bake for 10 minutes more, or until the muffins turn rich brown and a skewer inserted in the center of a muffin comes out clean.

5. Let the muffins sit until cool enough to handle. Carefully release the muffins from the tin, running an offset spatula or a paring knife along the edges if necessary. To finish the tops, use a pastry brush to paint each muffin with a thin layer of buckwheat honey while they're still warmish. The muffins will keep in an airtight container at room temperature for 2 to 3 days.

CHAPTER 2

BISCUITS AND SCONES

FROM TOP TO BOTTOM:
Pear, Chocolate, and Einkorn Scones (page 65);
Rhuberry Roly Polys (page 73);
Salted Butter Brown Scones (page 63);
Cream Scones (page 58)

> **Recipes**
>
> Buttermilk Whole-Grain Biscuits   53
> Parmesan-Rosemary Biscuits   56
> Cream Scones with Lemon Curd   58
> Cheddar and Jalapeño Cornmeal Scones   61
> Salted Butter Brown Scones   63
> Pear, Chocolate, and Einkorn Scones   65
> Herby Cottage Cheese Scones   67
> Brunch Red Pepper and Goat Cheese Scones   71
> Rhuberry Roly Poly   73

Like muffins, biscuits and scones belong to the quick bread family, though they could not be more different. Biscuits and scones start as a dough, rather than a batter. What's similar is that all three baked goods get their rise from artificial leaveners.

Both biscuits and scones are made using the cut-in method, which is best done by hand. In it, the way the butter is incorporated greatly affects the rising power and expansion of the pastries. The cut-in method requires pinching cold butter into the flour with your fingertips to form a mix of small pebbles and flakes. To do this well, chilled ingredients and efficiency are key. The goal is to create airy pockets and lift as chips of cold butter melt in the oven. Use cold butter and make sure it's cut to the right size. I avoid using the food processor when mixing biscuits or scones at home because it's far too easy to cut the butter too small.

Your choice of whole-grain flour is key for giving your pastries proper structure and texture, plus imbuing them with flavor. Lower-gluten flours are ideal, but don't rule out strong flours, which turn tender in combination with the amount of fat in biscuits and scones. My Salted Butter Brown Scones (page 63), made with hard red wheat, are a perfect example. To bring biscuits and scones together, use your hands to make a well in the center of the butter-flour mixture. Pour in the liquid and toss with both hands, as if tossing a salad, until a rough dough is formed.

Which liquid and how much of it goes into the recipe is an important consideration. Buttermilk is great for flavor and, depending on the rest of the ingredients, is the best all-around choice, but I also like cream, which helps tenderize bran-rich flour. Since too much liquid can have a detrimental effect on the pastries, you should also watch the moisture content of other mix-ins. This is why I prefer dried fruit over fresh. If using fresh fruit, I recommend freezing it in advance and incorporating it at the very last minute.

Speaking of mix-ins, incorporating flavorful ingredients into your pastries, especially scones, is half the fun. If you've ever been to the UK, you may have noticed that their scones don't have as many mix-ins as they do here in the US. British scones are usually plain or minimally adorned with humble black currants. That's because they're meant to be enjoyed with afternoon tea, split in half and accompanied with clotted cream and jam. They're more akin to American biscuits than American scones. I must admit, I really like our American take. At their best, American scones are crisp and slightly caramelized on the outside, with a soft interior. They highlight the goodies inside but are never too sweet.

Dressing up scones with delicious ingredients makes them a complete breakfast treat that doesn't need accompaniments and can be eaten on the go. Bakeries dream up tasty, creative variations full of fruits, grains, nuts, and spices, and sell tons of them on their pastry counters every day. I always feel a sense of comradery when I see a hurried customer on their way to work in the early morning, coffee and blueberry scone in hand. It makes me want to say, "Go ahead! Seize the day! American scones are built for that!"

Most of my biscuit and scone recipes are made with the cut-in method, but an alternative method is "dropping," in which lumps of dough are dropped directly on the baking sheet, as in my Cream Scones with Lemon Curd (page 58). This technique makes delectable scones or biscuits and is easy to master.

The most intricate scone in this chapter is the Rhuberry Roly Poly (page 73), which is assembled like a jelly roll, then sliced, and shouldn't be made in a rush.

Once you're ready to bake, preheating the oven to 400°F (205°C) is a must. Letting biscuits and scones bake at a lower temperature can cause them to expand sideways rather than lift upward. Also, be sure to space them sufficiently on the baking sheet. For most of the recipes in this chapter, you'll need two baking sheets placed on separate racks in the middle of the oven. Spacing the pastries generously will guarantee that each one develops a nice toasty exterior. It's also advisable to rotate the sheets and swap their positions halfway through the baking process to ensure that they bake evenly.

Leftover biscuits and scones keep for up to 2 days in an airtight container at room temperature or in the fridge. Make sure to reheat for a few minutes in the oven to bring them back to life.

WHAT'S THE DIFFERENCE BETWEEN BISCUITS AND SCONES?

They are both butter rich, but the butter in biscuits translates into defined flaky layers; in scones, it produces a tender, crumbly texture. Both are made with considerably less sugar than other quick breads, but biscuits are decisively unsweetened and have a more neutral or savory flavor profile, ready to be slathered with gravy or served with butter. In contrast, scones acquire sweet or savory personalities based on what other ingredients are thrown into the mix. Biscuits contain no eggs (except for an optional beaten egg varnish), whereas scones include them more often than not. Buttermilk is considered a prerequisite for a great biscuit, but there is more flexibility in scone recipes, where milk or cream is frequently the liquid of choice. As far as shape, traditional biscuits are cut with a round (aptly named) biscuit cutter, while scones are often sliced into wedges like a cake, which tends to mean they're larger.

BUTTERMILK WHOLE-GRAIN BISCUITS

MAKES 8 TO 10 BISCUITS

EQUIPMENT: 2½-inch (6.5 cm) biscuit cutter

3½ cups (455 g) whole-grain all-purpose wheat flour, such as Sonora or Frederick, plus extra for dusting

2 tablespoons sugar

1 tablespoon baking powder

1½ teaspoons baking soda

2 teaspoons kosher salt

1 cup (224 g/2 sticks/8 ounces) cold unsalted butter, cut into ½-inch (1.25 cm) cubes

1½ cups (360 ml) cold buttermilk

1 large egg, beaten

Is there anything more comforting than warm biscuits dabbed with butter? Though often made with bleached, self-rising flour, it's entirely possible to whole-grain-ify this American staple. You'll have to seek softer grains that are low in gluten. Sonora, Frederick, and Sirvinta are biscuit-ready soft wheat varieties (see My Favorite Flours, page 313). Avoid hard red and hard white wheats. If it's good for bread, it probably shouldn't be in your biscuits. Bakers who are new to whole-grain baking and would like a more mildly flavored biscuit can replace a portion of the whole-grain flour in the recipe with refined all-purpose flour as indicated in the variation that follows.

Technique is as crucial as flour selection. It comes down to the cut-in method, which ensures the bits of butter are small enough to melt throughout the dough during baking, creating steam that puffs up the layers. At the same time, artificial leaveners unleash their chemical powers, propelling the biscuits upward. Buttermilk is a must—its acidity reacts with artificial leavening to create lift while imbuing the biscuit with flavor. A little sugar encourages color, but we can certainly do without it. Far more important is salt, an essential for flavor. You should never reduce the amount, even if garnishing with more salt on top.

A clean, sharp biscuit cutter makes all the difference. It's important to wipe it off between biscuits, ensuring the cut occurs quickly and evenly. Doing this avoids compressing the dough's edges, which will inhibit rise. I bake biscuits at 400°F (205°C) on the middle rack of the oven, which helps them develop a crisp browned exterior. All these recommendations might sound overly fussy, but small details like these make all the difference! Once you're familiar with the biscuit-making process, you'll realize it's entirely possible to whip up a batch in no time. Nothing beats biscuits fresh out of the oven, but they keep well for a few days and taste good as new reheated in the oven.

continues

1. Place an oven rack in the middle position and preheat the oven to 400°F (205°C). Line a rimmed baking sheet with parchment paper.

2. Sift the flour, sugar, baking powder, baking soda, and salt into a mixing bowl. Add the butter cubes and toss to combine. Quickly cut the butter into the dry ingredients by pinching the butter with your fingertips—imagine you're snapping your fingers—until the mixture resembles a coarse meal with butter pieces the size of cornflakes.

3. Using your hands, make a well in the center of the mixture. Pour in the buttermilk and toss with both hands (as if tossing a salad) until a rough dough is formed.

4. Transfer the dough to a lightly floured surface. Using a rolling pin, flatten into a 12-by-10-inch (30 by 25.5 cm) rectangle. Fold the dough into thirds as if you were folding a business letter to insert in an envelope. Flatten once again into a 10-by-5-inch (25 by 13 cm) rectangle, dusting with additional flour as necessary.

5. Cut with a 2½-inch (6.5 cm) plain biscuit cutter, dipping the cutter in flour between cuts. Gather the scraps, knead gently until the dough comes back together, and cut a few additional biscuits. Discard anything left afterward; the dough is overworked and will likely yield tough biscuits.

6. Transfer the biscuits to the prepared baking sheet, placing them at least 2 inches (5 cm) apart. Brush with the beaten egg and bake for 10 minutes. Then rotate the baking sheet and bake for another 10 minutes, until the edges of the biscuits are golden. These biscuits are delicious while still warm, but you can also serve them at room temperature.

VARIATION

For lighter biscuits, replace the flour with 2½ cups (325 g) whole-grain all-purpose wheat flour, such as Sonora or Frederick, plus 1 cup (140 g) all-purpose flour.

Parmesan-Rosemary Biscuits

Buttermilk Whole-Grain Biscuits

PARMESAN-ROSEMARY BISCUITS

MAKES 10 TO 12 BISCUITS

- 2 cups (280 g) all-purpose flour, plus extra for dusting
- 2 cups (280 g) whole-grain durum wheat flour
- 2 tablespoons sugar
- 1 tablespoon baking powder
- 1½ teaspoons baking soda
- 1½ teaspoons kosher salt
- 1 cup (224 g/2 sticks/8 ounces) cold unsalted butter, cut into ½-inch (1.25 cm) cubes
- 2 cups loosely packed (112 g/4 ounces) finely grated Parmesan
- 1½ cups (360 ml) cold buttermilk
- 1 large egg, beaten
- 1 tablespoon fresh rosemary leaves

With its high protein content and density, durum is the hardest of all wheats—its name is, quite literally, Latin for "hard." These qualities make it a go-to choice in pasta production, and it plays an integral role in many bread and pizza recipes. It's believed to be one of the first domesticated grains, initially harvested sometime around 7000 BC. When ground, it's gritty and pale yellow, with a texture reminiscent of fine cornmeal. This powder is durum flour (see My Favorite Flours, page 313), and some mills produce it by double or triple grinding the entire kernel. Durum's endosperm, separated from the bran and germ, becomes semolina flour and, in theory, can be used in recipes calling for durum flour (and vice versa)—alas, with a lower fiber and nutrition content.

In this recipe, I blend durum flour with all-purpose flour for a more balanced biscuit. The durum adds sufficient structure, texture, and flavor, while refined flour softens the crumb and keeps the potent durum in check. To ensure the biscuits develop those all-important flaky layers, the dough is rolled and folded into thirds (this is the same technique as for Buttermilk Whole-Grain Biscuits, page 53), then cut into squares. Compressed or jagged edges can compromise the biscuits' height, so be sure to use your sharpest knife and slice cleanly, wiping the knife between cuts.

The biscuits are flavorful enough to enjoy plain but excellent with a smear of butter and thinly sliced ham or prosciutto. They taste fantastic next to soft scrambled eggs, or in a bread basket accompanying a meal.

1. Place an oven rack in the middle position of the oven and preheat the oven to 400°F (205°C). Line a rimmed baking sheet with parchment paper.

2. Combine the flours, sugar, baking powder, baking soda, and salt in a mixing bowl. Add the butter cubes and toss to combine. Quickly cut the butter into the dry ingredients by pinching the butter with your fingertips—imagine you're snapping your fingers—until the mixture resembles a coarse meal with butter pieces the size of cornflakes. Add the Parmesan and toss to combine.

3. Using your hands, make a well in the center of the mixture. Pour in the buttermilk and toss with both hands (as if tossing a salad) until a rough dough is formed.

4. Transfer the dough to a lightly floured surface. Using a rolling pin, flatten into a 12-by-10-inch (30 by 25.5 cm) rectangle. Fold the dough into thirds as if you were folding a business letter to insert in an envelope. Flatten once again into a 10½-by-4½-inch (27 by 11 cm) rectangle, dusting with additional flour as necessary.

5. Using a large chef's knife, trim ¼ inch (6 mm) of dough off the border to create a clean edge all around—clean edges will help the biscuits rise and grow tall. Cut the trimmed rectangle into ten 2-inch (5 cm) squares. Gather the scraps, knead gently until the dough comes back together, and cut a couple additional biscuits.

6. Transfer the biscuits to the prepared baking sheet, placing them at least 2 inches (5 cm) apart. Brush with the beaten egg and sprinkle with the rosemary leaves. Bake for 10 minutes. Then rotate the baking sheet and bake for another 10 to 14 minutes, until the tops of the biscuits are golden. These biscuits are delicious while still warm, but you can also serve them at room temperature.

VARIATIONS

Other herbs, such as fresh thyme or minced chives or parsley, work well. If you're feeling adventurous, stir a tablespoon of minced sun-dried tomatoes or mashed roasted garlic into the dough.

CREAM SCONES WITH LEMON CURD

MAKES 10 SCONES

- 2 cups plus 2 tablespoons (275 g) whole-grain hard red wheat flour, such as Turkey Red or Red Fife
- ¼ cup (50 g) sugar, plus extra for sprinkling
- 1 tablespoon baking powder
- 1 teaspoon kosher salt
- ½ cup (75 g) dried black currants
- 1½ cups (360 ml) heavy cream
- ½ cup (120 ml) Lemon Curd (recipe follows) or store-bought, for serving (optional)

These ultratender scones are a minimal-effort, maximum-reward bake. They rely on the richness of cream—no butter necessary—and a simple drop scone method: Toss the ingredients together, then "drop" the dough directly onto your baking sheet. They're meant to be made on a whim and with ease. This tried-and-true technique results in tender, buttery bundles with a craggy, slightly crunchy exterior. I love using dried black currants, but you could make these plain or stir in a different dried fruit, such as cranberries or golden raisins. The heavy cream is the hero. Never replace it with a leaner liquid. The fatty dairy softens the dough enough to make it droppable.

All sorts of flours work in this recipe, though I appreciate the earthy maltiness of red wheat (see My Favorite Flours, page 313). The cream hydrates its bran beautifully.

This is the scone I make when I want to run out the last few cups in a flour bag that has been hanging around my kitchen. It doesn't require planning ahead or shopping for fancy ingredients, so use what you have. It's more important that you make the scones than that you spend time and money looking for a particular flour.

Since these scones don't require working fat into flour or rolling and cutting dough, they're ideal for slow Sunday mornings when you're craving a warm pastry or crowd-pleasing brunch item but don't want to spend too much time in the kitchen. Paired with smooth lemon curd, the scones feel far fancier than the sum of their parts.

1. Place an oven rack in the middle position and preheat the oven to 400°F (205°C). Line a rimmed baking sheet with parchment paper.

2. Combine the flour, sugar, baking powder, salt, and black currants in a mixing bowl and toss to combine. Using your hands, make a well in the center of the dry ingredients. Pour the cream into the well and toss gently with both hands (as if tossing a salad) until a rough dough is formed.

3. To shape the scones, divide the dough into 10 equal lumps. Flour your hands and gently shape each lump into a rough ball or mound—don't aim for a perfect sphere; doing so would require overhandling the dough and will result in a tough scone. Place on the prepared baking sheet, spacing them at least 2 inches (5 cm) apart. Sprinkle generously with sugar.

4. Bake for 10 minutes, then rotate the baking sheet and bake for another 8 to 10 minutes, until the tops of the scones are golden. Serve warm or at room temperature alongside lemon curd, if desired.

LEMON CURD

MAKES 1 CUP

4 large egg yolks
½ cup (100 g) sugar
1 teaspoon finely grated lemon zest
½ cup (120 ml) lemon juice
¼ cup (55 g/½ stick/2 ounces) cold unsalted butter, cubed

Whisk the egg yolks and sugar vigorously in a nonreactive, heatproof bowl. Add the lemon zest and juice and whisk until well combined. Fill a medium pot halfway with water and place over low heat. When the water is barely simmering, fit the bowl on top, making sure the bottom of the bowl doesn't touch the simmering water. Cook for 30 minutes, whisking occasionally, until the curd thickens. Remove the bowl from the pot of water. Whisk in the butter cubes. Strain into a nonreactive container and let cool completely, then cover and refrigerate until ready to use, up to 1 month.

CHEDDAR AND JALAPEÑO CORNMEAL SCONES

MAKES 10 SCONES

¾ cup (95 g) whole-grain all-purpose wheat flour, such as Sonora or Frederick

¾ cup (105 g) all-purpose flour, plus extra for dusting

1 cup (160 g) medium or coarse yellow cornmeal

2 tablespoons sugar

1 tablespoon baking powder

1½ teaspoons baking soda

¾ teaspoon kosher salt

¾ cup (170 g/1½ sticks/6 ounces) cold unsalted butter, cut into ½-inch (1.25 cm) cubes

1 cup (100 g) shredded yellow cheddar

¼ cup (30 g) minced pickled jalapeños

½ cup plus 2 tablespoons (150 ml) buttermilk

1 large egg

I've tried this iconic flavor combination in every form imaginable. From sourdough loaves and brioche buns to bagels and pretzels, I've stuffed or topped almost everything with melty cheese and zingy jalapeños. If you've ever had a late-night hard-shell taco topped with a little cloud of shredded cheddar and a few slices of pickled jalapeño, you know exactly what I'm talking about. Fortunately, this scone is a great hangover cure—that is, if you manage to do any baking after a night out. They can also be baked in advance, then reheated in the morning. Unlike other scones, these are shaped into mounds, rather than rolled and cut.

Because the dough doesn't require patting and compacting, it yields fluffy, tender scones. You can certainly cut them in a more traditional way (as described on page 50), but their lumpy, imperfect shape is part of the charm. Next time you make a pot of chili, try serving these alongside it. The combination of whole-grain wheat and cornmeal is reminiscent of cornbread. Choose a neutral-flavored flour such as Sonora (see My Favorite Flours, page 313) that won't clash with the other ingredients. Medium or coarse cornmeal works well; use coarse if you like a bit more bite.

1. Place an oven rack in the middle position and preheat the oven to 400°F (205°C). Line a rimmed baking sheet with parchment paper.

2. In a large mixing bowl, combine the flours, cornmeal, sugar, baking powder, baking soda, and salt. Add the butter cubes and toss to combine. Quickly cut the butter into the dry ingredients by pinching the butter with your fingertips—imagine you're snapping your fingers—until the mixture resembles a coarse meal with butter pieces the size of cornflakes. Add the cheddar and jalapeños and toss to combine.

continues

3. Using your hands, make a well in the center of the mixture. Whisk together the buttermilk and egg and pour into the well. Toss with both hands (as if tossing a salad) until a rough dough is formed.

4. To shape the scones, divide the dough into 10 equal lumps. Flour your hands and gently shape each lump into a rough ball or mound—don't aim for a perfect sphere; doing so would require overhandling the dough and will result in a tough scone.

5. Transfer to the prepared baking sheet, spacing them at least 2 inches (5 cm) apart. Bake for 10 minutes. Then rotate the baking sheet and bake for another 8 to 10 minutes, until the tops of the scones are golden. These scones are delicious while still warm, but you can also serve them at room temperature.

SALTED BUTTER BROWN SCONES

MAKES 10 SCONES

2⅔ cups (360 g) whole-grain hard red wheat flour, such as Turkey Red or Red Fife, plus extra for dusting

½ cup (100 g) sugar, plus extra for sprinkling

1 tablespoon plus 1 teaspoon baking powder

1 cup (224 g/2 sticks/8 ounces) cold salted butter, such as Kerrygold

Finely grated zest of 1 orange

1 cup (240 ml) buttermilk

1 large egg, beaten

If you've never made classically shaped wedge scones before, start here: The dough comes together quickly and is very forgiving. The moniker "brown scones" implies that these goodies can and should be rustic. I still use a gentle touch, being mindful not to overmix. In Ireland, these are made with "wholemeal," or unsifted whole-grain flour. They're hearty, packed with malty, toasty flavor, and equally at home slathered with preserves or plunged into soup.

For this iteration, I recommend a boldflavored hard red wheat (see My Favorite Flours, page 313). Using a variety that produces tougher baked goods might seem counterintuitive, but the tenderizing ingredients—buttermilk, sugar, and butter—work together to soften the dough. Like many bakers, I favor unsalted butter. It's a clean slate, allowing for complete control over a recipe's salt content. In some cases, though, the rich savoriness of a nice salted butter simply can't be beat. This is one such case. And it's worth grabbing the good stuff, too. In general, high-quality butters have more butterfat, which translates to flavor. Aside from being extra creamy, quality butter supplies sweet, grassy, and milky notes, which bloom as it warms in your mouth. I tend to opt for Kerrygold, which is easy to find and not wildly expensive, and boasts a buttercup-yellow hue (the result of being made with milk from grass-fed cows). When serving these with a savory meal, I like to halve the amount of sugar; see the variation that follows.

1. Place an oven rack in the middle position and preheat the oven to 400°F (205°C). Line a rimmed baking sheet with parchment paper.

2. Combine the flour, sugar, and baking powder in a mixing bowl. Add the butter cubes and toss to combine. Quickly cut the butter cubes into the dry ingredients by pinching the butter with your fingertips—imagine you're snapping your fingers—until the mixture resembles a coarse meal with butter pieces the size of cornflakes. Add the orange zest and toss to combine.

continues

3. Using your hands, make a well in the center of the mixture. Pour the buttermilk into the well and toss gently with both hands (as if tossing a salad) until a rough dough is formed.

4. To shape the scones, transfer the dough to a lightly floured surface. Pat it down into a disk about 7 inches (18 cm) in diameter and 1 inch (2.5 cm) thick. Using a large chef's knife, slice the disk into 10 equal wedges (as you would a cake or a pie). Transfer each individual scone to the prepared baking sheet, placing them at least 2 inches (5 cm) apart. Brush with the beaten egg and sprinkle with sugar.

5. Bake for 10 minutes. Then rotate the baking sheet and bake for 10 to 14 minutes, until the tops of the scones are golden. These scones are delicious while still warm, but you can also serve them at room temperature.

VARIATION

To serve as an accompaniment to a savory meal, reduce the sugar to ¼ cup (50 g) and omit the orange zest.

PEAR, CHOCOLATE, AND EINKORN SCONES

MAKES 10 SCONES

1⅓ cups (165 g) whole-grain einkorn flour

1⅓ cups (165 g) all-purpose flour, plus extra for dusting

½ cup (100 g) sugar, plus extra for sprinkling

1 tablespoon plus 1 teaspoon baking powder

1 teaspoon kosher salt

1 cup (224 g/2 sticks/8 ounces) cold unsalted butter, cut into ½-inch (1.25 cm) cubes

¼ heaping cup (45 g) chopped bittersweet (65–80%) chocolate

1 cup (140 g) diced dried pears

¾ cup (180 ml) heavy cream, plus extra for brushing

The inspiration for these scones comes from poire belle Hélène, a dessert created in 1864 by culinary legend Auguste Escoffier and named after a famous operetta. It consists of pears poached in syrup, served with vanilla ice cream and chocolate sauce. To achieve the same harmony in a scone, I combine bitter dark chocolate, musky-sweet pears, and einkorn, a honey-hued ancient wheat whose flavor shines when paired with plenty of butter. Freeze the scones for at least 30 minutes before baking to keep them from spreading. Dehydrated pears, softer than most dried fruit, keep their texture in the oven and are easy to find in well-stocked grocery stores and online.

1. Place two oven racks in the middle positions and preheat the oven to 400°F (205°C). Line two rimmed baking sheets with parchment paper.

2. Combine the flours, sugar, baking powder, and salt in a mixing bowl. Add the butter cubes and toss to combine. Quickly cut the butter into the dry ingredients by pinching the butter with your fingertips—imagine you're snapping your fingers—until the mixture resembles a coarse meal with butter pieces the size of cornflakes. Add the chocolate and pears and toss to combine.

3. Using your hands, make a well in the center of the mixture. Pour the cream into the well and toss with both hands (as if tossing a salad) until a rough dough is formed.

4. To shape the scones, transfer the dough to a lightly floured surface. Pat it down into a disk about 7 inches (18 cm) in diameter and 1 inch (2.5 cm) thick. Using a large chef's knife, slice the disk into 10 equal wedges (as you would a cake or a pie). Put in the freezer for 30 to 60 minutes.

continues

5. Transfer the scones to the prepared baking sheets, placing them at least 2 inches (5 cm) apart. Brush with the cream and sprinkle generously with sugar.

6. Bake for 15 minutes. Then rotate the baking sheets, switch their positions, and bake for another 10 minutes, until the edges of the scones are golden. These scones are delicious while still warm, but you can also serve them at room temperature.

BISCUITS AND SCONES LOVE THE FREEZER

Bakers figured out long ago that many pastries bake better from frozen. This is because freezing prevents them from spreading. When a frozen biscuit or scone hits the oven, its butter chips melt rapidly. But because the dough is firm, its center doesn't become soft before the edges are sufficiently baked, reducing the risk of collapse or overexpansion. Freezing also gives us the ability to bake a wider variety of flavors without having to make them from scratch every morning. It allows us to plan ahead, producing larger quantities of pastries more efficiently—part of the "work smarter, not harder" mentality we subscribe to.

To make biscuits and scones for freezing, mix them, cut them, wrap them tightly with plastic, and freeze for up to 2 weeks. Then bake the pastries from frozen the day you plan to serve them. They will hold their shape better than the ones baked immediately after cutting. This time-saving tip makes biscuits and scones an ideal baked good for busy bakers who like to entertain. Just pretend they never went in the freezer to begin with, brush with heavy cream or beaten egg, and finish as the recipe indicates, adding 3 to 5 minutes to the baking time.

HERBY COTTAGE CHEESE SCONES

MAKES 10 SCONES

6 scallions

1 tablespoon olive oil

⅔ cup (85 g) whole-grain all-purpose wheat flour, such as Sonora or Frederick

⅔ cup (90 g) all-purpose flour, plus extra for dusting

½ cup (65 g) fine cornmeal

1 tablespoon sugar

1½ teaspoons baking powder

¼ teaspoon baking soda

1 teaspoon kosher salt

½ cup (112 g/1 stick/4 ounces) cold unsalted butter, cut into ½-inch (1.25 cm) cubes

2 tablespoons minced fresh dill

2 tablespoons minced fresh chives

1 teaspoon finely grated lemon zest

¼ teaspoon freshly cracked black pepper, plus extra to taste

1¼ cups (295 ml) 4% cottage cheese

1 large egg plus 1 large beaten egg for brushing

Dash of hot sauce, such as Tabasco

Coarse sea salt, such as Maldon, for sprinkling

These garden-inspired scones are a hit year round, but extra special in the spring and early summer when fragrant herbs grow rampant. I typically hydrate scones with cream or buttermilk, but in this case I use cottage cheese, giving the scones a sort of 1970s vintage feel. Cottage cheese is made by curdling milk with an acid, like vinegar or lemon juice, which separates the curds from the whey. The curds are then drained, rinsed to remove excess acidity, and sometimes mixed with cream. It may seem unusual to stir this retro breakfast staple into your scone dough, but it creates a tender, flavorful crumb that stays moist long after baking.

This is the kind of recipe that necessitates a mild-tasting flour such as Sonora wheat, ensuring nothing takes away from the delicate herbs. In addition to Sonora or other soft wheat flour (see My Favorite Flours, page 313), I use refined all-purpose flour and fine yellow cornmeal.

You'll find yourself mincing herbs to add to the mix. Make sure to use a sharp chef's knife that won't bruise the herby bits; this helps them retain their flavor and aroma. Roasting the scallions softens and caramelizes them a bit. I also add lemon zest and cracked black pepper. Both play a supporting role, never overpowering the herbs. To finish, garnish with a few flakes of crunchy salt, such as Maldon.

Smeared with butter, cream cheese, or even more cottage cheese, these scones are a dreamy addition to a weekend breakfast or afternoon tea. They also pair perfectly with smoked salmon or egg salad. For an elegant appetizer, they can be baked into smaller versions of themselves (see the variation that follows).

continues

1. Place an oven rack in the middle position and preheat the oven to 350°F (175°C).

2. Place the scallions on a rimmed baking sheet and drizzle with the olive oil. Roast until tender, 6 to 8 minutes. When the bulb part of a scallion can be easily pierced with a paring knife, the scallions are ready. Let them cool completely. Trim the roots and tops, leaving all the white part and 2 inches (5 cm) of the green part, and chop them roughly.

3. Increase the oven temperature to 400°F (205°C). Line another rimmed baking sheet with parchment paper.

4. Combine the flours, cornmeal, sugar, baking powder, baking soda, and salt in a mixing bowl. Add the butter cubes and toss to combine. Quickly cut the butter cubes into the dry ingredients by pinching the butter with your fingertips—imagine you're snapping your fingers—until the mixture resembles a coarse meal with butter pieces the size of cornflakes. Add the scallions, dill, chives, lemon zest, and black pepper and toss to combine.

5. Using your hands, make a well in the center of the mixture. Whisk the cottage cheese with the egg and hot sauce and pour into the well. Toss gently with both hands (as if tossing a salad) until a rough dough is formed.

6. To shape the scones, transfer the dough to a lightly floured surface. Pat it down into a disk about 6 inches (15 cm) in diameter and 1 inch (2.5 cm) thick. Using a large chef's knife, slice into 10 equal wedges (as you would a cake or a pie).

7. Transfer each individual scone to the prepared baking sheet, placing them at least 2 inches (5 cm) apart. Brush with the beaten egg, then season with a sprinkle of coarse sea salt and black pepper. Bake for 10 minutes, then rotate the baking sheet and bake for another 10 to 12 minutes, until the edges of the scones are golden. These are delicious while still warm, but you can also serve them at room temperature.

VARIATION

Cocktail Scones

To make cocktail scones, divide the dough into 3 equal portions and pat each down into a disk about 4 inches (10 cm) in diameter and ¾ inch (2 cm) thick. Cut each disk into 8 wedges. Finish as directed in the main recipe. You'll end up with 24 mini scones. Bake on two baking sheets for 12 minutes, then rotate the sheets and switch their positions in the oven. Bake for another 10 to 12 minutes, until golden.

BRUNCH RED PEPPER AND GOAT CHEESE SCONES

MAKES 15 SCONES

EQUIPMENT: 2-inch (5 cm) round biscuit cutter

- 1 cup (130 g) whole-grain all-purpose wheat flour, such as Sonora or Frederick, plus extra for dusting
- 1 cup (130 g) whole-grain spelt flour
- 1 tablespoon sugar
- 1½ teaspoons baking powder
- ¾ teaspoon baking soda
- 1½ teaspoons kosher salt
- 1 teaspoon smoked paprika
- ½ cup (112 g/1 stick/4 ounces) cold unsalted butter, cut into ½-inch (1.25 cm) cubes
- ½ cup (120 g) diced roasted red peppers, such as piquillo peppers
- 1 cup (130 g) crumbled fresh goat cheese
- 1 tablespoon minced fresh flat-leaf parsley
- ¾ cup (180 ml) buttermilk
- 1 large egg, beaten

When a beloved family member was granted Spanish citizenship, I decided to create a scone to celebrate. We were gathering for brunch, so a warm, savory treat seemed like just the thing. Naturally, the occasion called for Spanish ingredients: roasted piquillo peppers, fresh goat cheese, and spelt (see My Favorite Flours, page 313), an ancient relative of wheat currently experiencing a vigorous revival in the Iberian Peninsula. Inspired by the communal spirit of pull-apart breads, I cut the scones small, then placed them close together so they touched as they expanded while baking. The result was a real crowd pleaser: delicious and interactive. Serve these scones warm, right in the tray in which they were baked, allowing your guests to tear them off in a celebratory fashion.

1. Place an oven rack in the middle position and preheat the oven to 400°F (205°C). Line a rimmed baking sheet with parchment paper.

2. Combine the flours, sugar, baking powder, baking soda, salt, and smoked paprika in a mixing bowl. Add the butter cubes and toss to combine. Quickly cut the butter into the dry ingredients by pinching the butter with your fingertips—imagine you're snapping your fingers—until the mixture resembles a coarse meal with butter pieces the size of cornflakes. Add the peppers, goat cheese, and parsley and toss to combine.

3. Using your hands, make a well in the center of the mixture. Pour the buttermilk into the well and toss with both hands (as if tossing a salad) until a rough dough is formed.

continues

4. Transfer the dough to a lightly floured surface. Using a rolling pin, flatten into a rough rectangle that's about 1 inch (2.5 cm) tall. Using a 2-inch (5 cm) biscuit cutter, cut as many scones as possible, gather the scraps, knead back into a dough, flatten once again, and cut a few more scones. Repeat this process until you have no dough left; you should end up with 15 scones.

5. Transfer the scones to the prepared baking sheet, placing them ½ inch (1.25 cm) apart—close enough so they will touch as they expand in the oven. Brush with the beaten egg.

6. Bake for 12 minutes. Then rotate the baking sheet and bake for another 10 to 12 minutes, until the tops of the scones are golden. These scones are delicious while still warm, but you can also serve them at room temperature.

RHUBERRY ROLY POLY

MAKES 8 ROLY POLYS

- 1½ cups (195 g) whole-grain all-purpose wheat flour, such as Sonora or Frederick, plus extra for dusting
- ¼ cup (50 g) sugar, plus extra for sprinkling
- 2 teaspoons baking powder
- ½ cup (112 g/1 stick/4 ounces) cold unsalted butter, cut into ½-inch (1.25 cm) cubes
- ½ cup (75 g) chopped crystallized ginger (optional)
- ½ cup (120 ml) heavy cream, plus extra for brushing
- ⅓ cup (80 ml) Rhuberry Jam (page 76)

Roly poly is the whimsical name for a scone with sweet-tart jam woven throughout in a pinwheel pattern. To build the roly poly, you'll work the scone dough into a block, then roll it into a rectangle. From there, you'll spread jam over it, roll it like a jelly roll, and cut it into slices.

These call on a jam that combines raspberries and rhubarb—aka rhuberry. It's a Friends & Family favorite, made when the Southern California seasons bestow a wealth of ruby-red berries on the bakery. A touch of floral, tangy rhubarb keeps all the sweetness in check. Use a thick, well-set jam, which will hold its shape in the baked scone.

I often include crystallized ginger in the dough to complement the puckery jam. It does make slicing the roly polys somewhat challenging, but if you're up for it, make sure to use a sharp chef's knife. Even when the pinwheels are imperfect, they bake into delightful treats.

I like a mild-tasting whole-wheat flour for this recipe, one that won't take away from the fruitiness of the jam or the zing of the crystallized ginger. The flour can be on the softer side, like Sonora, Frederick, or Sirvinta (see My Favorite Flours, page 313). A harder or redder wheat would also work.

1. Line a rimmed baking sheet with parchment paper. Coat the parchment paper generously with nonstick spray. This step will prevent the jam-filled roly polys from sticking to the paper.

2. Combine the flour, sugar, and baking powder in a mixing bowl. Add the butter cubes and toss to combine. Quickly cut the butter cubes into the dry ingredients by pinching the butter with your fingertips—imagine you're snapping your fingers—until the mixture resembles a coarse meal with butter pieces the size of cornflakes. Mix in the crystallized ginger, if using.

3. Using your hands, make a well in the center of the mixture. Pour the cream into the well and toss with both hands (as if tossing a salad) until the mixture comes together. Transfer to a lightly floured surface and knead into a ball.

continues

4. Line a work surface with a sheet of parchment paper (or plastic wrap). Transfer the dough to the parchment paper. Using a rolling pin, flatten the dough into an 8-by-8½-inch (20 by 22 cm) rectangle. If the dough is too sticky, dust the rolling pin lightly with flour. Orient the dough so the longer side of the rectangle is parallel to your shoulders. Using an offset spatula, spread the jam over the dough, leaving a ½-inch (1.25 cm) border around the edges.

5. To roll, lift the bottom edge of the parchment paper and gently roll the jam-covered dough into a log away from you, as you would a jelly roll. Wrap the log tightly with the parchment paper and chill in the freezer for 1 hour, until firm but not completely frozen. This step will help with the slicing.

6. Place an oven rack in the middle position and preheat the oven to 400°F (205°C).

7. Unwrap the chilled log onto the work surface. Using a sharp chef's knife, trim ¼ inch (6 mm) off each end of the log, then slice into 8 even pinwheels, 1 inch (2.5 cm) thick. Be gentle when slicing to avoid the jam from squeezing out of the pinwheel and distorting the swirl pattern. If some of it does come out, don't fret—it will fall into place as the roly polys expand in the oven.

8. Place the roly polys jam side up on the prepared sheet, at least 2 inches (5 cm) apart. Using a pastry brush, coat the tops of each one with heavy cream and sprinkle generously with sugar. Bake for 10 minutes. Then rotate the baking sheet and bake for another 10 minutes, until the edges of the roly polys are golden.

9. Remove from the sheet while still warm. The jam may cause them to stick to the parchment paper, but a little coercing with an offset spatula will do the trick. Serve warm or at room temperature.

RHUBERRY JAM

MAKES ABOUT 1¼ CUPS (300 ML)

¾ cup (150 g) sugar
½ cup (120 ml) water
½ vanilla bean
2 cups (225 g) fresh or frozen raspberries
2 cups (225 g) rhubarb, cut into ½-inch (1.25 cm) pieces

Put the sugar in a medium saucepan. Add the water to moisten the sugar, but do not stir. Split the vanilla bean lengthwise with a paring knife, scrape out the sticky pulp with the back of the knife, and put both pulp and pod in the pot. Cook over high heat until the mixture comes to a boil. Lower the heat to medium and reduce the mixture to a thick syrup, 3 to 5 minutes. Add the raspberries and rhubarb and cook for 8 minutes while stirring vigorously with a wooden spoon. (Stirring is crucial because it breaks down the fruit while preventing overcaramelization, which may cause the jam to stick to the bottom of the pan.) To test the jam's readiness, chill a small plate in the freezer, spoon a bit of jam onto it, and run your finger through the jam. If your finger leaves a trace on the plate, the jam is ready. Transfer to a heatproof container and let it cool completely. Remove the vanilla bean and discard. The jam can be stored in the refrigerator for up to 1 month.

VARIATIONS

Raspberry Jam
Omit the rhubarb and use 4 cups (450 g) fresh or frozen raspberries.

Strawberry-Rhubarb Jam
Use 2 cups (300 g) fresh hulled and quartered strawberries instead of the raspberries. (Always use fresh strawberries for jam. Frozen strawberries tend to lack acidity and make a dull jam.)

Blackberry Jam with a Touch of Lime
Use 4 cups (480 g) fresh or frozen blackberries instead of the raspberry and rhubarb combo. When the jam is ready, stir in the finely grated zest and juice of 1 lime.

CLOCKWISE: Apricot Jam (page 297), Blackberry Jam, Strawberry-Rhubarb Jam, Rhuberry Jam

Banana Pancakes (page 88)

CHAPTER 3

PANCAKES AND FRIENDS

Recipes

Pancakes for Purists   84
Blueberry Pancakes   86
Banana Pancakes   88
Pumpkin Pancakes   89
Apple Upside-Down Pancakes   91
Gluten-Free Pancakes   94
Yeasted Pancakes   96
Sourdough Pancakes Two Ways   98
   Overnight Sourdough Pancakes   99
   Don't Wait Sourdough Discard Pancakes   100
Kaiserschmarrn (Austrian Soufflé Pancake)   101
Swedish Pancakes   103
1970s Multigrain Pancakes   106
Hearty Pancake Mix for Campers   107
Dutch Baby   108
Crispy Flax Seed Waffles   110
Sweet and Savory French Toasts   112
   Stuffed Ham, Cheddar, and Scallion French Toast   113
   Honey French Toast with a Touch of Cardamom and Orange   114

Pancakes of all shapes and sizes are a grain lover's best friend. Unlike more finicky flour-based goods, pancakes are forgiving. If push comes to shove, just slather 'em in butter, jam, or syrup. It's a delicious, low-pressure pursuit. That said, there are techniques and tips to keep in mind for pancake success. Let's get into it.

First and foremost, flour. Too much can make for dense pancakes; too little will result in a runny batter. If experimenting with a new-to-you grain, this may take trial and error. Don't be afraid to add more liquid if the batter feels overly thick, or more flour if it seems alarmingly loose; trust your intuition. And speaking of liquid, buttermilk reigns supreme. The cultured dairy stalwart adds tangy complexity, but also acid to activate the baking soda, helping the pancakes become their best, fluffiest selves. (To make nondairy buttermilk, just combine 1 tablespoon of lemon juice or apple cider vinegar with 1 cup of your go-to dairy substitute. Let it rest a few minutes before using; it will curdle slightly. Once combined with the remaining ingredients, the citrus or vinegar will play the same role as the lactic acid in the buttermilk.)

Butter in the batter is essential. It adds richness, tenderness, and, of course, a hit of buttery flavor. Melting beforehand ensures it will emulsify and incorporate easily into the batter. Eggs, meanwhile, bring both structure and moisture. As is always the case, use the best eggs and dairy you're comfortable purchasing. High-quality butter and buttermilk and fresh, golden-yolked eggs make for tastier pancakes.

From the hearty sourdough flapjacks made by Alaskan gold seekers to the cloudlike Austrian creation called Kaiserschmarrn, there's a pancake for every palate and occasion. In this chapter you'll find a wide array—yeasted, artificially leavened, sourdough, pan-fried, baked, and more, as well as recipes for crispy waffles and custardy French toasts.

Salt, vanilla extract, and sugar are flavor enhancers. Without them, your pancakes may be bland. Sugar also aids in browning and caramelization, so don't omit it! When it comes to leavening, I employ double the amount of baking powder as I do baking soda. The latter can turn batters metallic-tasting. Plus, too much baking soda will neutralize the tangy flavor of acidic ingredients such as lemon or buttermilk. Another thing to bear in mind is that soda contributes most to spread, while powder works more magic in the puffing department. A proper ratio seals the deal, maximizing the trinity: flavor, spread, and rise.

Now that your ingredients are ready to rock, remember: You mustn't overmix. It's why I insist on whisking together liquids before adding them to the dries. Gluten development isn't necessary here and will just make for tough flapjacks. Mix just until there are no visible dry patches or large lumps; a bit of an uneven consistency is fine.

Your batter is ready, your griddle is out; let's talk cookery. For me, the perfect pancake is 6 inches (15 cm) in diameter, made from roughly ½ cup (120 ml) of batter. However, at home, when you're cooking breakfast for more than one, it makes more sense to make them a little smaller: 4 inches (10 cm) in diameter, made from ¼ cup (60 ml) of batter. When making classic flapjacks, stovetop frying is key. Start by heating the pan or griddle over medium heat. When it's hot (a drop or two of water flicked onto it should sizzle), coat the surface with a small amount of oil and butter—butter brings the warm, toasty flavor, while oil ups the smoke point and nonstick properties. Ladle on the batter, using the back of the spoon to coax it into a circle. When small bubbles begin forming across the pancake's surface and the edges start to set, it's flipping time. Be confident and quick about it. Whatever you do, do not pat, smash, or squash the pancake to flatten it: We want tender, airy flapjacks, not dense, compressed ones!

The first pancake is an opportunity to adjust your heat level and cook time and shake off any pancake-flipping rustiness. Worst-case scenario? There's a misshapen, under- or overcooked cake, aka a snack for the hardworking flapjack flipper. Be sure to wipe the cooking surface with a paper towel between pancakes. That way, you won't pick up any burnt bits and can start fresh. Stash the finished pancakes on a baking sheet or heatproof dish covered with a lid or foil to keep them warm.

If you're dealing with slow risers or waiting on other breakfast components still coming together, don't stress. Slide the finished pancakes into a 275°F (135°C) oven, covered with foil or a lid. They may lose a bit of their fresh-off-the-griddle crispness, but they'll still be excellent, and likely smothered in syrup anyhow. The side of the pancake that first hits the griddle is typically more evenly browned and presentation-ready, so when serving up a stack, I ensure the pretty sides are face-up. All toppings are welcome: maple or fruit-based syrups, jams and jellies, seasonal fruit, and dollops of dairy. Want a pro tip? Slip a pat of butter between each pancake, so it melts with the warmth of the stack.

PANCAKE FAMILY TREE

Yeasted

This style of pancake employs commercial **yeast**, added directly to the batter or to a pre-ferment. They're a speedier affair than naturally leavened pancakes but take a bit longer than artificially leavened ones. They have an especially plush, pillowy texture thanks to the rising power of the yeast, and a complex, deep flavor as a result of the fermentation process.

Artificially Leavened

Artificially leavened pancakes rely on baking powder and/or baking soda, making them one of the quicker options. Think of your standard American diner pancakes and their relatives. This flapjack variety is light, fluffy, and almost always served in a stack.

Naturally Leavened

Naturally leavened pancakes get their lift from a wild yeast source, like sourdough starter. Just like sourdough bread, they require a long fermentation time, which gives the wild yeasts an opportunity to metabolize carbs and produce carbon dioxide. With the rise in popularity of sourdough bread in recent years, sourdough discard pancakes have also proliferated. Their batters typically combine natural and artificial leavening, since sourdough discard is past its prime. True naturally leavened pancakes are made without commercial yeast or rising agents.

Thin Versus Thick

Thin pancakes—think Indian dosas or French crepes, as well as similar offerings like Icelandic pönnukaka and Hungarian palacsinta—are delicate and lacy. Their thinness allows for quick, even cooking, which results in an extremely tender texture. The batter contains no leavening agents. This style of pancake lends itself well to stuffing with any number of sweet or savory fillings.

Thick pancakes, like the American diner-style ones, are fluffy and substantial. Their height usually comes from a leavening agent, which allows them to rise. This style of pancake is typically griddled or pan-fried to develop that soft-on-the-inside yet crisp-on-the-outside texture.

Pan-Fried Versus Baked

A defining characteristic of **pan-fried** pancakes, cooked on a stovetop griddle or in a skillet, is their golden-brown exterior. This method makes for a quick cook time and ample control over the process. It's used for both pancakes that are soft on the inside and have a thin, flavorful crust—like johnnycakes—and ones that are light and delicate, like blintzes.

Baked pancakes have a lofty presence. Oven heat comes at the batter from all angles, resulting in a more substantial rise than pan-frying. Depending on the style of pancake, baking can yield a thicker crust, too. One major benefit to baking pancakes, aside from the impressive height, is hands-off cooking. This makes them great for serving a crowd. Bake a large pancake to serve in wedges and avoid being glued to the griddle.

PANCAKES FOR PURISTS

MAKES 10 PANCAKES

EQUIPMENT: large nonstick skillet, cast-iron pan, or electric griddle

1 cup (130 g) whole-grain all-purpose wheat flour, such as Sonora or Frederick
2 tablespoons sugar
1½ teaspoons baking powder
¾ teaspoon baking soda
½ teaspoon kosher salt
1 cup (240 ml) buttermilk
2 large eggs
1 teaspoon vanilla extract
3 tablespoons unsalted butter, melted and cooled slightly, plus extra for pan-frying and serving
Vegetable oil for pan-frying
Maple syrup and/or other toppings for serving

For many of us, pancakes were the first thing we ever cooked. Tía Nena's recipe was also the first I ever wrote down. It called for one of everything: 1 cup flour, 1 cup milk, 1 egg, 1 teaspoon baking powder, 1 tablespoon sugar, and 1 tablespoon melted butter. The proud owner of an Oster blender, she threw everything in—no whisk needed—then poured the batter right from the pitcher. Her pancakes were flattish, not too fluffy, because the blender liquified them, but on a Saturday morning, I wanted nothing more.

The following recipe is my square one: classic buttermilk pancakes, perfect on their own. Small affairs make the difference: Don't overmix, find the sweet spot and pan-fry at a happy medium temperature, and stack the finished pancakes to keep them warm. The rest is up to you.

Keep in mind that pancakes are a perfect opportunity to get to know new flours. Next time you want to get acquainted with a grain but don't want to enter full baking mode, it's pancake time. Throw together a batter with any wheat—hard or soft, red or white, planted in the fall or the spring—and you'll get an excellent representation of the flour at hand. Even those with low or no gluten can yield fluffy pancakes when blended with other flours. With a riff for every mood, season, and grain, there's no need to relegate flapjack breakfast to Sundays.

1. Put the flour, sugar, baking powder, baking soda, and salt in a mixing bowl. Using your hands, make a well in the center of the dry ingredients. In a separate bowl, whisk together the buttermilk, eggs, and vanilla. Pour the liquid mixture into the well in the dry ingredients. Whisk slowly from the center out to draw the dry ingredients into the liquids. Add the melted butter and whisk to combine. The mixture will be slightly thicker than regular pancake batter.

2. Heat a pan or griddle over medium heat. Add a small amount of oil and a small lump of butter and swirl to coat the pan. Ladle ¼ cup (60 ml) of batter onto the hot surface, using the ladle to shape the batter into a circle. The ideal pancake will be 4 inches (10 cm) in diameter. Depending on the size of the pan, pour one or more pancakes. Flip when small bubbles start to form on top and the edges start setting, 2 to 3 minutes. Pan-fry on the other side until fully cooked, about 1 minute. Use your first pancake to nail the heat and cooking time, and adjust as necessary with the remaining pancakes.

3. Stash the finished pancakes on a baking sheet or heatproof serving dish and cover to keep them warm. Wipe the pan with a paper towel and repeat to make more pancakes. Serve warm with butter, maple syrup, or your favorite toppings.

BLUEBERRY PANCAKES

MAKES 10 PANCAKES

EQUIPMENT: large nonstick skillet, cast-iron pan, or electric griddle

- ¾ cup (100 g) whole-grain all-purpose wheat flour, such as Sonora or Frederick
- ¼ cup (40 g) medium or coarse blue or yellow cornmeal
- 2 tablespoons sugar
- 1½ teaspoons baking powder
- ¾ teaspoon baking soda
- ½ teaspoon kosher salt
- 1 cup (240 ml) buttermilk
- 2 large eggs
- 1 teaspoon vanilla extract
- ½ cup (65 g) frozen blueberries
- 3 tablespoons unsalted butter, melted and cooled slightly, plus extra for pan-frying and serving
- Vegetable oil for pan-frying
- Maple syrup for serving

I've volunteered at local edible gardens in the Los Angeles area for years, popping into their outdoor kitchens every now and again to whip up a recipe with young students. When my friend Julie Johnson, a cooking teacher at the local chapter of the Edible Schoolyard, asked me to cook with her ninth grade class one overcast morning last spring, I knew exactly what we'd make: blueberry blue cornmeal pancakes! The blue-on-blue concoction was a hit with the most curious, polite group of fourteen-year-olds I've ever met.

I often make these with a classic yellow cornmeal as well. I find the sunny yellow pancakes just as enticing as their more whimsical blue siblings. I like to use a medium grind, but you can certainly use a coarse cornmeal, which adds a fun toothy feel. The recipe calls for frozen blueberries. The cold berries chill the batter, making it thicker. When the pancakes hit the griddle they retain some height, creating pillowy pockets in which the berries can cook into tiny jam bombs. These are so flavor packed that you could skip butter and maple syrup, but then again, why would you?

1. Put the flour, cornmeal, sugar, baking powder, baking soda, and salt in a mixing bowl. Using your hands, make a well in the center of the dry ingredients. In a separate bowl, whisk together the buttermilk, eggs, and vanilla. Pour the liquid mixture into the well in the dry ingredients. Whisk slowly from the center out to draw the dry ingredients into the liquids. Add the melted butter and whisk to combine. Gently fold in the blueberries using a silicone spatula. The mixture will be slightly thicker than regular pancake batter.

2. Heat a pan or griddle over medium heat. Add a small amount of oil and a small lump of butter and swirl to coat the pan. Ladle ¼ cup (60 ml) of batter onto the hot surface, using the ladle to shape the batter into a circle. The ideal pancake will be 4 inches (10 cm) in diameter. Depending on the size of the pan, pour 1 or more pancakes.

3. Flip when small bubbles start to form on top and the edges start setting, 2 to 3 minutes. Pan-fry on the other side until fully cooked, about 1 minute. Use your first pancake to nail the heat and cooking time, and adjust as necessary with the remaining pancakes.

4. Stash the finished pancakes on a baking sheet or heatproof serving dish and cover to keep them warm. Wipe the pan with a paper towel and repeat to make more pancakes. Serve warm with butter and maple syrup.

BANANA PANCAKES

MAKES 11 TO 12 PANCAKES

EQUIPMENT: large nonstick skillet, cast-iron pan, or electric griddle

1 cup (130 g) whole-grain all-purpose or hard wheat flour, such as Sonora or Red Fife
2 tablespoons sugar
1½ teaspoons baking powder
¾ teaspoon baking soda
½ teaspoon kosher salt
1 cup (240 ml) buttermilk
2 large eggs
1 teaspoon vanilla extract
1 small banana (100 g/3½ ounces), grated, plus extra sliced bananas for serving (optional)
3 tablespoons unsalted butter, melted and cooled slightly, plus extra for pan-frying and serving
Vegetable oil for pan-frying
Maple syrup and/or other toppings for serving

Most banana pancakes are plain flapjacks with banana slices arranged on top during frying, and this works. However, I like adding grated bananas to the batter to maximize the fruit factor and create a fluffy banana bread–like texture. The bananas will still contribute moisture and sweetness, but you'll get shavings of fruit throughout. Whole-grain flours do well in high-hydration batters like this one; choose a flour with noticeable bran.

1. Put the flour, sugar, baking powder, baking soda, and salt in a mixing bowl. Using your hands, make a well in the center of the dry ingredients.

2. In a separate bowl, whisk together the buttermilk, eggs, vanilla, and banana. Pour the liquid mixture into the well in the dry ingredients. Whisk slowly from the center out to draw the dry ingredients into the liquids. Add the melted butter and whisk to combine. The mixture will be slightly thicker than regular pancake batter.

3. Heat a pan or griddle over medium heat. Add a small amount of oil and a small lump of butter and swirl to coat the pan. Ladle ¼ cup (60 ml) of batter onto the hot surface, using the ladle to shape the batter into a circle. The ideal pancake will be 4 inches (10 cm) in diameter. Depending on the size of the pan, pour 1 or more pancakes. Flip when small bubbles start to form on top and the edges start setting, 2 to 3 minutes. Pan-fry on the other side until fully cooked, about 1 minute. Use your first pancake to nail the heat and cooking time, and adjust as necessary with the remaining pancakes.

4. Stash the finished pancakes on a baking sheet or heatproof serving dish and cover to keep them warm. Wipe the pan with a paper towel and repeat to make more pancakes. Serve warm with butter, maple syrup, sliced bananas, or your favorite toppings.

PUMPKIN PANCAKES

MAKES 10 PANCAKES

EQUIPMENT: large nonstick skillet, cast-iron pan, or electric griddle

- 1 cup (130 g) whole-grain hard red wheat flour, such as Turkey Red or Red Fife
- 2 tablespoons sugar
- 1½ teaspoons baking powder
- ¾ teaspoon baking soda
- ½ teaspoon kosher salt
- 1½ teaspoons ground cinnamon
- ½ teaspoon freshly grated nutmeg
- ½ teaspoon ground cloves
- 1 cup (240 ml) buttermilk
- 2 large eggs
- 1 teaspoon vanilla extract
- ½ cup (165 g) Pumpkin Puree (page 90) or canned
- 3 tablespoons unsalted butter, melted and cooled slightly, plus extra for pan-frying and serving
- Vegetable oil for pan-frying
- Maple syrup and/or other toppings for serving

These pancakes are delicious with assertive red wheats. They can also be made with spelt, which gives them a rust-like hue. If you're feeling inspired, roast your own squash (see page 90). To serve, try a spoonful of browned butter instead of the customary butter lump or even softened cream cheese. These pancakes shine with a touch of sorghum syrup or other old-school fall staples like apple cider jelly, mincemeat, or pumpkin butter.

1. Put the flour, sugar, baking powder, baking soda, salt, cinnamon, nutmeg, and cloves in a mixing bowl.

2. Using your hands, make a well in the center of the dry ingredients. In a separate bowl, whisk together the buttermilk, eggs, vanilla, and pumpkin puree. Pour the liquid mixture into the well in the dry ingredients. Whisk slowly from the center out to draw the dry ingredients into the liquids. Add the melted butter and whisk to combine. The mixture will be slightly thicker than regular pancake batter.

3. Heat a pan or griddle over medium heat. Add a small amount of oil and a small lump of butter and swirl to coat the pan. Ladle ¼ cup (60 ml) of batter onto the hot surface, using the ladle to shape the batter into a circle. The ideal pancake will be 4 inches (10 cm) in diameter. Depending on the size of the pan, pour 1 or more pancakes. Flip when small bubbles start to form on top and the edges start setting, 2 to 3 minutes. Pan-fry on the other side until fully cooked, about 1 minute. Use your first pancake to nail the heat and cooking time, and adjust as necessary with the remaining pancakes.

4. Stash the finished pancakes on a baking sheet or heatproof serving dish and cover to keep them warm. Wipe the pan with a paper towel and repeat to make more pancakes. Serve warm with butter, maple syrup, or your favorite toppings.

PUMPKIN PUREE

MAKES ABOUT 2 CUPS

1 small (565 g/1¼ pounds) winter squash, such as butternut, kabocha, red kuri, or honeynut

Place an oven rack in the middle position and preheat the oven to 375°F (190°C). Halve the squash with a large chef's knife and scrape out the seeds. Put the halves on a roasting pan, cut sides down, add ½ cup (120 ml) water to the bottom of the pan, and cover with aluminum foil. Bake for 50 to 60 minutes, until very tender. To check if the squash is done, carefully invert one of the halves and press the flesh with the back of a fork—if it mashes easily, the squash is ready. Cool until safe to handle, but not completely—it will puree better while still warm. Carefully scoop out the flesh with a spoon, put it in a food processor, and puree until smooth. Depending on the size of your squash, you may have to work in batches. Let the puree cool completely, then refrigerate in an airtight container until ready to use. The chilled puree will keep for 1 week. You can also store it in the freezer for up to 2 months.

APPLE UPSIDE-DOWN PANCAKES

MAKES 10 PANCAKES

EQUIPMENT: large nonstick skillet, cast-iron pan, or electric griddle

FOR THE APPLE SLICES

1 firm apple, cored, cut in half lengthwise, and sliced into twenty ¼-inch (6 mm) half rings
2 tablespoons unsalted butter, melted
2 tablespoons packed dark brown sugar
¼ teaspoon ground cinnamon

FOR THE BATTER

¾ cup (100 g) whole-grain all-purpose wheat flour, such as Sonora or Frederick
¼ cup (40 g) whole-grain buckwheat flour
2 tablespoons granulated sugar
1½ teaspoons baking powder
¾ teaspoon baking soda
½ teaspoon kosher salt
1 cup (240 ml) buttermilk
2 large eggs
1 teaspoon vanilla extract
3 tablespoons unsalted butter, melted and cooled slightly, plus extra for pan-frying and serving
Vegetable oil for pan-frying
Maple syrup for serving

These pancakes are pretty darn magical. To start, thin slices of tart apple get tossed in a buttery brown sugar–cinnamon mixture. The apples are sautéed until just beginning to brown, covered with buckwheat batter, and griddled until golden. A few minutes later?

Hearty, whole-grain pancakes topped with spiced, caramelized apple rings. When the fall and winter holidays roll around, the recipe comes in handy; it's a fun project to do with younger cooks or houseguests. Let others help you slice and season the apples, put your best pancake maker in charge of pan-frying, and embrace the chaos of tag-teaming breakfast on a holiday morning.

Just like in the Buckwheat Joy Muffins (page 46), buckwheat's dual personality as a delicate, fine-textured grain with bold, earthy notes makes it a friend to apples. The buckwheat makes for a fluffy, custardy batter. Do note that this recipe can't be considered entirely gluten free. To change that, I recommend using Roxana's Whole-Grain Gluten-Free Flour (page 95) instead of whole-grain all-purpose flour and adding ¼ teaspoon xanthan gum, which helps the batter bind to prevent the pancakes from falling apart as you flip them.

When it comes to apple selection, opt for something just sweet enough. I recommend a baking apple such as Fuji, Pink Lady, Gala, Honeycrisp, Braeburn, or any heirloom variety that's firm enough to withstand cooking on a griddle.

continues

1. Toss the apple slices with the melted butter, brown sugar, and cinnamon in a bowl.

2. Put the flours, sugar, baking powder, baking soda, and salt in a mixing bowl. Using your hands, make a well in the center of the dry ingredients. In a separate bowl, whisk together the buttermilk, eggs, and vanilla. Pour the liquid mixture into the well in the dry ingredients. Whisk slowly from the center out to draw the dry ingredients into the liquids. Add the melted butter and whisk to combine. The mixture will be slightly thicker than regular pancake batter.

3. Heat a pan or griddle over medium-low heat. Add a small amount of oil and a small lump of butter and swirl to coat the pan. Lay 2 or 3 apple half rings on the hot surface and sauté for 1 minute on each side. The apples will soften and caramelize slightly.

4. Ladle ¼ cup (60 ml) of batter on top of the apples, using the ladle to spread the batter over the apples. The ideal pancake will be 4 inches (10 cm) in diameter. Depending on the size of the pan, pour 1 or more pancakes. Flip when small bubbles start to form on top and the edges start setting, 2 to 3 minutes. Pan-fry on the other side until brown and fully cooked, 1 minute. Use your first pancake to nail the heat and cooking time, and adjust as necessary with the remaining pancakes. Be sure to keep your temperature low or the apples can burn.

5. Stash the finished pancakes on a baking sheet or heatproof serving dish and cover to keep them warm. Wipe the pan with a paper towel and repeat to make more pancakes. Serve warm with butter and maple syrup.

GLUTEN-FREE PANCAKES

MAKES 10 TO 11 PANCAKES

EQUIPMENT: large nonstick skillet, cast-iron pan, or electric griddle

1 cup (145 g) Roxana's Whole-Grain Gluten-Free Flour (opposite)
2 tablespoons sugar
1½ teaspoons baking powder
¾ teaspoon baking soda
½ teaspoon kosher salt
¼ teaspoon xanthan gum (optional)
1 cup (240 ml) buttermilk
2 large eggs
1 teaspoon vanilla extract
3 tablespoons unsalted butter, melted and slightly cooled, plus extra for pan-frying and serving
Maple syrup for serving

This pancake recipe is made with my tried-and-true whole-grain, gluten-free flour blend. Mixing this pancake batter is identical to mixing any other pancake. Of course, there is no gluten to overwork, so overmixing is never an issue. To prevent pancakes from falling apart, xanthan gum—a natural binding substance commonly added to gluten-free recipes—can be whisked into the batter. However, a lot of people can be sensitive to gums (myself included). Luckily, this flour blend is firm enough to hold throughout the pan-frying process so you could leave it out. Be gentle with the flipping and don't get carried away making pancakes that are too large. Gluten-free batters don't keep well because the flours tend to dissolve, so I recommend pan-frying shortly after mixing.

1. Put the flour, sugar, baking powder, baking soda, salt, and xanthan gum (if using) in a mixing bowl. Using your hands, make a well in the center of the dry ingredients. In a separate bowl, whisk together the buttermilk, eggs, and vanilla. Pour the liquid mixture into the well in the dry ingredients. Whisk slowly from the center out to draw the dry ingredients into the liquids. Add the melted butter and whisk to combine.

2. Heat a pan or griddle over medium heat. Add a small amount of oil and a small lump of butter and swirl to coat the pan. Ladle ¼ cup (60 ml) of batter onto the hot surface, using the ladle to shape the batter into a circle. The ideal pancake will be 4 inches (10 cm) in diameter. Depending on the size of the pan, pour 1 or more pancakes. Flip when small bubbles start to form on top and the edges start setting, 2 to 3 minutes. Pan-fry on the other side until fully cooked, 1 minute. Use your first pancake to nail the heat and cooking time, and adjust as necessary with the remaining pancakes.

3. Stash the finished pancakes on a baking sheet or heatproof serving dish and cover to keep them warm. Wipe the pan with a paper towel and repeat to make more pancakes. Serve warm with butter and maple syrup.

ROXANA'S WHOLE-GRAIN GLUTEN-FREE FLOUR

MAKES 1 CUP (145 G) FLOUR

⅓ cup (50 g) brown rice flour
⅓ cup (50 g) whole-grain buckwheat flour
⅓ cup (45 g) whole-grain oat flour

When I came up with this flour, my focus was on flavor and versatility, acknowledging from the get-go that gluten-free flours have limitations. The goal was a formula universal enough to swap for all-purpose flour in a wide range of recipes, using only whole-grain ingredients—none of the modified starches and gums found in supermarket blends. I scored on my first try. Probably because I used three flours I've worked with extensively on their own: brown rice flour, oat flour, and buckwheat flour. All three were sourced from Anson Mills (see page 324). With great building blocks in hand, I only had to nail a ratio. I added them in equal amounts, whisked vigorously to combine, and whipped up some chocolate chip cookies. They were perfect!

Encouraged by my early success, I tried other recipes: muffins, biscuits, scones, cakes, and shortbread. Each flour fulfills a purpose. Oat adds malty notes and great absorption properties, since its bran readily retains moisture. Brown rice brings body and a fine particle size, yielding baked goods with a tender crumb. And buckwheat contributes character, depth, and gluelike binding properties.

1. Combine the flours in a bowl and whisk vigorously to combine.

2. Transfer to a ziplock bag or airtight container, write a label with the date, and store in a cool pantry, refrigerator, or freezer until ready to use. The flour will keep for up to 3 months at room temperature and up to 1 year in the refrigerator or freezer.

YEASTED PANCAKES

MAKES 10 PANCAKES

EQUIPMENT: instant-read thermometer; large nonstick skillet, cast-iron pan, or electric griddle

1 cup (240 ml) whole milk
1 teaspoon instant yeast
1 cup (130 g) whole-grain all-purpose or hard red wheat flour, such as Sonora or Red Fife
¾ teaspoon kosher salt
3 tablespoons unsalted butter, melted and cooled slightly, plus extra for serving
1 tablespoon honey
2 large eggs, separated
2 tablespoons sugar
Vegetable oil for pan-frying
Maple syrup for serving

Adding fermentation to the equation is a cool kitchen experiment for curious bakers. I originally developed these pillowy pancakes for the brunch menu at my old restaurant, Cooks County, where the line cooks had to keep the batter in the refrigerator to prevent the yeast from running amok.

As the batter ferments, the sponge produces lactic acid, which brings depth of flavor and a subtle tartness. My preferred flour is a bold wheat variety like Turkey Red (see My Favorite Flours, page 313); its robust flavor shines here. Because the batter has to ferment, strong flours, like those used in bread making, are ideal. Red wheats respond well, developing wheaty notes akin to freshly baked crusty bread. Interacting with the yeast will actually assuage the flour's glutinous powers, so don't fear, your pancake won't wind up tough.

To lighten it even further, the eggs are separated, then the whites are whipped until they resemble snow and folded into the batter. The result is a crispy pancake with fried buttery edges, a pillowy center, and a pleasant tang from the yeast. I love topping it with dollops of cider jelly or cinnamon-spiked apple compote.

1. Heat the milk in a small saucepan until lukewarm (98–105°F/37–41°C). Pour into a cup, sprinkle the yeast over the warm milk, stir with a spoon to help it dissolve, and let sit for 5 minutes.

2. Meanwhile, sift the flour and salt into a separate bowl. Using your hands, make a well in the center of the dry ingredients. Pour the dissolved yeast mixture, melted butter, honey, and egg yolks into the well and start whisking from the center out to draw the dry ingredients into the liquids. Once the mixture looks smooth, cover with a kitchen towel or plastic wrap and let rise for 1½ to 2 hours, until doubled in size.

3. Beat the egg whites until foamy in a separate bowl. Add the sugar and continue beating until soft peaks form.

4. Using a large silicone spatula, carefully fold the egg whites into the batter with wide, circular scoop-and-fold strokes. Resist the urge to stir rapidly, but do rotate the bowl as you fold to ensure the batter is evenly lightened. Cover and let it rest for another 20 minutes.

5. Heat a pan or griddle over medium heat. Add a small amount of oil and a small lump of butter and swirl to coat the pan. Ladle ¼ cup (60 ml) of batter onto the hot surface, using the ladle to shape the batter into a circle. The ideal pancake will be 4 inches (10 cm) in diameter. Depending on the size of the pan, pour 1 or more pancakes.

6. Flip when small bubbles start to form on top and the edges start setting, 2 to 3 minutes. Pan-fry on the other side until fully cooked, 1 minute. Use your first pancake to nail the heat and cooking time, and adjust as necessary with the remaining pancakes.

7. Stash the finished pancakes on a baking sheet or heatproof serving dish and cover to keep them warm. Wipe the pan with a paper towel and repeat to make more pancakes. Serve warm with butter and maple syrup.

SOURDOUGH PANCAKES TWO WAYS

There are two ways to make sourdough pancakes. The most popular one involves using your sourdough discard. For those of us who bake sourdough regularly, it's a perfect way to repurpose excess starter. Because the starter has lost most of its leavening capabilities, you'll still need to add baking powder and baking soda. It's also a good idea to use milk rather than buttermilk, because the discard is highly acidic. With enough discarded starter on hand, you're just a whiskful away from tender sourdough pancakes. See the recipe for Don't Wait Sourdough Discard Pancakes (page 100).

You can also make sourdough pancakes with a ripe starter at the top of its game, allowing it to be the pancakes' sole leavening source. However, like most legit sourdough recipes, the starter needs time to develop. You can start the process the night before by feeding the starter and letting it ferment overnight.

In the morning, simply add the remaining ingredients and let the batter rest for an hour so the sourdough culture can regain its oomph. This style of pancake descends from Yukon flapjacks, originally made by gold seekers in Alaska during the late nineteenth century. Perfumed with vanilla and leavened with tangy sourdough starter, these hearty flapjacks are chock-full of flavor. The sourdough gives them a uniquely satisfying texture, too: tender yet a bit chewy. I recommend topping these with a thick smear of salted butter and a layer of glossy marmalade. They're great with savory accouterments as well (skip the vanilla): Think herby cream cheese, salty gravlax, and a few fresh dill fronds.

You can use any kind of whole-grain wheat flour; I like a very soft all-purpose wheat, such as Sonora. The predominant flavor will come from the fermentation incited by the sourdough, and a creamy and neutral grain gets the job done.

OVERNIGHT SOURDOUGH PANCAKES

MAKES 10 PANCAKES

EQUIPMENT: large nonstick skillet, cast-iron pan, or electric griddle

FOR THE SPONGE

1 cup (130 g) whole-grain all-purpose wheat flour, such as Sonora or Frederick

¾ cup (180 ml) water

2 tablespoons (25 g) ripe sourdough starter (see page 240)

FOR THE BATTER

¼ cup (30 g) whole-grain all-purpose wheat flour, such as Sonora or Frederick

2 tablespoons sugar

¾ teaspoon kosher salt

¼ cup (60 ml) whole milk

2 large eggs

1 teaspoon vanilla extract

3 tablespoons unsalted butter, melted and cooled slightly, plus extra for pan-frying and serving

Maple syrup and/or other toppings for serving

1. To make the sponge, combine the flour, water, and starter in a bowl large enough to mix the pancake batter after the starter is fully fermented. Whisk to combine, cover with a kitchen towel or plastic wrap, and let it ferment at room temperature until doubled in size, 8 hours or overnight.

2. The next morning, make the batter: Add the flour, sugar, salt, milk, eggs, and vanilla to the sponge and whisk vigorously to combine. Stir in the melted butter, cover once again, and let it sit in a warm spot for 1 hour, or until bubbles appear on the surface.

3. Heat a pan or griddle over medium heat. Add a small amount of oil and a small lump of butter and swirl to coat the pan. Ladle ¼ cup (60 ml) of batter onto the hot surface, using the ladle to shape the batter into a circle. The ideal pancake will be 4 inches (10 cm) in diameter. Depending on the size of the pan, pour one or more pancakes. Flip when small bubbles start to form on top and the edges start setting, 2 to 3 minutes. Pan-fry on the other side until fully cooked, 1 minute. Use your first pancake to nail the heat and cooking time, and adjust as necessary with the remaining pancakes.

4. Stash the finished pancakes on a baking sheet or heatproof serving dish and cover to keep them warm. Wipe the pan with a paper towel and repeat to make more pancakes. Serve warm with butter, maple syrup, or your favorite toppings.

DON'T WAIT SOURDOUGH DISCARD PANCAKES

MAKES 10 TO 11 PANCAKES

EQUIPMENT: large nonstick skillet, cast-iron pan, or electric griddle

- ½ cup (65 g) whole-grain all-purpose flour, such as Sonora or Frederick
- 2 tablespoons sugar
- 1 teaspoon baking powder
- ¾ teaspoon baking soda
- ½ teaspoon kosher salt
- ¾ cup (150 g) sourdough starter discard (see page 240)
- ½ cup (120 ml) whole milk
- 2 large eggs
- 1 teaspoon vanilla extract
- 3 tablespoons unsalted butter, melted and cooled slightly, plus extra for pan-frying and serving
- Maple syrup and/or other toppings for serving

1. Put the flour, sugar, baking powder, baking soda, and salt in a mixing bowl. Using your hands, make a well in the center of the dry ingredients. In a separate bowl, whisk together the sourdough starter discard, milk, eggs, and vanilla. Pour the liquid mixture into the well in the dry ingredients. Whisk slowly from the center out to draw the dry ingredients into the liquids.

2. Add the melted butter and whisk to combine. The mixture will be slightly thicker than regular pancake batter.

3. Heat a pan or griddle over medium heat. Add a small amount of oil and a small lump of butter and swirl to coat the pan. Ladle ¼ cup (60 ml) of batter onto the hot surface, using the ladle to shape the batter into a circle. The ideal pancake will be 4 inches (10 cm) in diameter. Depending on the size of the pan, pour 1 or more pancakes. Flip when small bubbles start to form on top and the edges start setting, 2 to 3 minutes. Pan-fry on the other side until fully cooked, 1 minute. Use your first pancake to nail the heat and cooking time, and adjust as necessary with the remaining pancakes.

4. Stash the finished pancakes on a baking sheet or heatproof serving dish and cover to keep them warm. Wipe the pan with a paper towel and repeat to make more pancakes. Serve warm with butter, maple syrup, or your favorite toppings.

KAISERSCHMARRN (AUSTRIAN SOUFFLÉ PANCAKE)

MAKES ONE 10-INCH (25.5 CM) PANCAKE

EQUIPMENT: 10-inch (25.5 cm) oven-safe nonstick skillet, cast-iron pan, or pie pan

- 1 tablespoon unsalted butter at room temperature
- 6 tablespoons (75 g) granulated sugar
- 4 large eggs at room temperature, separated
- ½ cup (120 ml) sour cream
- 1 tablespoon dark rum or 2 teaspoons vanilla extract
- ¼ cup (35 g) whole-grain all-purpose wheat flour, such as Sonora or Frederick
- ¼ teaspoon cream of tartar
- Confectioners' sugar for dusting
- 2 cups (240 g) strawberries, sliced, for serving

This soufflé pancake is inspired by the legendary Kaiserschmarrn served at Spago in Los Angeles. The dish was made famous by my good friend Sherry Yard and continues to appear on Spago's dessert menu, currently curated by pastry chef Della Gossett—also a dear friend!

A large souffléed pancake of Austrian origin, Kaiserschmarrn means "the emperor's little nothing," potentially alluding to the whispery airiness of the pancake. To achieve its legendary height, you'll bake this pancake, rather than pan-fry it. One large pancake is enough for four, if not five people. Much like a soufflé, the pancake is baked in a buttered and sugared dish or skillet and lightened with beaten egg whites, so it must be enjoyed fresh out of the oven before it begins losing volume.

This pancake contains a minimal amount of flour, since the main players are the whipped eggs. Because so little goes in the recipe, you won't really be able to taste it, so don't choose your flour based on flavor. Just focus on using a whole-grain wheat that is super finely ground. The goal is for it to be easy to fold and distribute into the batter, ensuring it's stable enough to maintain its impressive height.

Though my friends serve this for dessert, I'd encourage you to make it for breakfast. Topped with fresh, peak-season strawberries, it's absolutely transcendent.

1. Place an oven rack in the middle position and preheat the oven to 400°F (205°C).

2. Using a paper towel, spread the soft butter all over the surface of a 10-inch (25.5 cm) nonstick oven-safe skillet, cast-iron pan, or pie plate. Sprinkle with 2 tablespoons of the sugar and shake and swirl to ensure it's completely covered. Tap out the excess and set aside.

continues

3. Beat the egg yolks with another 2 tablespoons sugar in a bowl with a whisk until the mixture is light and creamy, 2 minutes. Mix in the sour cream and rum. Sift the flour over the yolk mixture and fold with a silicone spatula until just combined.

4. In the bowl of a stand mixer fitted with the whisk attachment, whip the egg whites until foamy. Add the remaining 2 tablespoons sugar and the cream of tartar. Continue beating until it forms medium peaks, 2 to 3 minutes.

5. Using a large silicone spatula, carefully fold the egg whites into the egg yolk base with wide, circular scoop-and-fold strokes. Resist the urge to stir rapidly, but do rotate the bowl as you fold to ensure the batter is evenly lightened.

6. Transfer the mixture to the prepared pan. Bake for 15 minutes, then rotate the pan and continue to bake for 5 more minutes until puffed and browned. The center should be a bit jiggly while the edges are firm. Dust generously with confectioners' sugar and cut into wedges or spoon large scoops out of the hot pan. Serve immediately, topped with strawberries.

SWEDISH PANCAKES

MAKES 15 SWEDISH PANCAKES

EQUIPMENT: 6-inch (15 cm) nonstick or cast-iron pan

2 cups (480 ml) whole milk
¼ cup (55 g/½ stick/2 ounces) butter, plus extra for serving
½ cup (65 g) whole-grain or dark rye flour
½ cup (65 g) whole-grain all-purpose wheat flour, such as Sonora or Frederick
¾ teaspoon fine sea salt
2 large eggs
Strawberry-Rhubarb Jam (page 76) or store-bought, for serving
Sugar for sprinkling

These pancakes are inspired by a recipe from Brooklyn-based Swedish illustrator and cookbook author Johanna Kindvall. A version of Johanna's pancakes can be found in her stellar cookbook, *Fika: The Art of the Swedish Coffee Break*, where she also mentions a variation in which the pancakes are cooked into silver dollar versions using a cast-iron pan with indented circles known as a plett pan. Traditionally, these are made with refined wheat flour, but a thin, runny batter struck me as the ideal place to incorporate rye flour—one of Scandinavian baking's heavy hitters. I found that using equal amounts of wheat and rye yielded flavorful pancakes that flipped easily without falling apart. The rye also adds a pleasant acidity to the not-too-sweet pancake.

When making American-style pancakes, we avoid overmixing. But when making Swedish pancakes, you'll find yourself whisking vigorously to ensure the batter is lump-free. The milk and butter are heated gently, just enough to encourage the flours to gel. After all that agitation, it's important to let the batter rest, allowing any bubbles generated during the mixing process to dissipate.

Swedish pancakes can be made in advance and reheated before serving, but make sure to cover them with a kitchen towel or plastic wrap so that the edges don't dry out. They can also be made ahead, then stacked, wrapped, and stored in the fridge or freezer until ready to eat.

These are almost always served the same way, smeared with butter and strawberry or lingonberry jam while still warm. As with many Scandinavian preparations, there are slightly different variations across countries in the region. From our Danish baker Maja, who has been working at Friends & Family for almost as long as we've been open, we learned that Danes sprinkle the pancakes with sugar after spreading on the jam, then roll them like a cigar (see photo, page 105). I love this version—the sugar adds great texture.

continues

1. Heat the milk and butter in a small sauté pan over medium-low heat until the butter is completely melted, about 2 minutes. Remove from the heat.

2. Combine the flours and salt in a large mixing bowl. Using your hands, make a well in the center of the dry ingredients. In a separate bowl, whisk the eggs and slowly add the warm milk mixture while whisking vigorously. Pour the liquid mixture into the well in the dry ingredients. Whisk slowly from the center out to draw the dry ingredients into the liquids. Then whisk vigorously to get rid of any lumps.

3. Cover with plastic wrap and let the batter rest in the refrigerator for at least 2 hours and up to 3 days. The mixture will be thinner than regular pancake batter.

4. To make the pancakes, preheat a 6-inch (15 cm) nonstick or cast-iron pan over medium-high heat. Lightly coat with nonstick spray or add a small amount of oil and butter and swirl to coat. Ladle about 2 tablespoons of batter into the hot skillet, swirling immediately so a thin layer of batter coats the entire surface. Cook for 1 minute, then flip with a spatula. Cook for another minute. Use your first pancake to nail the heat and cooking time, and adjust as necessary with the remaining pancakes. Repeat until all the batter has been used.

5. Stash the finished pancakes on a plate or container and cover to prevent the edges from becoming dry and brittle. Serve while still warm or at room temperature, and encourage everyone at the table to schmear their pancake with jam, sprinkle it with sugar, and roll it like a cigar before biting into it.

1970S MULTIGRAIN PANCAKES

MAKES 10 PANCAKES

EQUIPMENT: large nonstick skillet, cast-iron pan, or electric griddle

⅔ cup (90 g) whole-grain hard red wheat flour, such as Turkey Red or Red Fife
3 tablespoons old-fashioned rolled oats
1½ teaspoons baking powder
¾ teaspoon baking soda
½ teaspoon kosher salt
2 teaspoons flax seeds
2 teaspoons sesame seeds
2 tablespoons sunflower seeds
1 cup (240 ml) buttermilk
2 large eggs
2 tablespoons honey
2 tablespoons vegetable oil, plus extra to pan-fry the pancakes
⅓ cup (60 g) cooked short-grain brown rice
Unsalted butter at room temperature for pan-frying and serving
Maple syrup for serving

These multigrain pancakes take inspiration from the flapjacks one might find at a 1970s-style health-food joint. Approach them with an everything-but-the-kitchen-sink mentality. The harder, redder, and coarser the whole-wheat flour you use, the better. To push the grain quotient, oats and cooked brown rice are thrown into the mix.

1. Combine the flour, oats, baking powder, baking soda, and salt with the flax, sesame, and sunflower seeds in a mixing bowl. Using your hands, make a well in the center of the dry ingredients. In a separate bowl, whisk together the buttermilk, eggs, honey, and oil. Pour the liquid mixture into the well and whisk slowly from the center out to draw the dry ingredients into the liquids. Then whisk vigorously to ensure the batter is well combined. Stir in the cooked rice. Let the batter rest at room temperature for 20 minutes to allow the oats to hydrate.

2. Heat a pan or griddle over medium heat. Add a small amount of oil and a small lump of butter and swirl to coat. When the butter is melted, ladle ¼ cup (60 ml) of batter onto the hot surface, using the ladle to shape the batter into a circle. The ideal pancake will be 4 inches (10 cm) in diameter. Depending on the size of the pan, pour 1 or more pancakes. Flip when small bubbles start to form on top and the edges start setting, 2 to 3 minutes. Pan-fry on the other side until fully cooked, 1 minute. Use your first pancake to nail the heat and cooking time, and adjust as necessary with the remaining pancakes.

3. Stash the finished pancakes on a baking sheet or heatproof serving dish and cover to keep them warm. Wipe the pan with a paper towel and repeat to make more pancakes. Serve warm with butter and maple syrup.

HEARTY PANCAKE MIX FOR CAMPERS

MAKES 1 QUART DRY PANCAKE MIX, ENOUGH FOR 10 TO 12 PANCAKES

EQUIPMENT: 1-quart/1-liter mason jar

- ½ cup plus 2 tablespoons (85 g) whole-grain hard red wheat flour, such as Turkey Red or Red Fife
- ½ cup (70 g) oat flour
- ¼ cup (25 g) buttermilk powder
- 1 teaspoon baking powder
- ¾ teaspoon baking soda
- ½ teaspoon kosher salt
- ¼ teaspoon ground cinnamon
- 2 tablespoons sugar
- 2 tablespoons chia seeds

Featuring robust red wheat, toasty oat flour, and crunchy chia or sesame seeds, this mix is ideal for packing in a 1-quart (1-liter) mason jar to bring on your next camping trip. Oat flour swells when hydrated, making the pancakes moist and tender. What really makes this mix a success is the buttermilk powder, which is exactly that—buttermilk that has been dehydrated to a fine powder, retaining all its acidic qualities and reconstituted easily with water. It is inexpensive and easy to find online from brands like King Arthur and Bob's Red Mill. To finish the mix, you'll need water, eggs, oil, and a good shake. Don't forget to label the jar with quantities and instructions reminding you what to do. It makes a stellar gift for the outdoors enthusiast in your life. It's also a sweet housewarming present, and a cool care package add-on for any young adult off to college. Young cooks will love the immediate satisfaction of shaking a jar and making their own pancakes. The recipe yields enough batter for 10 to 12 pancakes or 4 or 5 happy campers. The mix is shelf-stable, but keep in mind that baking powder and baking soda begin losing their effectiveness after 6 months.

1. Sift the flours, buttermilk powder, baking powder, baking soda, salt, cinnamon, and sugar in a bowl. Whisk well to combine. Add the chia seeds and whisk to distribute thoroughly throughout the mix. Use a funnel to pack the dry mix in a 1-quart (1-liter) mason jar. Cover and label. Store in a dark pantry.

Write a label with important ingredient information as well as instructions to prepare the pancake mix. For example:

CAMPING PANCAKE MIX (MAKES 10 TO 12 PANCAKES)

Add to the jar 1 cup water, 2 eggs, and 3 tablespoons oil. Secure the lid and shake vigorously. Heat some oil in a pan. Pour the pancake batter on the hot pan directly from the jar.

Allergens: wheat, oats, seeds, dairy

DUTCH BABY

SERVES 4

EQUIPMENT: 10-inch (25.5 cm) oven-safe skillet or cast-iron pan

3 large eggs at room temperature
¼ cup (35 g) whole-grain all-purpose or hard white wheat flour, such as Sonora or Starr
½ cup (120 ml) whole milk
2 tablespoons granulated sugar
Pinch of kosher salt
2 tablespoons unsalted butter
2 tablespoons confectioners' sugar, for dusting
½ lemon cut into thin wedges, for serving

A Dutch baby is the coolest science project in the breakfast world. The batter for this crepe-pancake-popover hybrid comes together quickly; the trick is in starting the pancake on the stove, then finishing it in a ripping-hot oven where it can puff into its characteristic shape. Once out of the oven, it will deflate into custardy-yet-crisp perfection that should be eaten right away.

To achieve a successful puff, the eggs and milk must be at room temperature. Whisking power and high heat are your best allies, and the agents that will give your Dutch baby lift. You can't possibly overmix the batter because there isn't much gluten. You actually need to whisk somewhat aggressively to encourage a good puff. Stronger wheats, like Starr and Red Fife, make this pancake expand higher. I prefer using a cast-iron pan, but you can use any type of oven-safe skillet. The whole process is fairly quick: just over 25 minutes from start to finish.

This showstopper can be served for breakfast, brunch, or even dessert. A Dutch baby won't require shopping for any specialty ingredients—just the forethought of leaving the eggs and milk at room temperature an hour or two before baking.

1. Place an oven rack in the middle position and preheat the oven to 425°F (220°C).

2. In a medium bowl, whisk vigorously the eggs, flour, milk, granulated sugar, and salt.

3. Heat a 10-inch (25.5 cm) cast-iron pan or other oven-safe skillet over medium heat. Add the butter, carefully swirling the pan to ensure the entire surface is well coated. Add all the batter at once and transfer to the oven. Bake for 20 minutes.

4. Remove from the oven, score into quarters directly in the pan, put the confectioners' sugar in a sifter or fine-mesh sieve to dust over the surface, and serve immediately with the lemon wedges.

CRISPY FLAX SEED WAFFLES

MAKES FOUR TO FIVE 7-INCH (18 CM) WAFFLES

EQUIPMENT: instant-read thermometer, electric waffle iron

1 teaspoon instant yeast
1 cup (240 ml) lukewarm (98–105°F/37–41°C) whole milk
1 tablespoon honey
1 cup (135 g) whole-grain hard red wheat flour, such as Turkey Red or Red Fife
2 tablespoons flax meal
3 tablespoons granulated sugar
1 teaspoon kosher salt
2 large eggs, separated
1 teaspoon vanilla extract
¼ cup (55 g/½ stick/2 ounces) unsalted butter, melted and cooled slightly, plus extra for cooking the waffles and serving
⅓ cup (80 ml) Belgian beer
2 tablespoons confectioners' sugar, for dusting
Toppings as desired for serving (optional)

There are two primary routes for making light, crispy waffles. The more unconventional one involves adding a sparkling liquid, such as sparkling water or cider, to the batter at the last minute, promoting an airy interior and thin crust. It's a bit of a shortcut, yielding fantastic results and allowing for waffle-making at a moment's notice; I certainly recommend it. But the more traditional, well-known method was made famous by the Belgians. Belgian waffles' most distinctive feature is that they're made with yeast rather than artificial leaveners like baking powder and baking soda. This waffle iteration was introduced to the United States at the 1962 Century 21 Exposition in Seattle, thanks to Belgian businessman Walter Cleyman, then again by Maurice Vermersch at the New York World's Fair in 1964. At both events, the waffles were served with whipped cream and strawberries, much like we see them today in diners and coffee shops across the country.

This recipe is a departure from what we've come to identify as the quintessential American waffle, yet just as enticing. Since the batter is leavened with yeast, I use robust wheat flours—think Turkey Red or Yecora Rojo—to make a full-flavored waffle with more personality. To accentuate its bread-like flavor profile (and pay homage to the waffles' ancestors), I finish the batter with a splash of Belgian beer. With their nutty and toasty qualities, ground flax seeds are a great addition to the recipe. I grind the flax into a coarse meal, but you can use the ready-made flax meal available in grocery stores.

1. In a bowl large enough to allow for the batter to rise, sprinkle the yeast over the lukewarm milk. Add the honey, stir with a spoon to help it dissolve, and let sit for 5 minutes. Whisk in the flour, ground flax, 1 tablespoon of the granulated sugar, salt, egg yolks, and vanilla. Add the melted butter and whisk to combine. Cover the bowl with a kitchen towel or plastic wrap and let sit at room temperature for 1½ hours, until doubled in volume.

2. Stir the beer into the risen batter with a silicone spatula. Don't overmix! You don't want to deflate the gassy batter.

3. In the bowl of a stand mixer fitted with the whisk attachment, beat the egg whites with the remaining 2 tablespoons granulated sugar until soft to medium peaks form. Using a large silicone spatula, carefully fold the egg whites into the batter with wide, circular scoop-and-fold strokes. Resist the urge to stir rapidly, but do rotate the bowl as you fold to ensure the batter is evenly lightened.

4. To make the waffles, preheat a waffle iron. Lightly brush the surface with melted butter. Pour in about ¾ cup (180 ml) of the batter and use a spatula to gently spread it over the entire surface. Close the lid and cook according to the manufacturer's instructions until golden. Make three to four more waffles with the remaining batter.

5. To keep warm, line a plate with a kitchen towel, stash the waffles on top, and fold the kitchen towel over the waffles. Keep the plate in a warm spot such as beside the stovetop or in a 200°F (90°C) oven.

6. Put the confectioners' sugar in a sifter or fine-mesh sieve and shake over the surface of the waffles to create a thin, even layer. Serve with butter and your favorite toppings. Freeze leftovers for up to 2 weeks, tightly wrapped in plastic, and reheat in the toaster oven.

SWEET AND SAVORY FRENCH TOASTS

The secret to a great French toast is in the soak. I'd love to believe that simply dipping stale bread into beaten egg and frying it yields an excellent breakfast, but many depressing, dried-out, and unpleasantly eggy French toasts have taught me otherwise. It's true that foamy breads, such as challah and brioche, make the best French toast, but you'll have to invest some time in preparing a well-balanced, custardy bath to wind up with French toast worthy of your time and effort. To score beautifully browned exteriors and a custard-like center, it's ideal to approach French toast the way you would bread pudding.

I couldn't choose between a sweet or savory French toast in this book, so I've included both. The sweet one will make a lasting impression, whether you serve it for breakfast—topped with butter and maple syrup, crème fraîche and strawberries, or mascarpone and honey—or for dessert, with seasonal fruit and a scoop of ice cream. My stuffed savory French toast is equally delicious. It's basically a ham and cheddar sandwich dipped in savory custard, cut in half, and pan-fried.

Milk and Honey Brioche (page 217) is the main building block in this recipe. Made with 100 percent whole-grain flour, milk instead of water, and honey instead of sugar, it is rich and buttery, with a feathery structure that will absorb the custard nicely. You could also use challah or another egg-enriched bread.

STUFFED HAM, CHEDDAR, AND SCALLION FRENCH TOAST

MAKES 8 SAVORY FRENCH TOASTS

EQUIPMENT: large nonstick skillet or cast-iron pan

4 slices smoked ham
4 slices white cheddar
8 (½-inch/1.25 cm thick) slices Milk and Honey Brioche (page 217) or store-bought brioche or challah
1 cup (240 ml) heavy cream
1 teaspoon kosher salt
¼ teaspoon ground white pepper
Pinch freshly grated nutmeg
1 bay leaf
5 large eggs
1 scallion, white and light green parts thinly sliced
Vegetable oil for pan-frying
Butter and berry jam for serving (optional)

1. Make four sandwiches by placing a slice of ham and a slice of cheddar in between two slices of brioche. Arrange the assembled sandwiches in a roasting pan where they can soak.

2. Combine the cream, salt, white pepper, nutmeg, and bay leaf in a small saucepan. Bring to a boil over medium heat, stirring occasionally, then remove from the heat.

3. Whisk the eggs in a mixing bowl to break them up. Temper the eggs by slowly adding a ladleful of the hot cream while whisking the eggs vigorously. Continue adding the hot cream to the eggs until you've added all of it.

4. Strain through a fine-mesh sieve directly over the brioche. Sprinkle with the scallion, scattering all over the sandwiches so little rings stick to them. Soak the sandwiches in the warm liquid, turning them a few times until they are fully saturated, 1 to 2 minutes on each side. Be gentle! The bread will become fragile as it soaks in the liquid.

5. Heat a nonstick skillet or cast-iron pan over medium heat. Drizzle with oil. Working in batches, put two sandwiches at a time on the hot surface and cook until brown, about 2 minutes. Your goal is to cook until the cheese is melty. Flip using a wide spatula and cook the other side for 2 minutes longer. Carefully transfer each sandwich to a cutting board and cut in half on a diagonal.

6. Transfer to a serving dish and cover to keep warm while you finish the remaining sandwiches. Serve the stuffed French toasts as is or with butter and a side of berry jam. Leftovers keep well in an airtight container in the refrigerator for up to 2 days. To bring them back to life, reheat on a baking sheet covered with foil in a 350°F (175°C) oven until warm all the way through.

HONEY FRENCH TOAST WITH A TOUCH OF CARDAMOM AND ORANGE

MAKES 8 FRENCH TOASTS

EQUIPMENT: large nonstick skillet or cast-iron pan

4 (1-inch/2.5 cm thick) slices Milk and Honey Brioche (page 217) or store-bought brioche or challah

1 cup (240 ml) heavy cream

2 tablespoons honey

2 tablespoons sugar

1 cinnamon stick

8 cardamom pods, crushed in a mortar and pestle or with a rolling pin

Peel of 1 orange

5 large eggs

Vegetable oil for pan-frying

Butter, maple syrup, and/or other toppings for serving (optional)

1. Cut the brioche slices in half diagonally to end up with 8 triangles. Arrange the pieces in a roasting pan where they can soak.

2. Combine the cream, honey, sugar, cinnamon stick, cardamom pods, and orange peel in a small saucepan. Bring to a boil over medium heat, stirring occasionally, then remove from the heat. Let the mixture steep for 5 minutes.

3. Whisk the eggs in a mixing bowl to break them up. Temper the eggs by slowly adding a ladleful of the warm cream while whisking the eggs vigorously. Continue adding the cream to the eggs until you've added all of it.

4. Strain through a fine-mesh sieve directly over the sliced brioche. Soak the brioche in the warm liquid, turning the slices a few times until they are fully saturated, 1 to 2 minutes on each side. Be gentle! The slices will become fragile as they soak in the liquid.

5. Heat a nonstick skillet or cast-iron pan over medium-low heat. Drizzle with oil. Working in batches of 2 to 3 slices at a time, add the soaked bread to the skillet and cook until brown, 2 minutes. Flip using a spatula and continue to cook until brown on the other side, 2 minutes longer.

6. Transfer the French toasts to a serving dish and cover to keep warm while you finish the remaining toasts. Serve the French toasts with butter, maple syrup, or your favorite toppings. Leftovers keep well for up to 2 days if stored in an airtight container in the refrigerator. To bring them back to life, reheat on a baking sheet covered with foil in a 350°F (175°C) oven until warm all the way through.

CHAPTER 4

DOUGHNUTS AND FRITTERS

Sour Cream Cake Doughnuts (page 132)

Recipes

Glazed or Sugared Doughnuts   121
   Chocolate Glaze   126
   Peanut Butter Glaze   126
   Maple-Brown Butter Glaze   127
   Pink Glaze   127
Jelly Doughnuts   129
Pineapple Fritters   130
Sour Cream Cake Doughnuts   132
Fried Blueberry Hand Pies   135
   Fried Peach Hand Pies   137
   Fried Onion Hand Pies   137

My ideal doughnut has a balanced, barely sweet flavor, with a good ratio of thin crust exterior to soft, yielding interior. Doughnuts can be classified into two main categories: raised and cake. The main difference between them is the way in which each is leavened. Cake doughnuts are made with artificial leaveners like baking powder and baking soda, while raised doughnuts contain yeast. Raised doughnut dough is very similar to enriched sweet roll dough and goes through the same cycle: The dough ferments in bulk for about 2 hours and is then cut into individual portions that must proof before frying. In contrast, cake doughnuts don't require rising time and can be cut and fried shortly after mixing. The different methodologies yield two distinct types of doughnuts. While raised doughnuts are airy and billowy with a thin, crispy exterior, cake doughnuts have a creamy density and compact crumb with a thicker crust.

A few principles apply to all fried dough confections. First, it's critical to ensure the dough has a proper moisture level. Moisture makes it into the dough through the addition of liquids such as milk or buttermilk, eggs, and butter (which contains about 16 percent water). A moist dough makes for doughnuts that will cook more evenly. When heated, moisture generates steam, in turn creating a degree of separation between the dough and the hot oil and allowing a crusty, caramelized layer to form around the doughnut without letting it absorb too much fat.

Choice of flour is also an important consideration. Doughnuts and fritters made with whole-grain flours behave differently than those made with refined flours. The bran in the flour can make the dough somewhat porous and more prone to absorbing oil. Adding more flour can solve the problem, but it can also make the doughnuts denser. To prevent this, I blend soft whole wheat flour, such as Sonora wheat, with refined all-purpose flour. The whole-grain flour brings its delicious nutty flavor and tender texture, while the refined flour gives the dough more gluten and a lighter touch, creating a wholesome yet airy doughnut. To roll and cut the dough into doughnuts, additional flour is required. Remember, with all that moisture, doughnut dough is loose and sticky, and flouring your work surface generously before rolling and cutting is a must. Use any of the flours that went into the dough for this purpose.

Doughnut recipes tend to be undersweetened for good reason. Sugar is important because it encourages browning, but too much will make the dough compact and cause it to caramelize too quickly while frying. Plus, the dough itself should be somewhat subdued, allowing finishing touches like sparkly sugar, glistening glaze, and colorful sprinkles to sweeten the deal.

A few basic pieces of equipment are required to make most doughnut recipes. Using a stand mixer simplifies making the dough for raised doughnuts, but cake doughnuts are easily mixed by hand. Once either dough is ready to be cut, a rolling pin is best to flatten the dough evenly. Specialty doughnut cutters are available in cooking stores or online; however, a conventional set of round cutters can mimic the doughnut shape fairly easily.

Lastly, a word about deep-frying, which can be intimidating to do at home. Start with a neutral vegetable oil, such as canola or safflower, and the right kind of pot. You should always fry doughnuts in a heavy-bottomed pot that can hold 3 inches (7.5 cm) of oil without being more than halfway full. It is essential to use an oil thermometer to gauge the right temperature and prevent the oil from overheating. The ideal temperature is 360°F (182°C); frying at a lower temperature will make the doughnuts overly greasy. To drop a doughnut in oil safely, hold a single doughnut close to the surface and gently lay it in the hot oil. Use a pair of kitchen tongs or a heat-safe spider skimmer to flip it, then remove it when ready. A skewer is helpful to confirm if the doughnut is cooked through. Use your first doughnut to calculate cooking time. Doughnuts, like all fritters, should always be enjoyed fresh. Their shelf life expires 4 to 6 hours after frying.

This chapter includes raised doughnuts—sugared, glazed, and more complexly shaped fritters filled with fruit or jam—as well as old-fashioned cake doughnuts and fried hand pies. The Glazed or Sugared Doughnuts (page 121) take longer than the Sour Cream Cake Doughnuts (page 132), but the dough itself isn't more complicated. If you're new to doughnut making, I recommend starting with one of those two.

GLAZED OR SUGARED DOUGHNUTS

MAKES ABOUT 15 DOUGHNUTS WITH THEIR HOLES

EQUIPMENT: instant-read thermometer, 3-inch (7.5 cm) doughnut cutter or 3-inch (7.5 cm) and ¾-inch (2 cm) plain round cutters

FOR THE DOUGH

½ cup (120 ml) whole milk

1½ teaspoons instant yeast

2½ cups (325 g) whole-grain all-purpose wheat flour, such as Sonora or Frederick

1¼ cups (175 g) all-purpose flour, plus extra for dusting

1½ teaspoons kosher salt

¾ cup (170 g) sour cream

3 large eggs

⅓ cup (65 g) granulated sugar

6 tablespoons (85 g/¾ stick/3 ounces) unsalted butter at room temperature

1 teaspoon vanilla extract

Vegetable oil for frying (1 to 2 quarts/liters, depending on the size of your pot)

FOR THE CREAM GLAZE, OPTIONAL (SEE VARIATIONS ON PAGES 126–127)

1¼ cups (145 g) confectioners' sugar, sifted

¼ cup (60 ml) heavy cream

2 tablespoons butter, melted and cooled slightly

½ teaspoon vanilla extract

FOR THE SUGAR COATING, OPTIONAL

1 cup (200 g) granulated sugar

1 teaspoon ground cinnamon

This is the master risen doughnut recipe from which all variations stem. Sugared, glazed, or filled, it doesn't matter: They all start here. I've made them so much throughout my career, I've unintentionally memorized the recipe. Whether it is for fried-to-order doughnuts with fancy sauces and ice creams at a restaurant or for Doughnut Friday at Friends & Family, I could make this dough with my eyes closed. Get acquainted with this recipe and you'll open the door to a world of fried possibilities.

Since doughnuts take a bit of time to make, they're best left for weekends or holidays. The process can be shortened by preparing the dough the night before, then leaving the cutting, proofing, and frying for the following day. It's important to knead the dough into a nice uniform ball on the work table once you're done with the mixer, giving it structure before it begins to rise. Use flour somewhat liberally when working with the doughnut dough—this includes kneading, rolling, cutting, and even sprinkling the tray in which you'll let them proof before frying.

Always use soft wheats, such as Sonora or Frederick, for the lightest dough possible. How you dress your doughnuts is a matter of taste—choose between dipping them in the glaze of your choice (pages 126 to 127) or rolling them in sparkly cinnamon sugar.

continues

1. Start with the doughnut dough. Warm the milk in a small saucepan over medium heat until lukewarm (98–105°F/37–41°C), about 2 minutes. Transfer the warm milk to the bowl of a stand mixer, then sprinkle the yeast over the milk. Stir to dissolve and let sit for 5 minutes.

2. Add the flours, salt, sour cream, eggs, granulated sugar, butter, and vanilla to the dissolved yeast mixture. Fit the mixer with the dough hook attachment and combine on low speed until the ingredients just come together, 3 minutes. Stop the mixer, scrape down the sides of the bowl with a silicone spatula, and mix on medium speed for 2 minutes. The dough will be loose and sticky. Transfer the dough to a well-floured work surface, dust additional flour on top of the dough, and knead gently into a ball.

3. Coat a bowl with nonstick spray and place the dough in it—the bowl should be large enough to let the dough double in size. Cover with plastic wrap and let it rise at room temperature for 2 hours, until the dough doubles in volume.

4. Gently punch the dough in the middle to release its gases, wrap the bowl tightly with plastic, and refrigerate overnight.

5. The next morning, remove the dough from the refrigerator and turn it out onto a well-floured work surface. Dust more flour on top of the dough.

6. Line a rimmed baking sheet with parchment paper and dust it generously with flour. Roll the dough with a rolling pin until it is ½ inch (1.25 cm) thick.

7. Cut as many doughnuts as possible with a 3-inch doughnut cutter or plain round cutter. Make sure to dip the cutter in flour in between cuts to prevent the dough from sticking. If using a round cutter, cut a smaller inner circle from each doughnut with a ¾-inch (2 cm) cutter. Gather the scraps into a ball, let rest for 30 minutes, reroll, and cut a few more doughnuts and holes. You can discard the leftover scraps or fry the random pieces after you fry the doughnuts later—they will be funny looking but just as delicious.

8. Place the doughnuts and holes on the prepared baking sheet, cover with a kitchen towel, and let rise for 1 hour.

9. While the doughnuts are rising, prepare the toppings. If you're going to use the glaze, whisk the confectioners' sugar, cream, melted butter, and vanilla together in a mixing bowl until smooth. Transfer the glaze to a small, deep bowl where you can comfortably dip the doughnuts. If you're planning on skipping the glaze and rolling the doughnuts in cinnamon sugar, combine the granulated sugar and cinnamon in a small bowl and reserve to coat the doughnuts later.

10. Fill a large pot with vegetable oil, 3 inches (7.5 cm) deep, and place over medium heat until the oil reaches 360°F (182°C) on an instant-read thermometer. (Alternatively, fill a countertop fryer with vegetable oil and heat to 360°F/182°C.) Line a rimmed baking sheet with paper towels.

11. Working in batches, carefully drop a few doughnuts into the hot oil, one a time. Fry until the doughnuts are golden brown, 1 to 2 minutes, then flip over and fry the other side, about 1 more minute. To test for doneness, pierce a doughnut with a skewer; if the skewer comes out clean, the doughnut is done. You can choose a sacrificial doughnut and cut in the middle to ensure it's cooked through. When the doughnuts are done, remove them from the oil with a slotted spoon and place on the paper towel–lined baking sheet. Repeat until all the doughnuts are fried.

12. Carefully put all the holes in the frying oil at once, stir continuously with a wooden spoon so they fry evenly, and remove from the hot oil when they're golden brown. The holes will fry much faster than the doughnuts. Drain on paper towels.

13. If using the glaze, put a cooling rack on a rimmed baking sheet. While the doughnuts are still a bit warm, gently dip their tops in the glaze, one at a time. Transfer to the cooling rack and let the excess glaze drip, wait 5 minutes, and dip one more time. Let the double-dipped doughnuts rest on the cooling rack until the glaze is set. If the glaze thickens, you can heat it over a warm bath or in the microwave for a few seconds until loosened.

14. If choosing to skip the glaze, roll the doughnuts and their holes, one at a time, in the cinnamon sugar. Serve immediately, preferably while still warm. Once glazed or sugared, they'll keep well for 4 to 6 hours at room temperature.

FROM LEFT TO RIGHT:
Chocolate-Glazed Doughnuts, Maple-Glazed Doughnuts, Cream-Glazed Doughnuts, Peanut Butter–Glazed Doughnuts, Berry-Glazed Doughnuts

GLAZE VARIATIONS

CHOCOLATE GLAZE

MAKES ABOUT 1 CUP (240 ML)

¼ cup (40 g) bittersweet (65–80%) chocolate chips
1¼ cups (145 g) confectioners' sugar, sifted
¼ cup (60 ml) heavy cream
2 tablespoons butter, melted and cooled slightly
¼ teaspoon vanilla extract

1. Put the chocolate in a small heatproof bowl. Fill a small saucepan a quarter of the way with water and place over low heat. When the water is barely simmering, fit the bowl with the chocolate on top, making sure the bottom of the bowl doesn't touch the simmering water.

2. Stir occasionally with a silicone spatula until the chocolate is completely melted.

3. Whisk the confectioners' sugar, cream, melted butter, and vanilla together in a mixing bowl until smooth. Stir in the melted chocolate. Put the glaze in a small, deep bowl, where you can comfortably dip the doughnuts. If the glaze thickens, you can heat it over a warm bath or in the microwave for a few seconds until loosened. After dipping, refrigerate or freeze any leftover glaze to use later.

PEANUT BUTTER GLAZE

MAKES ABOUT 1 CUP (240 ML)

¼ cup (60 ml) boiling water
¼ cup (60 g) smooth peanut butter
1¼ cups (145 g) confectioners' sugar, sifted
¼ teaspoon vanilla extract
¼ teaspoon kosher salt

1. Whisk the boiling water and peanut butter in a medium bowl until smooth. Whisk in the confectioners' sugar, vanilla, and salt until well incorporated. Transfer the glaze to a small, deep bowl where you can comfortably dip the doughnuts. After dipping, refrigerate or freeze any leftover glaze to use later.

MAPLE–BROWN BUTTER GLAZE

MAKES ABOUT 1 CUP (240 ML)

¼ cup (55 g/½ stick/2 ounces) unsalted butter
9 tablespoons (135 ml) maple syrup, warm
1¼ cups (350 g) confectioners' sugar, sifted

1. Put the butter in a small saucepan. Melt over medium-low heat and cook until the butter is deep golden brown, 3 to 4 minutes. Keep a watchful eye; butter can burn easily if left unattended. Turn off the heat and add the maple syrup to warm it up slightly.

2. Transfer the butter and syrup mixture to a mixing bowl and whisk in the confectioners' sugar until smooth. Put the glaze in a small, deep bowl where you can comfortably dip the doughnuts. After dipping, refrigerate or freeze any leftover glaze to use later.

PINK GLAZE

MAKES ABOUT 1 CUP (240 ML)

1¼ cups (145 g) confectioners' sugar, sifted
¼ cup (60 ml) whole milk
2 tablespoons butter, melted and cooled slightly
1 tablespoon freeze-dried raspberry or strawberry powder

If berry powder isn't available, you can purchase the freeze-dried fruit in pieces, put them in a plastic bag, and crush to a powder with a rolling pin.

1. Whisk the confectioners' sugar, milk, melted butter, and berry powder together in a mixing bowl until smooth. Transfer the glaze to a small, deep bowl where you can comfortably dip the doughnuts. If the glaze thickens, you can heat it over a warm bath or in the microwave for a few seconds until loosened. After dipping, refrigerate or freeze any leftover glaze to use later.

JELLY DOUGHNUTS

MAKES 15 DOUGHNUTS

EQUIPMENT: 3-inch (7.5 cm) round cutter, pastry bag with a plain round tip

1 batch dough for Glazed or Sugared Doughnuts (page 121)

Vegetable oil for frying (1 to 2 quarts/1 to 2 liters, depending on the size of your pot)

2 cups (480 ml) Strawberry-Rhubarb Jam (page 76) or store-bought

Granulated sugar for coating

Confectioners' sugar for dusting

We fry tons of these jelly doughnuts every spring at Friends & Family as soon as we make our first batch of strawberry-rhubarb jam. Once the doughnuts are fried, use a paring knife to make an incision, move the knife from side to side to create a pocket for the jam, then use a pastry bag with a plain round tip to squeeze the jam inside.

1. Roll out the dough and cut the doughnuts following the instructions on page 122, but skip cutting the centers out of the doughnuts. Proof and fry as directed, then drain on paper towels.

2. Put the jam in a pastry bag fitted with a plain round tip. Insert a paring knife three-quarters of the way in on one side of a doughnut, then gently move it from side to side to create a cavity. Insert the tip of the jam-filled pastry bag into the doughnut and fill it with 1 to 2 tablespoons of jam, until it feels full and heavy. Repeat with the rest of the doughnuts.

3. Put the granulated sugar in a small bowl and roll each of the filled doughnuts until completely coated. Use a sifter to dust the confectioner's sugar over the doughnuts. Serve immediately. Once filled, they'll keep well for 4 to 6 hours at room temperature.

PINEAPPLE FRITTERS

MAKES 15 FRITTERS

EQUIPMENT: instant-read thermometer

1 small pineapple, peeled, cored, and cut into ½-inch (1.25 cm) chunks (about 4 cups)

⅓ cup (65 g) granulated sugar

⅓ cup packed (70 g) dark brown sugar

¼ cup (55 g/½ stick/2 ounces) unsalted butter, melted and cooled slightly

½ teaspoon kosher salt

1 tablespoon ground cinnamon

2 tablespoons cornstarch

⅓ cup (80 ml) water

1 batch dough for Glazed or Sugared Doughnuts (page 121)

Vegetable oil for frying (1 to 2 quarts/1 to 2 liters, depending on the size of your pot)

1 batch Cream Glaze (page 121)

These pineapple fritters are a delicious riff on the traditional apple fritter. Because the pineapple filling is made identically to its apple iteration, you could substitute if you'd like to stick to the classic fritter. The fruit filling can be made ahead of time, up to 3 days in advance. You will need a batch of the basic doughnut recipe and a batch of the cream glaze, both of which can be made the day before. To shape the fritters, you'll roll the entire batch of dough into a rectangle, fill it with the fruit filling, roll it like a jelly roll, and slice twice over into chunks. Then you'll gather the chunks into clumps and fry them. Once out of the fryer, you'll coat them generously with the cream glaze.

1. To make the pineapple filling, place an oven rack in the middle position and preheat the oven to 350°F (175°C).

2. Combine the pineapple, sugars, melted butter, salt, and cinnamon in a large bowl. In a small bowl, stir the cornstarch into the water until there are no lumps. Add the cornstarch slurry to the pineapple mixture and mix well. Transfer to a large roasting pan. Roast for 15 minutes, stir the filling with a wooden spoon, and roast for another 15 minutes. Let cool completely to room temperature. You can use the filling once it is cool or refrigerate it until you're ready to assemble the fritters.

3. To assemble the fritters, line two rimmed baking sheets with parchment paper and dust generously with flour. Transfer the dough to a well-floured surface. Using a rolling pin, roll the dough into a 13-by-10-inch (33 by 25.5 cm) rectangle. With a spatula, spread enough of the filling to evenly cover the dough all the way to the edges (you may not use it all). Using both hands, roll the dough away from you to form a log (as you would a jelly roll). Rock the log back and forth to tighten and elongate a bit.

4. Using a sharp chef's knife, cut the log at a slight angle into 1-inch (2.5 cm) slices. Without moving the slices, cut again at a slight angle in the opposite direction at 1-inch (2.5 cm) intervals to end up with oblique pieces.

5. Divide the irregular pieces into 15 lumps and compress each with your hands to shape it into a tight clump. Place the clumps on the prepared baking sheets 2 inches (5 cm) apart, cover with a kitchen towel, and let rise for 30 minutes.

6. Fill a large pot with vegetable oil, 3 inches (7.5 cm) deep, and place over medium heat until the oil reaches 360°F (182°C) on an instant-read thermometer. (Alternatively, fill a countertop fryer with vegetable oil and heat to 360°F/182°C.) Line a rimmed baking sheet with paper towels.

7. Working in batches, flour your hands to lift one fritter at a time. Carefully press it together one more time before dropping it into the hot oil. Fry until the bottom side is golden brown, 1 to 2 minutes, then flip over and fry the other side, about 1 more minute. To test for doneness, choose a sacrificial fritter and cut in the middle to ensure it's cooked through. When the fritters are done, remove them from the oil with a slotted spoon and place on the paper towel–lined baking sheet. Repeat until all the fritters are fried.

8. Put a cooling rack on a rimmed baking sheet. While the fritters are still a bit warm, gently dip their tops in the glaze, one at a time. Transfer to the cooling rack and let the excess glaze drip, wait 5 minutes, and dip one more time. Let the double-dipped fritters rest on the cooling rack until the glaze is set. If the glaze thickens, you can heat it over a warm bath or in the microwave for a few seconds until loosened. Serve immediately. Once glazed, they'll keep well for 4 to 6 hours at room temperature.

SOUR CREAM CAKE DOUGHNUTS

MAKES ABOUT 12 DOUGHNUTS

EQUIPMENT: instant-read thermometer, 3-inch (7.5 cm) doughnut cutter or 3-inch (7.5 cm) and ¾-inch (2 cm) plain round cutters

¾ cup (180 ml) whole milk

1½ teaspoons instant yeast

3 cups (390 g) whole-grain all-purpose wheat flour, such as Sonora or Frederick

1 cup (140 g) all-purpose flour, plus extra for dusting

¾ cup (150 g) granulated sugar, plus extra for coating

1 teaspoon baking powder

¾ teaspoon baking soda

1½ teaspoons kosher salt

1 tablespoon freshly grated nutmeg

1 cup (225 g) sour cream

3 large eggs

1 tablespoon vanilla extract

1 cup (115 g) confectioners' sugar, for dusting

Vegetable oil for frying (1 to 2 quarts/1 to 2 liters, depending on the size of your pot)

As a young pastry cook at Campanile, I fried a batch of these cake doughnuts, created by my mentor Nancy Silverton, every morning to sell next door at its sister company La Brea Bakery. If you're craving doughnuts and don't have the time to make a risen dough, which can take up to 2 hours, this recipe is for you. Cake doughnuts rely on baking powder and baking soda to puff up, forgoing the lengthy fermentation period. They can be made in one morning without much forethought.

Freshly grated nutmeg gives these doughnuts their characteristic old-fashioned flavor, so don't leave it out, even if you think you aren't fond of nutmeg. Always grate your own nutmeg right before using and avoid the store-bought ground stuff. Use a soft whole-wheat for this recipe, such as Sonora. Successful cake doughnuts require a very sticky dough, not unlike cake batter. Flour your work surface and cutter generously with the same flour that you used in the dough (some will inevitably get worked in), but resist the urge to incorporate more flour into the dough while mixing. Tossed in sugar and sprinkled with confectioners' sugar, these are everything a cake doughnut should be: light as a feather, crunchy on the outside, tangy from the sour cream, and warm with nutmeg.

1. In a small saucepan, heat the milk until it is lukewarm (98–105°F/37–41°C). Pour into a cup, sprinkle the yeast on top of the milk, stir with a spoon to dissolve, and let it sit for about 5 minutes.

2. In the meantime, sift the flours, granulated sugar, baking powder, baking soda, salt, and nutmeg into a mixing bowl. Using your hands, make a well in the center of the dry ingredients.

3. In a separate bowl, whisk together the dissolved yeast mixture, sour cream, eggs, and vanilla. Pour the liquid mixture into the well in the dry ingredients and stir to combine using a silicone spatula. The dough should be uniform but very sticky.

4. Line a rimmed baking sheet with parchment paper and dust generously with flour. Transfer the dough to a well-floured work surface. Dust the dough surface generously with flour and pat down with the palms of your hands until it is ½ inch (1.25 cm) thick. Cut as many doughnuts as possible with a 3-inch (7.5 cm) doughnut cutter or plain round cutter. Make sure to dip the cutter in flour in between cuts to prevent the dough from sticking. If using a round cutter, cut a smaller inner circle from each doughnut with a ¾-inch (2 cm) cutter. Gather the scraps into a ball, pat down again, and cut a few more doughnuts and holes. You can discard the leftover scraps or fry the random pieces after you fry the doughnuts later—they will be funny looking but just as delicious. Place the doughnuts and holes on the prepared baking sheet, cover with a kitchen towel, and let them rest for 30 minutes.

5. Fill a large pot with vegetable oil, 3 inches (7.5 cm) deep, and place over medium heat until the oil reaches 360°F (182°C) on an instant-read thermometer. (Alternatively, fill a countertop fryer with vegetable oil and heat to 360°F/182°C.) Line a rimmed baking sheet with paper towels.

6. Working in batches, carefully drop a few doughnuts into the hot oil, one a time. Fry until the doughnuts are golden brown, 1 to 2 minutes, then flip over and fry the other side, about 1 more minute. To test for doneness, choose a sacrificial doughnut and cut in the middle to ensure it's cooked through. When the doughnuts are done, remove them from the oil with a slotted spoon and place on the paper towel–lined baking sheet. Repeat until all the doughnuts are fried. Carefully put all the holes in the frying oil at once, stir continuously with a wooden spoon so they fry evenly, and remove from the hot oil when they're golden brown. The holes will fry much faster than the doughnuts. Drain on paper towels.

7. Toss the fried doughnuts and holes in a bowl of granulated sugar while still warmish. Put confectioners' sugar in a fine-mesh sieve and dust generously over the sugared doughnuts. Serve immediately, preferably while still warm. They'll keep for 4 to 6 hours at room temperature.

FRIED BLUEBERRY HAND PIES

MAKES 6 HAND PIES

EQUIPMENT: instant-read thermometer

FOR THE FILLING
3 cups (390 g) fresh or frozen blueberries
¾ cup (150 g) sugar
½ vanilla bean
3 tablespoons cornstarch
⅓ cup (80 ml) water
¼ cup (55 g/½ stick/2 ounces) unsalted butter, cut into cubes

FOR THE PIE DOUGH
1 cup (130 g) whole-grain hard white wheat flour, such as Starr or Edison
1 cup (105 g) all-purpose flour, plus extra for rolling
1 tablespoon sugar
½ teaspoon kosher salt
¾ cup (170 g/1½ sticks/6 ounces) cold unsalted butter, cut into ½-inch (1.25 cm) cubes
¾ cup (170 g/6 ounces) cold cream cheese, cut into ½-inch (1.25 cm) cubes
¼ cup (60 ml) ice water

FOR FRYING
Vegetable oil for frying (1 to 2 quarts/1 to 2 liters, depending on the size of your pot)
1 cup (200 g) sugar
1 teaspoon ground cinnamon

The secret to fried pies is in how far you work the dough. You have to manipulate it enough to build some strength, ensuring the gluten holds its own in the fryer, but you also don't want to overdo it, which would prevent the pies from being light and flaky. I've played this Goldilocks game countless times over the years and am pleased to report that the following recipe has the variables dialed in. You will be making a standard cream cheese pie dough, but handling it a little more to ensure it doesn't fall apart in the fryer. To do this, you will roll the dough twice, refrigerating it in between rolls to ensure it develops the proper structure. The cream cheese is an added bonus and will make your dough tender, malleable, and tasty to boot. A soft whole-wheat flour such as Sonora works really well, but because we want a dough that holds during frying, it wouldn't hurt to use a wheat with more strength, like a hard white. If desired, the lightly sweetened fruit filling can be made ahead of time. The pies hold well and are equally tasty at room temperature, but the jammy blueberries are magical when the fritter is still warm.

1. Place an oven rack in the middle position and preheat the oven to 350°F (175°C).

2. To make the filling, combine the blueberries with the sugar in a small roasting pan. Cut the vanilla bean in half lengthwise with a paring knife, scrape out the sticky pulp with the back of the knife.

continues

3. Add both pulp and pod to the blueberries. In a cup, dissolve the cornstarch in the water and add to the berries. Dot the berries with the cubes of butter, cover with foil, and bake for 15 minutes. Take off the foil, stir with a silicone spatula, and continue to bake until the juices start to thicken, 10 more minutes. Remove from the oven and let it cool completely. Once cool, the filling should be the consistency of jam.

4. To make the pie dough, combine the flours, sugar, and salt in a medium bowl. Toss the cold butter cubes and cream cheese cubes in the flour. Quickly cut the butter and cream cheese into the dry ingredients by pinching the cubes with your fingertips until the mixture resembles a coarse meal with crumbs the size of hazelnuts. Using your hands, make a well in the center of the dry ingredients. Pour the ice water into the well. Mix gently with your hands until a raggedy dough forms; don't worry if bits of butter or cream cheese are still visible. Transfer to a lightly floured surface and knead briefly into a ball. Flatten into a disk and wrap tightly with plastic. Refrigerate for at least 30 minutes and up to 2 days.

5. Using a rolling pin, roll the dough into a rough 18-by-10-inch (45 by 25.5 cm) rectangle, dusting additional flour over the work surface if needed. Fold the dough into thirds as if you were folding a business letter to insert in an envelope and wrap it tightly with plastic.

6. Refrigerate for 30 minutes. Repeat this step one more time, including the refrigeration time. The purpose of rolling and folding the dough a couple of times is to build strength so it doesn't fall apart in the fryer while keeping it flaky and tender.

7. Line a rimmed baking sheet with parchment paper and sprinkle lightly with flour.

8. Roll out the dough on a lightly floured surface into a 19-by-12-inch (50 by 30 cm) rectangle about ¼ inch (6 mm) thick. Use a 6-inch (15 cm) plate as a guide to trace and cut six circles with a paring knife. Gather the scraps, roll them out, and cut two more circles, dusting the surface with more flour as needed. Brush the edges of the circles lightly with water. Put 3 to 4 tablespoons of filling in the center of each dough circle, fold in half to form a half-moon, and press with a fork around the edges to seal. Transfer the shaped pies to the prepared baking sheet.

9. Fill a large pot with vegetable oil, 3 inches (7.5 cm) deep, and place over medium heat until the oil reaches 360°F (182°C) on an instant-read thermometer. (Alternatively, fill a countertop fryer with vegetable oil and heat to 360°F/182°C.) Line a rimmed baking sheet with paper towels.

10. Combine the sugar and cinnamon in a bowl large enough to toss the finished pies one at a time.

11. Working in batches, carefully drop two or three pies into the hot oil, one at a time. Fry until the pies are golden brown, 5 to 6 minutes. Remove the fried pies from the oil with a slotted spoon and place on the paper towel–lined baking sheet.

12. Repeat until all the pies are fried. Gently toss each pie in the cinnamon sugar. The pies should be enjoyed within an hour of frying while still warm or at room temperature.

VARIATIONS

Fried Peach Hand Pies

To make fried peach hand pies, use 4 medium to large ripe peaches instead of the blueberries. Fill a medium pot with water and bring to a boil over high heat. With a paring knife, score an X on the skin of each peach. Gently drop two peaches at a time into the boiling water. Blanch for 1 minute, remove with a slotted spoon, and place in a large bowl until cool enough to handle. Remove the skins—they should come off easily—and chop the peaches into 1-inch (2.5 cm) chunks. Combine the peach chunks with the rest of the ingredients for the filling and roast as directed. Follow the instructions to assemble and fry as for the main recipe.

Fried Onion Hand Pies

This deeply savory variation is inspired by a delicious cheese and onion Cornish pasty I had at Hart's Bakery while visiting friends in Bristol, UK. The familiar and comforting combination of long-cooked onions, mild melty cheese, and a touch of caraway seeds makes this hand pie a sustaining breakfast for colder days. To make the filling, slice 2 large onions and cook with 1 thyme sprig, 1 bay leaf, and ½ teaspoon caraway seeds in 3 tablespoons olive oil over medium-low heat until softened, 8 to 10 minutes. Season with kosher salt and ground black pepper to taste, let cool, and remove the thyme sprig and bay leaf. Combine the onion mixture with 1 cup (100 grams) shredded aged white cheddar. Follow the instructions to assemble and fry as for the main recipe.

CHAPTER 5

WHOLE-GRAIN CROISSANTS

Recipes

Hybrid Croissant Dough 145
    Whole-Grain Croissant Dough 147
Salted Honey Croissants 152
Pistachio-Almond Croissants 155
Espresso Pains au Chocolat 157
Smoked Ham and Gruyère Croissants 159
Bacon and Onion Blossoms 161
Prosciutto en Croûte 164
Berries 'n' Cream Puffs 166
Raspberry Fairies 169
Potato Dillies 170
Cherry Tomato Crests 172
Morning Buns 175
Blackberry Swirls 179
Strawberry Poppies 180
Pineapple Suns 181
Crunchy Bites 184

Making croissants from scratch is no doubt one of the most rewarding projects a baker can undertake. There's nothing quite like marveling at paper-thin layers of butter and dough post-lamination, knowing that they'll proof and bake into ethereally flaky pastries. Adding whole grains to the equation brings its own slew of challenges, but with a bit of planning and preparedness, baking beautiful and flavor-packed whole-grain croissants at home is entirely possible.

My early tests revealed that a great whole-grain croissant requires a combination of strong and soft flours. The strength of high-gluten wheat allows the dough to withstand the intense lamination process and ensures that the pastries hold their shape, while softer, less glutinous wheat makes the dough malleable and easier to work with—an important consideration when you account for all the hand rolling involved in croissant making.

Even if you've made laminated dough before, I recommend starting with the Hybrid Croissant Dough (page 145), which blends refined bread flour with whole-grain flours to make the process a bit more predictable and manageable. Refined bread flour's gluten content is far more consistent than that in whole-grain flours, therefore, it's easier to anticipate how it will behave, reducing the need for troubleshooting as you go. Once you're comfortable with this recipe, take it to 100 percent with the Whole-Grain Croissant Dough (page 147), which calls for 50 percent hard white wheat flour, such as Starr or Edison, 45 percent all-purpose whole-wheat flour, such as Sonora or Frederick, and 5 percent spelt to add a darker hue and flavor complexity.

The rest of the ingredients in the croissant dough are common and easy to find. I include a small amount of barley malt syrup to encourage yeast performance and improve rise and caramelization. Barley malt syrup, also known as malt extract, is a common additive in pastry and bread making, and is easy to find in well-stocked grocery stores, health food stores, and online.

Do keep in mind that lamination is a lengthy process, best completed over the course of multiple days. My preference is to schedule most of the lamination work for the first day, then execute the shaping, rolling, and baking on the second day. At its most basic, the process involves placing a block of butter atop your dough, folding the dough over the butter and rolling it out, then folding the butter-filled dough over itself. Rolling and folding are repeated with refrigerated rests in between, building the pastry's characteristic flaky structure. To make things easier on yourself, it's best to clear a shelf in the fridge before getting started; this ensures you'll have a clean landing place for the dough to rest between folds.

You'll need a ruler, trusty rolling pin, and pastry wheel cutter. Rolling pins are made from different materials, from marble to hardwood, aluminum, and silicone. I choose wooden ones, although a marble rolling pin, which is heavy and remains cool, is a great laminating tool. Many bakers prefer them with handles, but I favor a French dowel without handles. The length of your rolling pin is an important consideration. An 18- to 19-inch (45 to 50 cm) professional rolling pin is most appropriate. It could be difficult to flatten your dough as far as it is necessary with a peewee one. Similar to a pizza cutter, a pastry wheel cutter will enable you to score and cut the dough cleanly.

The more you laminate, shape, proof, and bake croissants, the more insight you'll gain into fine-tuning the process. Once you're comfortable with the two traditional shapes—classic croissants and pains au chocolat—there's endless opportunity for creativity, both in shaping the laminated dough and dressing it up with exciting fillings and toppings.

Croissants should be enjoyed the day they're baked. Leftovers can be put to excellent use for sandwiches, bread pudding, or French toast. You'll notice that the cutting and shaping instructions ask you to trim the dough's edges. This may seem wasteful, but it's an important step: Trimming the edges exposes the layers of dough and butter, helping the pastry grow taller as it proofs and bakes. Not to worry, though; there are plenty of ways to ensure your time is well spent and the process yields zero waste. Save all your raw dough scraps to make Crunchy Bites (page 184).

WHAT COULD POSSIBLY GO WRONG?

Croissant making is a multifaceted craft one learns and develops over time. As one of the most technically challenging projects in the pastry kitchen, it trains you, through trial and error, to become aware of a multiverse of factors that determine the quality of your pastry. As challenging as it is, paying attention to the following critical points will bring you a few steps closer to croissant success.

STARTING TEMPERATURE AND CONSISTENCY: Several croissant issues ensue when the croissant dough and the butter block are too dissimilar in temperature and consistency. Before starting to laminate, the dough needs to be cold and firm enough. To reach the ideal point, you must refrigerate it for 1 hour or longer after mixing. This will allow the gluten to relax and the dough to chill. A good way to see if the dough has spent enough time in the refrigerator is to check the temperature with an instant-read thermometer, which should read between 65°F and 68°F (18°C and 20°C). If the dough has gotten too cold, leave it out to temper. The butter has to be the right temperature as well—malleable enough so it can be rolled without oozing all over the place, but not so solid that it breaks when pressed between layers of dough. To check if the butter is in the sweet spot, I press a corner with my index finger: The butter should resist you, but your finger should leave an imprint, like a footstep in the sand.

REST IN BETWEEN FOLDS: Resting the dough between folds for a stint of 30 minutes is key to ensure that the gluten in the dough has relaxed enough to withstand more rolling, but not so much that the butter inside has hardened to the point that it may chip or break in the next fold. If the butter starts to chip as you roll, press pause, let the dough temper at room temperature for 15 to 20 minutes, and then resume rolling.

ROLL WITH LESS FLOUR: Whenever I train a new baker to laminate, I always insist they roll the dough with as little flour as possible—enough to prevent the dough from sticking, but not so much that it can be absorbed, making the croissants tougher, drier, and flat tasting. Use as much flour as you need to roll properly, but sweep it off with your hand or pastry brush when you're done.

USE GREAT BUTTER: The quality of your butter greatly influences the croissants' flavor. Look for unsalted European-style butter with a higher fat content (83 to 84 percent butterfat). Popular and easy-to-find brands include Kerrygold, Plugrà, and Danish Creamery.

MONITOR THE ROOM'S TEMPERATURE: Croissant nightmares usually involve a kitchen that is too warm or too cold. A warm room will make the task of rolling your dough almost impossible, promoting the dough to warm up too quickly and causing the butter to become melty and oily. On the other side of the temperature spectrum, a cold kitchen may cause the butter to harden, making it difficult to roll it thinly in between layers of dough without breaking it. To preserve the integrity of the butter, it is crucial to work at cool room temperature, between 68°F and 75°F (20°C and 24°C). Once the croissants are shaped, a cold environment can also slow down the proofing, letting the croissants dry out before they even hit the oven, while a warm kitchen can cause the butter to leak, which translates into bready croissants with less-defined layers.

PROOFING AND BAKING: There are a few tricks to create a moist and warm ambient environment in which your croissants can proof happily. A popular one involves letting them rise in the oven (which should be turned off) and putting a pan of warm water in the bottom to generate steam. This is a good move for those of us in places with low humidity. If you live in a warm region with more moisture, your croissants can also rise in a warm corner of the kitchen with a thin towel, such as a flour sack, covering them. Discerning when the croissants are properly proofed is a bit of a guessing game. Look for expansion in between the layers and a little bit of a wobble if you shake the tray gently. If you were to press one of the croissants, it shouldn't spring back. For maximum shine, I brush my croissants with egg wash twice, letting the first coat dry for 10 minutes before applying the second one. Always bake the croissants in a preheated 375°F (190°C) oven on the middle rack. For optimal results, bake one sheet of croissants at a time, rotating the sheet halfway through the baking process to ensure that the croissants bake evenly. Go for a bold, deep golden brown—an undercooked croissant will be doughy in the center and will likely collapse. Croissants benefit from baking with a bit of steam. The results are nuanced but definitely noticeable. To set up a steam bath in your oven, follow the directions on page 211.

AVOID SHAPING MISHAPS: Once you've cut the laminated dough into pieces ready to be shaped, you must continue to treat them with care and attention. Sure, lamination is the most technical part, but shaping is how you show off your hard work. To set yourself up for success, make sure to have equipment such as baking sheets and a pastry wheel cutter, as well as your fillings of choice, ready to go. Keep the pieces cold as you work so the last one you shape is as good as the first one. This is particularly important if you have warm hands. Ironically the most difficult shape is the classic crescent. I find that the most common problems are a result of how you place the croissant on the baking sheet. Once you coil your dough triangle, it's important to make sure it is sitting on its tail in such a way that you can see the tip of the tail on the back of the croissant. As it expands in the oven, it will uncoil slightly and the tail will end up under the crescent. But don't overdo it! If too much of the tail is exposed, your croissant might look funny, like it has a turtle tail. If you sit the croissant directly on the tail and aren't able to see the tip, it could flip and cause the croissant to come undone. Thankfully, other shapes deriving from rectangles and squares are more straightforward.

HYBRID CROISSANT DOUGH

MAKES ABOUT 16 PIECES

EQUIPMENT: instant-read thermometer, plain pastry wheel cutter

FOR THE DOUGH
1½ teaspoons instant yeast

½ cup (120 ml) lukewarm (98–105°F/37–41°C) water

2 cups (260 g) whole-grain all-purpose wheat flour, such as Sonora or Frederick

2 cups (270 g) refined bread flour, plus extra for dusting

½ cup (65 grams) whole-grain spelt flour

3 tablespoons sugar

1 tablespoon plus 1½ teaspoons kosher salt

1 cup (240 ml) whole milk

1 tablespoon barley malt syrup

1 tablespoon unsalted butter at room temperature

FOR THE BUTTER BLOCK
2 cups (455 g/4 sticks/1 pound) cold unsalted butter

1. Start with the dough. Sprinkle the yeast over the lukewarm water in a small bowl. Stir with a spoon to dissolve and let it rest for 5 minutes.

2. In the bowl of a stand mixer fitted with the dough hook attachment, combine the flours with the sugar, salt, milk, barley malt syrup, butter, and dissolved yeast mixture. Mix on low speed until well combined, 2 to 3 minutes, stopping to scrape the sides of the bowl with a silicone spatula if necessary. Increase the speed to medium and mix for 2 minutes to develop the gluten further.

3. Transfer the dough to a lightly floured surface and knead into a ball. Lightly coat a medium bowl with nonstick spray and place the dough in it. Cover with plastic wrap and refrigerate for 1 hour.

4. Meanwhile, for the butter block, lay the butter sticks side by side in between two sheets of parchment paper. Let the butter sit at room temperature for 20 minutes to temper until malleable but not overly soft. Then flatten with a rolling pin to form an 8-inch (20 cm) square. In lamination, this butter packet is known as a butter block. If needed, you may use an offset spatula to help shape the butter block into the specified size. Refrigerate the butter block until the dough is finished resting.

continues

5. At this point, the butter block and the dough should be about the same consistency. To laminate, it's important that the butter not be too cold or it will crack and be hard to spread evenly over the dough. Soft, warm butter is equally problematic, because it will tend to leak out of the dough. To test the butter's readiness, press with your finger; if it resists but leaves an imprint, it is the right temperature.

6. Transfer the refrigerated dough to a lightly floured surface. Using a rolling pin, roll the dough into a 16-inch (40.5 cm) square and put the butter block in the middle. Gently fold the excess dough on the sides over the butter, then fold the excess dough on the bottom and top toward the center until they meet in the middle. Seal in the butter by pinching the two flaps of excess dough together. Now you have a nice package of dough with a butter block inside it. We call this step "locking in the butter."

7. Next, do the first fold. Carefully roll the dough into an 18-by-10-inch (45 by 25.5 cm) rectangle, dusting additional flour over the work surface if needed. The easiest way to roll the dough is to flatten it with your rolling pin using a back-and-forth motion until the dough is 10 inches (25.5 cm) long. Then rotate it 90 degrees and flatten the dough with the same back-and-forth motion until it is 18 inches (45 cm) long. Fold the rectangle into thirds as if you were folding a business letter to insert in an envelope, wrap tightly with plastic, and refrigerate for 30 minutes. You just put in the first turn. If butter squirts out in some patches of dough, dust the surface with flour so it doesn't stick to the rolling pin.

8. Second fold: After the dough has chilled, roll it into another 18-by-10-inch (45 by 25.5 cm) rectangle, dusting additional flour over the work surface if needed. To do so, orient the dough so that the long end that resembles a book spine is parallel to your shoulders and closest to you. Flatten the dough with a rolling pin using a back-and-forth motion until it is 10 inches (25.5 cm) long. Then rotate it 90 degrees and flatten the dough using the same back-and-forth motion until it is 18 inches (45 cm) long. Fold into thirds like a business letter one more time. Refrigerate for another 30 minutes.

9. Third and fourth folds: Repeat this process two more times, refrigerating for 30 minutes in between folds for a total of four folds. Let the dough rest in the refrigerator for 2 hours after the last fold.

10. Remove the dough from the refrigerator and roll into a 16-by-10-inch (40.5 by 25.5 cm) rectangle. Using a pastry wheel cutter, cut the rectangle in half to end up with two 8-by-10-inch (20 by 25.5 cm) rectangles. Wrap each portion tightly with plastic and freeze overnight.

11. Transfer the dough portions from the freezer to the refrigerator and let them thaw completely. Keeping the dough chilled is key. It slows down fermentation and makes the dough more collaborative during shaping. Before you start cutting the dough, make sure you have all your tools, fillings, and garnishes handy to prevent the dough from warming. You will be able to cut eight pieces from each dough portion. Follow the instructions on pages 148 to 149 to make your desired pastry.

> ## VARIATION
>
> ### Whole-Grain Croissant Dough
>
> Refined bread flour makes the Hybrid Croissant Dough more user friendly, but for bakers willing to take things further, this is my go-to 100 percent whole-grain formula. Replace the flour combination on page 145 with the following:
>
> 1½ cups (195 g) whole-grain all-purpose wheat flour, such as Sonora or Frederick
> 2 cups (260 g) whole-grain hard white wheat flour, such as Starr or Edison
> ½ cup (65 g) whole-grain spelt flour

CROISSANT CUTTING GUIDE

To cut classic croissant **triangles** for Salted Honey Croissants (page 152) and Pistachio-Almond Croissants (page 155): Roll one portion of dough into a 14-by-10-inch (35.5 by 25.5 cm) rectangle using a rolling pin. Next, cut into isosceles triangles (both long sides are equal in length) that are 3 inches (7.5 cm) at the base and 9 inches (23 cm) long: Orient the dough rectangle so that one of the long sides is parallel to your shoulders and directly in front of you on the work surface. Score very small notches every 1½ inches (3.8 cm) along the edge of the long side closest to you. Repeat to score notches every 1½ inches (3.8 cm) along the edge of the other long side. Now use a pastry wheel cutter to cut from the bottom left corner on a diagonal upward to the first notch on the top edge, which should be 1½ inches (3.8 cm) in from the left side. Use a ruler to guide the pastry wheel cutter and make neat, straight cuts. Then cut down the second notch on the bottom edge (3 inches/7.5 cm in from the left side). Continue cutting in this zigzag pattern, using the 1½-inch (3.8 cm) notches to create eight triangles.

To cut croissant dough **rectangles** for Espresso Pains au Chocolat (page 157), Smoked Ham and Gruyère Croissants (page 159), and Bacon and Onion Blossoms (page 161): Roll one portion of dough into a 12½-inch (32 cm) square using a rolling pin. Trim ¼ inch (6 mm) of dough from the edges of the dough with a pastry wheel cutter. Cut into four 3-by-12-inch (7.5 by 30 cm) strips and then cut each strip into two 3-by-6-inch (7.5 by 15 cm) rectangles. Use a ruler to guide the pastry wheel cutter and make neat, straight cuts. You should end up with eight rectangles.

For the **Prosciutto en Croûte** (page 164), which is baked as a large pastry to be cut and shared after it is baked, roll one portion of dough into a 10½-by-12½-inch (27 by 32 cm) rectangle. Use a ruler to guide the pastry wheel and trim ¼ inch (6 mm) of dough around all four edges.

To cut croissant dough **squares** for Berries 'n' Cream Puffs (page 166), Raspberry Fairies (page 169), Strawberry Poppies (page 180), Potato Dillies (page 170), Cherry Tomato Crests (page 172), and Pineapple Suns (page 181): Roll one portion of the dough into an 8½-by-16½-inch (22.5 by

42 cm) rectangle using a rolling pin. Trim ¼ inch (6 mm) of dough from the edges of the dough with a pastry wheel cutter. Cut into two 4-by-16-inch (10 by 40.5 cm) strips and then cut each strip into four 4-inch (10 cm) rectangles. You should end up with eight squares.

To cut croissant dough **strips** for Morning Buns (page 175) and Blackberry Swirls (page 179): Roll one portion of the dough into a 12½-by-13½-inch (30 by 35 cm) rectangle using a rolling pin. Trim ¼ inch (6 mm) of dough from the edges of the dough with a pastry wheel cutter. Orient the dough rectangle so the narrower ends are parallel to your shoulders. Cut into eight 1½-by-13-inch (3.8 by 33 cm) strips. Use a ruler to guide the pastry wheel cutter and make neat, straight cuts. You should end up with eight strips.

CHOC.

EN CROÛTE

H/C

X-SANT

BLOSSOM

SWIRL

MORNING BUN

DILLY

POPPY

PUFF

FAIRY

CREST

SUN

SALTED HONEY CROISSANTS

MAKES 8 CROISSANTS

1 portion Hybrid Croissant Dough (page 145) or Whole-Grain Croissant Dough (page 147), rolled and cut into 8 classic croissant triangles (see page 148)

1 large egg

1 tablespoon heavy cream

¼ cup (60 ml) honey

Coarse sea salt, such as Maldon to garnish

This nutty, salty-sweet flavor combination was inspired by the honey-glazed Croissant Integral at Panadería Rosetta in Mexico City. Finished with a few flakes of sea salt, they're delicious alongside a cup of steaming-hot café con leche.

Croissants are so quotidian in bakeries, coffee shops, and even grocery stores that it's easy to forget how much care goes into making them from scratch. Every baker who has stood in front of a baker's bench faced with the task of transforming freshly cut dough triangles into beautiful croissants knows that this shape, more than any other, requires practice. In time, every croissant maker develops their own style, making choices that will determine the look of the final product, from stretching the triangle a bit longer to obtain a few more coils, to elongating the middle to get wider croissants, to pointing the ends forward so the croissants have a quintessential arched shape. When I teach a new baker how to make our croissants at the bakery, I point out how other small details also count. Once you've cut your dough into triangles, you should monitor the dough's temperature diligently and find a pace that allows you to work with each piece without letting it get too warm or soft. If this happens, press pause, refrigerate them for 20 to 30 minutes, and then resume shaping. You should also make sure the shaped croissant sits firmly on the baking sheet in such a way that you're able to see the very tip of the triangle behind the croissant, ensuring it doesn't uncoil while proofing and baking. Always space the croissants far enough apart on the baking tray so they have enough room to grow—they will triple or quadruple in size. And above all, give yourself grace, knowing that with each imperfect croissant, you're becoming a more skilled shaper.

1. Line two rimmed baking sheets with parchment paper.

2. To shape the croissants, gently stretch one dough triangle at a time with both hands to elongate it slightly. Roll the base of the triangle toward the tip and press the tip to the bottom of the croissant to secure the coil. Place the shaped croissants on the prepared baking sheets, spaced at least 3 inches (7.5 cm) apart.

3. Cover loosely with a kitchen towel and let them rise at room temperature for 2 to 3 hours, until puffy and soft to the touch or until they no longer bounce back when you press gently with a moistened index finger.

4. Place two oven racks in the middle positions and preheat the oven to 375°F (190°C).

5. Beat the egg and cream together. Brush the proofed croissants thoroughly with the egg and cream mixture. Let the egg wash dry for 10 minutes, then brush the croissants one more time.

6. Bake for 15 minutes. Rotate the baking sheets, switch their positions in the oven, and bake for 10 to 15 minutes more, until the croissants are deep golden brown.

7. Heat the honey in a small saucepan until lukewarm; careful, this happens quickly—the honey will become thinner as it warms up. Brush each croissant with honey generously and sprinkle with a few flakes of sea salt. Let them cool completely. Enjoy on the day prepared.

PISTACHIO-ALMOND CROISSANTS

MAKES 8 CROISSANTS

FOR THE ROSE SYRUP
½ cup (100 g) sugar
½ cup (120 ml) boiling water
2 tablespoons rose water

FOR THE PISTACHIO-ALMOND FILLING
¼ cup (35 g) whole raw almonds
¼ cup (35 g) whole raw pistachios plus 2 tablespoons finely chopped for decorating
2 tablespoons sugar
6 tablespoons (85 g/¾ stick/3 ounces) unsalted butter, at room temperature
¾ cup (50 g) marzipan or almond paste
1 large egg
1 teaspoon almond extract
8 classic croissants, baked as per Salted Honey Croissants recipe (page 152), but without salted honey topping, or 8 unfilled pains au chocolat (see headnote)

After investing a long weekend making croissants at home, I find it hard to imagine that anyone would have leftover croissants. But if you did, do what most cost-efficient bakeries do and turn them into twice-baked pastries. Almond croissants come to mind, but I would suggest trying something different and new like these pistachio-almond croissants.

Alternatively, you could do what we do at Friends & Family: Instead of going through the trouble of making classic croissants, we cut croissant dough rectangles (page 148) and shape them like pains au chocolat, but skip the chocolate. These unfilled croissants are easier to assemble and can accommodate a good amount of pistachio filling.

Originally developed as a nod to Turkish delight, these pistachio-almond croissants are filled with nutty-rich cream, brushed generously with fragrant rose water syrup, and topped with a sprinkle of vibrant pistachios. You'll start by splitting the already baked croissants in half, brushing them with the syrup, and then filling them with the pistachio-almond filling before baking them once more.

1. Place an oven rack in the middle position and preheat the oven to 350°F (175°C). Line a rimmed baking sheet with parchment paper.

2. To make the rose syrup, add the sugar to the boiling water and stir until it is completely dissolved. Add the rose water and let cool completely.

3. Make the pistachio-almond filling next. In a food processor, grind the almonds, whole pistachios, and sugar to a fine meal. Add the butter and marzipan and mix until creamy. Add the egg and almond extract and mix to incorporate. Transfer to a bowl and keep at room temperature until ready to use.

continues

4. To assemble the pistachio-almond croissants, carefully cut the croissants in half horizontally with a serrated knife, as if you were slicing a bagel.

5. Place the bottom halves cut side up on a work surface and brush them generously with the rose syrup. Using an offset spatula, cover each bottom with the pistachio-almond filling (about 2 tablespoons per piece). Put the top pieces back on and brush the exterior generously with additional rose syrup. Space the finished croissants a few inches apart on the prepared baking sheet. You can fit all 8 croissants in one sheet since they won't expand any further in the oven.

6. Bake for 10 minutes. Then rotate the baking sheet and bake for 10 minutes more.

7. Remove from the oven. While the croissants are still warm, brush the tops with a very light stroke of rose syrup (the right amount will serve as just enough glue, while too much will make them soggy) and sprinkle with the chopped pistachios. Let cool completely. Enjoy at room temperature.

ESPRESSO PAINS AU CHOCOLAT

MAKES 8 PAINS AU CHOCOLAT

EQUIPMENT: instant-read thermometer

8 espresso beans

½ cup (90 g) bittersweet (65–80%) chocolate chips

1 portion Hybrid Croissant Dough (page 145) or Whole-Grain Croissant Dough (page 147), rolled and cut into 8 croissant dough rectangles (see page 148)

1 large egg

1 tablespoon heavy cream

Combining crushed dark-roasted coffee beans and bittersweet chocolate is a simple way to create your own flavored batons, packed with toasty, earthy notes and unparalleled crunch. You could fill the croissants with regular chocolate chips, if desired, but making your own flavored chocolate is a lot easier than it sounds. I love melting chocolate and infusing it with the rich flavor of espresso. You could get creative and play with this concept if espresso isn't your cup of tea. Great additions are crushed freeze-dried raspberries, finely ground Earl Grey tea, or crushed cocoa nibs (see the variations that follow). Rolled into pains au chocolat and baked, they're a subtle twist on the classic, making for one very special croissant.

1. In a mortar and pestle, crush the espresso beans into coarse bits no larger than a grain of rice. (Alternatively, you can press the coffee beans against a cutting board with the bottom of a mug or a rolling pin.)

2. Using a ruler, trace an 8-by-3-inch (20 by 7.5 cm) rectangle with a marker in the center of a sheet of parchment paper. Invert the parchment and place on a rimmed baking sheet. Put the chocolate chips in a medium heatproof bowl. Fill a medium pot a quarter of the way with water and place over low heat. When the water is barely simmering, fit the bowl on top, making sure the bottom of the bowl doesn't touch the simmering water. Stir occasionally with a silicone spatula until the chocolate is completely melted.

3. Remove the bowl from the heat. Stir in the crushed espresso beans and continue stirring with the spatula until the chocolate thickens and reaches 90°F (32°C). Pour the chocolate on the parchment sheet with the traced rectangle and use an offset spatula to encourage the chocolate to stay within the border. The chocolate layer should be ¼ inch (6 mm) thick. Refrigerate until almost solid. Using a chef's knife, score the chocolate into sixteen ½-inch (1.25 cm) strips. Put back in the refrigerator until completely firm. Transfer the solid chocolate to a cutting board and cut the strips along your score lines. Transfer to a container and keep refrigerated.

continues

4. To shape the croissants, line two rimmed baking sheets with parchment paper. Orient the rectangles so that the shorter sides are parallel to your shoulders. Put two chocolate strips on each rectangle, one on the bottom edge and another 2 inches (5 cm) up. Roll as you would a jelly roll. Place the shaped croissants seam side down on the prepared baking sheets, spaced at least 3 inches (7.5 cm) apart.

5. Cover loosely with a kitchen towel and let them rise at room temperature for 2 to 3 hours, until puffy and soft to the touch or until they no longer bounce back when you press gently with a moistened index finger.

6. Place two oven racks in the middle positions and preheat the oven to 375°F (190°C).

7. Beat the egg and cream together. Brush the proofed croissants thoroughly with the egg and cream mixture. Let the egg wash dry for 10 minutes, then brush the croissants one more time. Bake for 15 minutes. Then rotate the baking sheets, switch their positions in the oven, and bake for 10 minutes more, until the croissants are deep golden brown. Let cool for a few minutes. Though delicious warm, the espresso beans are crunchiest at room temperature.

VARIATIONS

Chocolate Raspberry Pains au Chocolat
Crush 2 tablespoons freeze-dried raspberries to a powder in a mortar and pestle or a spice grinder. Stir into the melted chocolate instead of the espresso beans.

Chocolate Earl Grey Pains au Chocolat
Crush 1 teaspoon loose-leaf Earl Grey tea to a powder in a mortar and pestle or a spice grinder. Stir into the melted chocolate instead of the espresso beans.

Cocoa Nib Pains au Chocolat
Toast 2 tablespoons cocoa nibs in a skillet over medium-low heat until they begin to release their aroma, about 1 minute. Make sure to swirl the skillet nonstop, which will prevent them from burning. Cool completely, then stir into the melted chocolate instead of the espresso beans.

SMOKED HAM AND GRUYÈRE CROISSANTS

MAKES 8 CROISSANTS

1 portion Hybrid Croissant Dough (page 145) or Whole-Grain Croissant Dough (page 147), rolled and cut into 8 croissant dough rectangles (see page 148)

8 slices smoked ham

1 cup (120 g/4½ ounces) grated Gruyère

1 large egg

1 tablespoon heavy cream

Smoky-sweet ham plus gooey cheese, both encased in flaky, subtly sweet pastry... need I say more? It's a timeless classic. There are two ways to make this famous savory croissant. The first involves taking a flat croissant dough rectangle, filling it with thinly sliced ham and a chunk of Gruyère, and rolling it into a tight cylinder, just like pain au chocolat. The second one is a lot simpler (and a little bit of a cheat): You split an already baked croissant, fill it with sliced ham and cheese, and bake until melty. For me, the former is the real way to make them.

Choose a mild cheese and it will go unnoticed against the buttery richness of the croissant. My go-to is a deeply savory and pungent Gruyère: the stinkier, the better. To ensure the cheese melts adequately, I recommend grating it, then using your hands to compress it into a log that covers the width of the dough rectangle. Equally important is ham choice. I prefer smoked ham over a sweet ham, taking the croissant in a more savory direction. Ask any of the bakers at Friends & Family and they will wax poetic about the importance of using the right amount of ham. By the time the croissant is fully proofed, there should be enough ham for every bite. Be sure to form a tight cylinder that won't uncoil while proofing or baking. When spacing the croissants on the baking sheet, anticipate that some melty cheese will ooze from their sides. This cheese skirt, which we like to call the "cheese-charrón," is the best part of eating a ham and cheese croissant. How long should you bake a ham and cheese croissant for, you ask? Until the cheese-charrón is crispy! Ham and cheese croissants hold (and reheat) very well.

1. Line two rimmed baking sheets with parchment paper.

2. To shape the croissants, orient the rectangles so that the shorter sides are parallel to your shoulders. Then lay a slice of ham on each rectangle; don't worry if the ham slice is wider than the rectangle. Press a handful of grated Gruyère (about 2 tablespoons) into your hand to form an elongated clump resembling a cigar.

continues

Put the cigar at the bottom of the rectangle and roll as you would a jelly roll, applying pressure as you roll to keep the croissant from uncoiling. Place the shaped croissants seam side down on the prepared baking sheet, spaced at least 3 inches (7.5 cm) apart.

3. Cover loosely with a kitchen towel and let them rise at room temperature for 2 to 3 hours, until puffy and soft to the touch or until they no longer bounce back when you press gently with a moistened index finger.

4. Place two oven racks in the middle positions and preheat the oven to 375°F (190°C).

5. Beat the egg and cream together. Brush the proofed croissants thoroughly with the egg and cream mixture. Let the egg wash dry for 10 minutes, then brush the croissants one more time.

6. Bake for 15 minutes. Then rotate the baking sheets, switch their positions in the oven, and bake for 10 to 15 minutes more, until the croissants are deep golden brown. Let cool for a few minutes. You can enjoy these croissants at room temperature, but they're extra special when still warm from the oven.

BACON AND ONION BLOSSOMS

MAKES 8 BLOSSOMS

1 portion Hybrid Croissant Dough (page 145) or Whole-Grain Croissant Dough (page 147), rolled and cut into 8 croissant dough rectangles (see page 148)

1 batch Caramelized Onions (page 162)

2 slices thick-cut bacon, cooked and cut into lardons or ¼-inch (6 mm) strips

1 large egg

1 tablespoon heavy cream

Caramelization turns otherwise sharp, intense onions into an aromatic and savory jam that can be used in a million ways. It took me a few tries to successfully develop a pastry garnished with caramelized onions. The onions are fully cooked by the time they go into the pastry, so I had to engineer the right shape, allowing the dough to bake properly without burning the onions. This blossom-like, tart-inspired shape was just the thing. I also lowered the oven temperature to 350°F (175°C) to ensure the onions wouldn't go over. Not only is it beautiful, but it holds the right amount of each of the ingredients. Smoky bacon lardons offset the sweetness of the onions in a pleasant way. These must be eaten soon after being baked or slightly warmed up so the fats around the bacon lardons won't congeal and look dull.

1. Line two rimmed baking sheets with parchment paper.

2. To shape the blossoms, orient the dough rectangles so that the shorter sides are parallel to your shoulders. Make a 4-inch (10 cm) slit lengthwise down the middle of each rectangle, stopping 1-inch (2.5 cm) short of the top and bottom. Slip the bottom end of the rectangle through the slit to form a bow.

3. Lay the blossoms flat on the prepared baking sheets at least 3 inches (7.5 cm) apart. Cover loosely with a kitchen towel and let them rise at room temperature for 2 hours, until puffy and soft to the touch or until they no longer bounce back when you press gently with a moistened index finger.

4. Place two oven racks in the middle positions and preheat the oven to 350°F (175°C).

5. Combine the caramelized onions with the bacon in a bowl.

6. Beat the egg and cream together. Brush the blossoms thoroughly with the egg and cream mixture. Let the egg wash dry for 10 minutes, then brush the blossoms one more time. Put a generous spoonful of the onion and bacon mixture right in the middle of each.

continues

7. Bake for 15 minutes. Rotate the baking sheets, switch their positions in the oven, and bake for 10 minutes more, until the blossoms are deep golden brown. Let cool for a few minutes. Enjoy at room temperature or slightly warm.

CARAMELIZED ONIONS

MAKES 1 CUP

3 tablespoons olive oil
2 medium onions, thinly sliced
1 thyme sprig
1 teaspoon kosher salt
½ teaspoon freshly ground black pepper

1. Heat the oil in a medium pan over high heat. Add the onions, thyme, salt, and pepper. Cook, stirring constantly with a wooden spoon, until the onions are translucent, 5 minutes. Reduce the heat to medium-low and continue to cook, stirring occasionally, until the onions look jammy and have developed a deep caramel color, 10 to 15 minutes.

2. If the onions begin to stick to the bottom of the pan as they cook, add 1 to 2 tablespoons water and stir, scraping the caramelized bits from the bottom of the pan. Remove from the heat.

3. Taste and add more salt if necessary. Discard the thyme sprig and let cool completely.

FROM TOP TO BOTTOM, LEFT TO RIGHT: Smoked Ham and Gruyère Croissant (page 159), Bacon and Onion Blossom (page 161), Potato Dilly (page 170), Cherry Tomato Crest (page 172), Individual Prosciutto en Croûte (page 165)

PROSCIUTTO EN CROÛTE

SERVES 8

1 portion Hybrid Croissant Dough (page 145) or Whole-Grain Croissant Dough (page 147), rolled into large rectangle (see page 148)
16 slices prosciutto or speck
1½ cups (170 g/6 ounces) grated fontina
1 large egg
1 tablespoon heavy cream
Freshly cracked black pepper as needed

If you're cooking breakfast for someone you want to impress, mark this page. This pastry is easy to put together, but it looks as if you've spent hours in the kitchen. The trick is in scoring a pattern on the dough that serves a dual purpose: It allows the pastry to open up and elongate, and also provides a little window into the delicious filling inside. With prosciutto slices and shredded fontina, this creation is actually an Italianesque version of a ham and cheese croissant. Because the prosciutto is baked in the dough and surrounded by melty cheese, it is unnecessary to opt for top-of-the-line prosciutto. However, if available, try it with speck—a cured then smoked prosciutto from Northern Italy—for a little bit more depth. Serve it with coffee or, if the occasion calls for it, a bellini. It's delicious served warm or at room temperature. Be sure to top with plenty of freshly cracked black pepper, which brings woodsy notes and bold heat. Prosciutto en croûte can also be baked in individual portions; see the variation that follows.

1. Line a rimmed baking sheet with parchment paper.

2. Orient the 10-by-12-inch (25.5 by 30 cm) rectangle so that the wider side is parallel to your shoulders. Use a paring knife to create a lattice pattern: Starting at the left edge of the dough, cut five 1-inch (2.5 cm) slits lengthwise, spacing them ½ inch (1.25 cm) apart. Right next to that, cut four more slits the same way, so they're slightly offset from the first set. Keep repeating this five-then-four pattern across the dough until you reach the other side. Gently pull from the left and right sides to expand the rectangle like an accordion; it will be about 14 inches (35.5 cm) wide.

3. Lay the prosciutto slices lengthwise on the rectangle. Scatter the grated fontina over the prosciutto. Roll the dough upward as you would a jelly roll. Place the roll seam side down on the prepared baking sheet.

4. Cover loosely with a kitchen towel and let it rise at room temperature for 2 to 3 hours, until puffy and soft to the touch or until it no longer bounces back when you press gently with a moistened index finger.

5. Place an oven rack in the middle position and preheat the oven to 375°F (190°C).

6. Beat the egg and cream together. Brush the proofed prosciutto en croûte thoroughly with the egg and cream mixture. Let the egg wash dry for 10 minutes, brush one more time, and sprinkle generously with black pepper.

7. Bake for 15 minutes. Rotate the baking sheet and bake for 10 to 15 minutes more, until it's deep golden brown. Let cool for a few minutes. Slice into 8 portions with a serrated knife. Enjoy at room temperature or slightly warm.

VARIATION

Individual Prosciuttos en Croûte

For individual portions, cut the rolled-out dough portion into 8 rectangles (see page 148). Orient each rectangle so that the shorter side is parallel to your shoulders. Use a paring knife to create a lattice pattern: Starting at the left edge of the dough, cut three 1-inch (2.5 cm) slits lengthwise, spacing them ½ inch (1.25 cm) apart. Right next to that, cut two more slits the same way, so they're slightly offset from the first set. Keep repeating this three-then-two pattern across the dough until you reach the other side. Gently pull from the left and right sides to expand the rectangle like an accordion. Lay 2 prosciutto slices on each rectangle. Scatter 2 tablespoons of grated fontina over the prosciutto. Roll each rectangle upward as you would a ham and cheese croissant. Follow the instructions in the main recipe for proofing and baking.

BERRIES 'N' CREAM PUFFS

MAKES 8 PASTRIES

EQUIPMENT: 2½-inch (6.5 cm) plain round cutter

1 portion Hybrid Croissant Dough (page 145) or Whole-Grain Croissant Dough (page 147), rolled and cut into 8 croissant dough squares (see page 148)

1 cup (190 g) fresh blueberries

1 tablespoon granulated sugar, plus extra for sprinkling

1 teaspoon cornstarch

1 tablespoon water

1 large egg

1 tablespoon heavy cream

½ batch Cream Cheese Filling (recipe follows)

Confectioners' sugar for dusting

Inspired by plush, old-fashioned, creamy cheese danishes, each of these flaky puffs is topped with lightly sweetened cream cheese and a hefty spoonful of macerated blueberries. The striking contrast of off-white filling and dark, velvety berries makes for an especially beautiful pastry. To separate the outside of the pastry from the filled center, you'll use a biscuit cutter to create a circular score in each dough square. Be careful not to cut all the way through. You want to make a clear indentation but keep the pastry intact. Keep in mind that since this pastry isn't coiled, it will proof and bake faster than other pastries in this chapter. You'll know the puffs are done baking when the cheese filling starts to develop a tan hue.

1. Line two rimmed baking sheets with parchment paper.

2. Place the dough squares on the prepared baking sheets, spaced at least 3 inches (7.5 cm) apart. Using a 2½-inch (6.5 cm) plain round cutter, punch a circle in the middle of the square, pressing just enough to score the dough without cutting all the way through.

3. Cover loosely with a kitchen towel and let them rise at room temperature for 2 to 3 hours, until puffy and soft to the touch or until they no longer bounce back when you press gently with a moistened index finger.

4. While the puffs are rising, toss the blueberries with the granulated sugar, cornstarch, and water in a bowl. Let them macerate at room temperature while the puffs are proofing.

5. Place two oven racks in the middle positions and preheat the oven to 375°F (190°C).

6. Beat the egg and cream together. Brush the proofed puffs thoroughly with the egg and cream mixture. Let the egg wash dry for 10 minutes, then brush the puffs one more time.

7. Spoon a dollop of cream cheese filling (about 1 tablespoon) to cover half of the circle on each puff, then put a generous spoonful of macerated blueberries right next to the cream cheese filling. Sprinkle generously with granulated sugar.

8. Bake for 15 minutes. Then rotate the baking sheets, switch their positions in the oven, and bake for 10 to 15 minutes more, until the puffs are golden brown. Let cool completely. Put the confectioners' sugar in a fine-mesh sieve and dust the edges decoratively. Enjoy on the day prepared.

CREAM CHEESE FILLING

MAKES 1 HEAPING CUP

1 cup (225 g/8 ounces) cream cheese at room temperature
¼ cup (50 g) sugar
1 tablespoon cornstarch
1 large egg yolk

In a small bowl, mix together the cream cheese and sugar until they form a uniform paste. Add the cornstarch and mix to combine. Add the egg yolk and mix until smooth. Transfer to a small container, cover, and refrigerate until ready to use. The filling can be made up to 2 days in advance.

FROM TOP TO BOTTOM, LEFT TO RIGHT:
Blackberry Swirl (page 179),
Pineapple Sun (page 181),
Raspberry Fairy (page 169),
Strawberry Poppy (page 180),
Blueberries 'n' Cream Puff (page 166)

RASPBERRY FAIRIES

MAKES 8 PASTRIES

1 portion Hybrid Croissant Dough (page 145) or Whole-Grain Croissant Dough (page 147), rolled and cut into 8 croissant dough squares (see page 148)

1 large egg

1 tablespoon heavy cream

⅓ cup (80 ml) Raspberry Jam (page 76) or store-bought

1 cup (120 g) raspberries

Granulated sugar for sprinkling

Confectioners' sugar for dusting

This playful shape is one of my all-time favorites. Why? Because it gives the pastry wings! (Hence the name.) Making this shape feels like origami. Start with a dough square, score a border on the two opposite corners with a paring knife, then fold them over so you end up with a diamond.

1. Line two rimmed baking sheets with parchment paper.

2. To shape the fairies, fold a dough square in half diagonally to form a triangle. This creates a crease to guide your cuts. With the fold at the bottom, make two 2-inch (5 cm) diagonal cuts along the open edges of the triangle, creating a ½-inch (1.25 cm) border. Unfold the dough triangle back into a square. You'll see a smaller diamond shape in the center with flaps on either side. Now, pull up one of the outer flaps and fold it inward until the tip meets the cut line. Then fold the opposite flap the same way. You should end up with a diamond shape, with two neat "wings" on each end.

3. Place the fairies on the prepared baking sheets, spaced at least 3 inches (7.5 cm) apart. Cover loosely with a kitchen towel and let them rise at room temperature for 2 to 3 hours, until puffy and soft to the touch or until they no longer bounce back when you press gently with a moistened index finger.

4. Place two oven racks in the middle positions and preheat the oven to 375°F (190°C).

5. Beat the egg and cream together. Brush the proofed fairies thoroughly with the egg and cream mixture. Let the egg wash dry for 10 minutes, then brush the fairies one more time. Spoon a dollop of jam (about 1 tablespoon) in the middle of each fairy and top it with 3 or 4 raspberries. Sprinkle generously with granulated sugar.

6. Bake for 15 minutes. Then rotate the baking sheets, switch their positions in the oven, and bake for 10 to 15 minutes more, until the fairies are golden brown. Let cool completely.

7. Put the confectioners' sugar in a fine-mesh sieve and dust the edges decoratively. Enjoy on the day prepared.

POTATO DILLIES

MAKES 8 PASTRIES

1 portion Hybrid Croissant Dough (page 145) or Whole-Grain Croissant Dough (page 147), rolled and cut into 8 croissant dough squares (see page 148)

2 teaspoons kosher salt

1 cup (170 g/6 ounces) fingerling potatoes (about 8 thumb-size potatoes)

½ cup (120 ml) crème fraîche or sour cream

1 large egg yolk plus 1 whole large egg

1 tablespoon minced dill

1 tablespoon heavy cream

The classic combination of dill and potatoes makes our dillies a favorite savory pastry at Friends & Family. The bright, grassy herb is a natural friend to earthy tubers, which here are enriched with crème fraîche. Keep in mind that this shape tends to unfold during proofing. Feel free to gently push the corners back into place with your fingers. Once the filling is on top, they won't come undone.

1. Line two rimmed baking sheets with parchment paper.

2. To shape the dillies, cut 1½-inch (3.8 cm) lines at a 45-degree angle on each corner of the dough square, making sure they don't meet in the middle. Fold up the corners until they touch in the center. You should end up with a smaller 3-inch (7.5 cm) square. Press each square assertively with the palm of your hand to secure the folded corners in the center.

3. Place the dillies on the prepared baking sheets at least 3 inches (7.5 cm) apart. Cover loosely with a kitchen towel and let them rise at room temperature for 2 to 3 hours, until puffy and soft to the touch or until they no longer bounce back when you press gently with a moistened index finger.

4. While the dillies are proofing, make the filling. Fill a medium saucepan with water. Bring to a boil over high heat. Season with 1 teaspoon of the salt, add the potatoes, and cook until tender, 10 to 15 minutes. To check if the potatoes are ready, pierce one with a paring knife; if it releases easily, the potatoes are done. If not, cook for a few more minutes. Drain the potatoes and let them cool completely. Cut into ½-inch (1.25 cm) thick rounds.

5. In a small bowl, whisk together the crème fraîche and egg yolk. Stir in the dill and season with the remaining 1 teaspoon salt. Using a silicone spatula, toss in the potato slices. Cover and refrigerate until ready to use.

6. Place two oven racks in the middle positions and preheat the oven to 375°F (190°C).

7. Beat the whole egg and cream together. Brush the proofed dillies thoroughly with the egg and cream mixture. Let the egg wash dry for 10 minutes, then brush the dillies one more time. (If the folds come a bit undone while proofing, gently push them back toward the middle.) Put a generous dollop of the potato filling in the center of each square.

8. Bake for 15 minutes. Then rotate the baking sheets, switch their positions in the oven, and bake for 10 to 15 minutes more, until the dillies are golden. Let cool completely. Enjoy on the day prepared.

CHERRY TOMATO CRESTS

MAKES 8 PASTRIES

1 portion Hybrid Croissant Dough (page 145) or Whole-Grain Croissant Dough (page 147), rolled and cut into 8 croissant dough squares (see page 148)

3 cups (450 g) assorted cherry tomatoes

2 tablespoons olive oil

½ teaspoon kosher salt

1 large egg

1 tablespoon heavy cream

2 tablespoons Basil Pesto (recipe follows) or store-bought

¼ cup (20 g) grated Parmesan

As soon as summer approaches, Friends & Family regulars begin inquiring about the whereabouts of our cherry tomato crests. Topped with jammy oven-roasted tomatoes, lemony basil pesto, and plenty of Parmesan, it's no wonder. Good thing Southern California's tomato season is nice and long! Beyond summer, I like filling the crests with sautéed mushrooms coated with béchamel, or chunks of sweet potato or butternut squash roasted with plenty of olive oil and a touch of minced sage.

1. Line two rimmed baking sheets with parchment paper.

2. To shape the crests, start by folding a dough square in half diagonally to form a triangle. This creates a crease to guide your cuts. With the folded edge at the bottom, make two 2-inch (5 cm) diagonal cuts along the open sides of the triangle, creating a ¾-inch (2 cm) border. Unfold the dough triangle back into a square. You'll now see a smaller diamond in the center with two triangular flaps on each side. Pull one flap, lift it up, fold it down, and thread the tip through the nearest cut. Gently pull it inward and lay the tip flat on top of the inner diamond. Repeat with the opposite flap. This lift-fold-and-tuck motion creates a twisted frame around the center, forming a crest-like shape, similar to a decorative seal or emblem.

3. Place the crests on the prepared baking sheets at least 3 inches (7.5 cm) apart. Cover loosely with a kitchen towel and let them rise at room temperature for 2 to 3 hours, until puffy and soft to the touch or until they no longer bounce back when you press gently with a moistened index finger.

4. While the dough is proofing, make the filling. Place two oven racks in the middle positions and preheat the oven to 350°F (175°C).

5. Scatter the cherry tomatoes on a rimmed baking sheet or roasting pan. Drizzle with the olive oil and salt and toss with your hands just to coat.

6. Roast for 5 minutes, or until the tomatoes just start to blister. Remove from the oven and let them cool completely.

7. Increase the oven temperature to 375°F (190°C).

8. Beat the egg and cream together. Brush the proofed crests thoroughly with the egg and cream mixture. Let the egg wash dry for 10 minutes and brush the crests one more time. Top the middle of each crest generously with roasted cherry tomatoes.

9. Bake for 15 minutes. Then rotate the baking sheets, switch their positions in the oven, and bake for 10 to 15 minutes more, until golden. Let cool completely.

10. Drizzle the tomatoes generously with pesto and sprinkle with Parmesan. Enjoy on the day prepared.

BASIL PESTO

MAKES ABOUT ¾ CUP

2 tablespoons pine nuts
1 cup packed (40 g) fresh basil leaves
1 garlic clove, peeled and crushed
½ cup (120 ml) extra-virgin olive oil
2 tablespoons grated Parmesan
1 tablespoon fresh lemon juice
Kosher salt to taste

1. Toast the pine nuts in a skillet over medium-low heat until they begin releasing their nutty aroma, 3 to 4 minutes. Make sure to swirl the skillet nonstop to prevent them from burning. Let the pine nuts cool completely.

2. Using a food processor, puree the basil and garlic with the olive oil and toasted pine nuts. You may need to stop every so often to scrape the sides of the bowl and help the basil puree evenly. Blend in the Parmesan. Season with the lemon juice and salt to taste. Pesto will keep for 3 days in the refrigerator and leftovers freeze well.

MORNING BUNS

MAKES 8 PASTRIES

EQUIPMENT: 8-mold mini loaf pan (3½-by-2¼-inch/9 by 5.5 cm cavity size)

6 tablespoons (85 g/¾ stick/3 ounces) unsalted butter at room temperature

2 tablespoons Cara Cara Orange Marmalade (page 177) or store-bought orange marmalade

1 cup (200 g) sugar

1 teaspoon ground cinnamon

1 teaspoon ground cardamom

1 portion Hybrid Croissant Dough (page 145) or Whole-Grain Croissant Dough (page 147), rolled and cut into 8 croissant dough strips (see page 149)

Morning buns are a modern-day American bakery staple, combining buttery croissant dough with the sugary filling of a cinnamon roll. They're traditionally shaped like snails and baked in muffin tins. It's widely believed that they were invented in the San Francisco Bay area, where they're still ubiquitous. Some disagree, asserting that they originated in Wisconsin. Birthplace aside, they're undoubtedly a West Coast thing. Here, every bakery worth its salt makes them. The pretty snail shape has a great ratio of crusty, caramelized exterior to gooey interior, but they tend to grow out of their tins and collapse in the center. When I started making them at Friends & Family, I grew tired of troubleshooting this issue. I decided to shape them like a squiggle and bake them in mini loaf pans instead. The squiggle is a lot of fun to make and the balance between crunchy outside and soft inside is still there. I like to think of the shape as a morning bun on psychedelics, enhanced by butter seasoned with orange marmalade and a coating of spiced sugar.

1. Coat a mini loaf pan generously with nonstick spray.

2. To make the orange butter, in a small bowl, stir together the butter and marmalade.

3. Combine the sugar, cinnamon, and cardamom in a bowl and mix by hand until well combined.

4. Line the work surface with parchment paper. Place the dough strips side by side on the parchment. Using an offset spatula, spread two-thirds (about 6 tablespoons) of the orange butter over the strips. Sprinkle the strips generously with the spiced sugar. Flip each of the strips, spread with the remaining one-third (about 2 tablespoons) of the orange butter, and sprinkle once again with the spiced sugar. Reserve the remaining sugar.

5. To shape the morning buns, fold each strip four times in a zigzag pattern, making sure the side of the strip with the least amount of butter is facing outward. The resulting shape should resemble an accordion in which each fold is identical to the next.

continues

6. Transfer the morning buns to the prepared mini loaf pan. Cover loosely with a kitchen towel and let them rise at room temperature for 2 to 3 hours, until puffy and soft to the touch or until they no longer bounce back when you press gently with a moistened index finger.

7. Place an oven rack in the middle position and preheat the oven to 375°F (190°C).

8. Put the mini loaf pan on a rimmed baking sheet to catch the drips. Bake for 15 minutes. Then rotate the baking sheet and bake for 10 minutes more, until golden.

9. Let cool for 5 minutes. Use an offset spatula to remove the morning buns from the mold. Be careful. They will be very hot. You must unmold before they cool or the molten sugar may cause them to stick to the pan. Transfer the warm morning buns to a cooling rack and let them cool completely.

10. Toss each morning bun in the remaining spiced sugar. Enjoy on the day prepared.

CARA CARA ORANGE MARMALADE

MAKES 2 CUPS

- 5 medium (2 pounds/900 g) Cara Cara oranges, plus a few extra to juice if needed
- 2 cups (400 g) sugar
- ½ cup (120 ml) water
- 1 vanilla bean
- 1 cup (240 ml) unsweetened Applesauce (page 31) or store-bought

Cara Cara oranges have a rosy, pinkish interior and floral-sweet flavor, reminiscent of red fruit like cranberries and cherries. Naturally low in acid and bitter pith, Cara Caras make for an exceptionally well-balanced marmalade. Blanching the zest multiple times ensures it's free of bitterness and soft enough to maintain a pleasant texture in the finished preserve. I like to add unsweetened applesauce to give the marmalade body. It's rich in pectin, so it aids in making a yielding, spreadable marmalade without overtaking the citrus.

1. Trim a thin sliver from each end of the oranges. The flat surface will allow them to stand and be easier to cut. With a sharp chef's knife and following the curve of the fruit, slice strips of peel from top to bottom. Slice each strip into thin slivers. Put the cut peels in a medium saucepan and cover with cold water. Bring to a boil over high heat. Drain the peels over the kitchen sink, discarding the blanching water. Repeat two more times with fresh water each time.

2. Juice the peeled oranges. You should end up with 1 cup (240 ml) juice. If necessary, supplement with juice from other oranges to complete the 1 cup (240 ml).

3. Put the sugar in a medium saucepan. Add the water to moisten the sugar, but do not stir. Split the vanilla bean lengthwise with a paring knife, scrape out the sticky pulp with the back of the knife, and put both pulp and pod into the pot. Cook over high heat until the mixture comes to a boil. Lower the heat to medium and reduce the mixture to a thick syrup, 3 to 5 minutes.

4. Add the blanched orange peels, juice, and applesauce and cook for 15 minutes while stirring constantly with a wooden spoon. (Stirring is crucial because it breaks down the peels while preventing overcaramelization, which may cause the jam to stick to the bottom of the pot.) To test the marmalade's readiness, chill a small plate in the freezer, spoon a bit of marmalade onto it, and run your finger through the marmalade. If your finger leaves a trace on the plate, the marmalade is ready.

5. Transfer to a bowl and let cool completely. Remove the vanilla bean and discard. The marmalade can be stored in the refrigerator for up to 1 month.

BLACKBERRY SWIRLS

MAKES 8 PASTRIES

EQUIPMENT: plain pastry wheel cutter

1 portion Hybrid Croissant Dough (page 145) or Whole-Grain Croissant Dough (page 147), rolled and cut into 8 croissant dough strips (see page 149)

1 large egg

1 tablespoon heavy cream

½ cup (120 ml) Blackberry Jam (page 76) or store-bought

1 cup (150 g) fresh blackberries

Granulated sugar for sprinkling

Confectioners' sugar for dusting

This swirly, S-shaped pastry is a real show-stopper. Fun to eat and simple to master, it's definitely one to keep in your back pocket. The swirl provides a higher ratio of dough to filling than other croissant shapes, so I also like pairing it with bright, punchy offerings. These are finished with lime-spiked blackberry jam and a smattering of fresh fruit, but orange marmalade or cranberry jam would also work. With the jam safely tucked in its designated spot, the swirls aren't as delicate as other pastries and can be packed in a lunch box or picnic basket.

1. Line two rimmed baking sheets with parchment paper.

2. Using a pastry wheel cutter, cut out a triangle from both ends of each dough strip at a 30-degree angle.

3. Form an "S" by coiling both ends inward in opposite directions until they meet in the middle. Place the swirls on the prepared sheets at least 3 inches (7.5 cm) apart. Cover loosely with a kitchen towel and let them rise at room temperature for 2 to 3 hours, until puffy and soft to the touch or until they no longer bounce back when you press gently with a moistened index finger.

4. Place an oven rack in the middle position and preheat the oven to 375°F (190°C).

5. Beat the egg and cream together. Brush the proofed swirls thoroughly with the egg and cream mixture. Let the egg wash dry for 10 minutes, then brush the swirls one more time.

6. Press the center of the two coils in each swirl with your thumb to create two craters. Spoon a dollop of blackberry jam (about 1 tablespoon) in the center of each crater and top each one with a blackberry. Sprinkle generously with granulated sugar.

7. Bake for 15 minutes. Then rotate the baking sheets, switch their positions in the oven, and bake for 10 to 15 minutes more, until golden. Let cool completely. Put the confectioners' sugar in a fine-mesh sieve and dust the tops decoratively. Enjoy on the day prepared.

STRAWBERRY POPPIES

MAKES 8 PASTRIES

1 portion Hybrid Croissant Dough (page 145) or Whole-Grain Croissant Dough (page 147), rolled and cut into 8 croissant dough squares (see page 148)

1 large egg

1 tablespoon heavy cream

½ cup (120 ml) Cream Cheese Filling (page 167)

¼ cup (60 ml) Strawberry-Rhubarb Jam (page 76) or store-bought

6 to 8 strawberries, sliced

Granulated sugar for sprinkling

Confectioners' sugar for dusting

If strawberry cheesecake woke up one day a flaky, buttery pastry, it would be these poppies—so named because their shape reminds me of wildflowers. Filled with tangy-sweet cream cheese, strawberry-rhubarb jam, and fresh strawberries, they're totally irresistible.

1. Line two rimmed baking sheets with parchment paper and coat with nonstick spray.

2. To shape the poppies, cut 1½-inch (3.8 cm) lines at a 45-degree angle on each corner of the dough square, making sure they don't meet in the middle. Fold up the corners until they touch in the center. You should end up with a smaller 3-inch (7.5 cm) square.

3. Place the poppies on the prepared baking sheets at least 3 inches (7.5 cm) apart. Invert them so that the folded corners are facing down. Cover loosely with a kitchen towel and let them rise at room temperature for 2 to 3 hours, until puffy and soft to the touch or until they no longer bounce back when you press gently with a moistened index finger.

4. Place two oven racks in the middle positions and preheat the oven to 375°F (190°C).

5. Beat the egg and cream together. Brush the proofed poppies thoroughly with the egg and cream mixture. Let the egg wash dry for 10 minutes, then brush the poppies one more time. Press the center of each poppy with your thumb to create a crater. Spoon a generous dollop of cream cheese filling (about 1 tablespoon) into the crater, follow with a spoonful of jam (about 1 tablespoon), and top with 5 to 6 strawberry slices, keeping the filling in the center. Sprinkle generously with granulated sugar.

6. Bake for 15 minutes. Then rotate the baking sheets, switch their positions in the oven, and bake for 10 minutes more, until the poppies are golden.

7. Let cool completely. Put the confectioners' sugar in a fine-mesh sieve and dust the edges decoratively. Enjoy on the day prepared.

PINEAPPLE SUNS

MAKES 8 PASTRIES

1 portion Hybrid Croissant Dough (page 145) or Whole-Grain Croissant Dough (page 147), rolled and cut into 8 croissant dough squares (see page 148)
1 large egg
1 tablespoon heavy cream
½ cup (120 ml) Pastry Cream (page 182)
1 cup (165 g) chopped fresh pineapple (¼-inch/ 6 mm pieces)
Granulated sugar for sprinkling
Confectioners' sugar for dusting

Not a fan of pineapple? Hard to believe! But if that's the case, you could use thin slices of peach, apricot, or nectarine macerated with a sprinkle of sugar.

1. Line two rimmed baking sheets with parchment paper.

2. To shape the suns, make a 2½-inch (6.5 cm) diagonal cut from each corner toward the center, angled at roughly 30 degrees from the edges. This creates four tapered "arms" at each side of the square. To form the sun shape, take the tip of one arm and gently tuck it underneath the base (or "armpit") of the next arm. Rotating clockwise around the square, continue tucking each tip under the next armpit until all four are tucked in place. The result should resemble a stylized sun, with four rays radiating from a central point.

3. Place the suns on the prepared baking sheets at least 3 inches (7.5 cm) apart. Cover loosely with a kitchen towel and let them rise at room temperature for 2 to 3 hours, until puffy and soft to the touch or until they no longer bounce back when you press gently with a moistened index finger.

4. Place two oven racks in the middle positions and preheat the oven to 375°F (190°C).

5. Beat the egg and cream together. Brush the proofed suns thoroughly with the egg and cream mixture. Let the egg wash dry for 10 minutes, then brush the suns one more time.

6. Spoon a dollop of pastry cream (about 1 tablespoon) in the center of each sun and top it with a few pieces of pineapple, keeping the filling in the center. Sprinkle generously with granulated sugar.

7. Bake for 15 minutes. Then rotate the baking sheets, switch their positions in the oven, and bake for 10 to 15 minutes more, until golden. Let cool completely.

8. Put the confectioners' sugar in a fine-mesh sieve and dust the edges decoratively. Enjoy on the day prepared.

PASTRY CREAM

MAKES 1 CUP

1 cup (240 ml) whole milk
½ vanilla bean
½ cup (100 g) sugar
3 tablespoons all-purpose flour or whole-grain all-purpose wheat flour, such as Sonora or Frederick
3 large egg yolks
2 tablespoons unsalted butter
1 teaspoon vanilla extract
Pinch of kosher salt

1. Put the milk in a small saucepan. Cut the vanilla bean in half lengthwise with a paring knife, scrape out the sticky pulp with the back of the knife, and add both pulp and pod to the saucepan. Add the sugar and flour and cook over medium heat while whisking continuously until the mixture has come to a boil.

2. Cook for 2 more minutes, whisking non-stop to prevent the cream from sticking to the bottom of the pan. Turn off the heat.

3. Working quickly, whisk the yolks to break them up. Add a spoonful of the warm cream to the yolks and whisk vigorously. Pour the tempered yolks back into the saucepan and cook for 2 minutes over medium heat while whisking vigorously.

4. Strain through a fine-mesh sieve into a bowl. Stir in the butter, vanilla, and salt until the butter is completely melted and fully incorporated. Let cool completely. Keep the pastry cream in a covered container in the refrigerator until ready to use. It will keep for up to 2 days.

Pineapple Suns (page 181)

CRUNCHY BITES

MAKES AS MUCH AS YOU HAVE

1 cup (200 g) sugar
1 teaspoon ground cinnamon
Pinch of kosher salt
Croissant dough scraps, cut into 1-inch (2.5 cm) pieces

It's no secret that preparing laminated dough requires a good deal of time and effort, so save those scraps. Here's an easy and quick way to repurpose them. These crunchy, buttery tidbits bring cinnamon-sugar pretzel bites to mind. Croissant scraps can be frozen for up to 1 week; allow them to thaw fully before proceeding with the recipe.

1. Place an oven rack in the middle position and preheat the oven to 350°F (175°C). Line a rimmed baking sheet with parchment paper.

2. Combine the sugar, cinnamon, and salt in a bowl and mix by hand until well combined.

3. Toss the croissant dough pieces in the cinnamon sugar, making sure the pieces are coated on all sides. Scatter the pieces on the prepared sheet. Cover loosely with a kitchen towel and let them rise at room temperature for 1 hour, until puffy and soft to the touch.

4. Sprinkle some of the leftover cinnamon sugar on the pieces and bake for 15 minutes, until golden and crispy. Remove from the oven and let cool completely. Enjoy on the day prepared.

CHAPTER 6

WHOLE-GRAIN BREADS

Recipes

FLATBREADS 192
Multigrain Crackers 193
Za'atar Flatbreads 195
Swiss Chard, Feta, and Egg Pide 197
Heirloom Masa Tortillas 200
Hybrid Tortillas 202
Tortillas Aliñadas 205

YEASTED BREADS 207
Khorasan Baguettes 209
Rosemary Sandwich Loaf 212
Durum Ciabatta 214
Milk and Honey Brioche 217
Cinnamon-Raisin Brioche 221
Brioche Jam Buns 223
Brioche à la Crème 227
Potato Nigella Buns 230
Finnish Malt Bread 232
   Clark Street Bakery's Nordic Breakfast Plate 234
Dark Rye Rolls 237

SOURDOUGH BREADS 239
Make Your Own Sourdough Starter 240
Basic Sourdough Bread 244
Benched Sourdough Rolls 248
   Seeded Benched Sourdough Rolls 249
Apple Levain 250
Pumpkin Spelt Bread 254
   Open-Face Carrot Sandwich 257
Dill, Chive, and Black Pepper Loaf 260
Caramelized Onion, Comté, and Nigella Boule 263
Sprouted Grain Loaf 266
   Friends & Family Famous Hippie Sandwich 271
Chocolate-Cherry Pan Loaf 273

Aside from a quick and superficial bread-making week in culinary school, I didn't dive seriously into the stuff until I'd been working in the industry for almost a decade. My first focus was dessert making and, even after working at La Brea Bakery and Campanile under none other than Nancy Silverton, Los Angeles's undisputed bread mother, it took a significant shift in my career to afford me the time and space to delve into bread. The reasons were mostly circumstantial: None of the restaurants I worked in had a bread oven, the white bread flour we used was generic and uninspiring, and most restaurateurs didn't allocate resources to bread at the time.

My first breads were functional, made using the no-knead method I had read about in the immensely popular book *My Bread: The Revolutionary No-Work, No-Knead Method* by Jim Lahey. The no-knead method called for minimal yeast and a lot more water than I had ever used. The results were dramatically positive. It was only a matter of time before I concocted my own sourdough starter and went down the naturally leavened rabbit hole. I was hooked, and I was not alone. Bread-focused bakeries flourished around the country, cookbooks on the subject were published one after the other, and the community grew at such a rate that we started having baking parties. With this support system, plus good flour and new formulas, I started to develop breads on my own. These days, the vast majority of the breads I make are whole-grain sourdoughs, though I still use commercial yeast in many other products.

When we opened Friends & Family, we knew that bread would be the backbone of our breakfast and lunch menus. With this in mind, we tailored our breads to be right for the jobs we were assigning them. A potato roll engineered to be fluffy and tender, yet strong enough to support eggs, bacon, and cheese, for example. Or a seed-heavy sprouted loaf created to bring big flavor and texture to our ultimate vegetarian sandwich.

The bread station is always thinking ahead since it takes 3 days to complete most of the recipes. A meticulous list that looks more like a spreadsheet guides the crew through the steps of scaling on day 1, mixing and shaping on day 2, and finally baking on day 3. To the benefit of home bakers, it's easy to mimic these practices at home.

Whether a soft roll, crisp cracker, or hearty sourdough, all the breads in this chapter are excellent on their own, but they also shine as the starting points of tasty, energy-filled morning offerings, and in learning to bake them, you will have the makings of excellent meals as well.

This chapter is divided into three sections: Flatbreads, Yeasted Breads, and Sourdough Breads. Flatbreads include fun projects like Multigrain Crackers (page 193) and my favorite recipes for tortillas, the kind of flatbread many of us eat the most. Then we move on to Yeasted Breads, which run the gamut from practical Rosemary Sandwich Loaf (page 212) to indulgent Milk and Honey Brioche (page 217). The last section encompasses a sourdough bread–making guide. It begins with instructions for making your own sourdough starter, then moves on to a handful of sourdough bread recipes that I like making at home and at the bakery. If you're new to bread, following the recipes in sequence is a good way to learn in a logical order, but more adventurous bakers can skip to the more advanced recipes if that's what speaks to them.

I share bread-making concepts that have improved my breads greatly, and that I think can do the same for you. The coolest one is perhaps the autolyse—a widely used technique in which the flour is hydrated, without leavening or salt, and allowed to rest for as little as 20 minutes and as long as overnight. This resting period encourages the gluten in the flour to develop elasticity, fires up enzymatic activity, and lays the foundation for better caramelization, flavor, and aroma. I will also walk you through the equally important step of folding the dough to encourage a strong structure. This requires grabbing a section of the dough at a time, stretching it, and then folding it onto itself. When done repeatedly at set intervals, the folds will build a stronger loaf that springs upward in the oven.

Expect flour choice to play a key role in all these recipes. But don't be shocked to see refined bread flour in some of the recipes—it's there to support the whole-grain flour. Like everything I bake, the emphasis is on flavor and texture rather than appearance. And, above all, always remember that a wonky loaf is just as tasty as a beautifully shaped one.

BREAD-MAKING TOOLS

Certain pieces of equipment are essential to make bread; however, most are also easy to find and affordable. A beginner's equipment set includes:

Digital Scale

I recommend a digital scale with weights in grams and ounces and a capacity of at least 5 or even 10 pounds. I find it useful when the scale is large enough (approximately 6 square inches/15 square cm) to fit a medium bowl on top. Taylor, Escali, and XOX make durable, affordable, and easy-to-find scales with these characteristics.

Bench Knife

This is the best tool to cut and divide bread dough. You can also use it to scrape the dough stuck to the work table, making cleanup a lot easier.

Dutch Oven

A lidded 4½- or 5½-quart/liter cast-iron Dutch oven provides a perfect environment for breads to develop open crumbs and crusty exteriors. The lid traps the steam released by the loaf in the hot environment, keeping the exterior of the bread supple so it may expand and reach a desirable oven spring. If you don't already own one, I recommend starting with an affordable brand, such as Lodge, and, in time, upgrading to the Challenger Bread Pan (see page 324), a highly functional cast-iron pan designed specifically for superior bread baking at home.

Instant-Read Thermometer

This is a must to ensure ingredients are at the right temperature, especially liquids. It's also key to determining whether a loaf of bread is done by checking its internal temperature. They're affordable and easy to find. Just make sure yours reads temperatures from 75° to 400°F (24° to 205°C).

Lame

This slashing tool, composed of a blade attached to a handle, is used to score the tops of bread loaves. A lame can be used to make decorative designs, but its main purpose is to create a vent on the surface for the bread to release pressure as it expands in the oven. Lames are cheap and easy to find, but in a pinch a sharp paring knife will do.

Lidded Glass Jar

I recommend a 1-quart/liter mason jar or Weck jar (see page 325) to hold your starter. Glass jars are the most durable and sanitary. This size is roomy enough to allow the starter to ferment exponentially, yet small enough to fit in the fridge in between bakes.

Loaf Pan and Banneton

The standard 8½-by-4½-inch (22 by 11 cm) loaf pan is easy to find and very practical to bake a sandwich loaf. As I do with other pans, I prefer coated ones to prevent sticking and guarantee easy release. Used for proofing bread dough, bannetons are baskets made from different materials (from rattan and wicker to plastic) in a wide variety of shapes. I recommend an 8- to 9-inch (20 to 23 cm) round banneton, which can fit a loaf ranging from 1 to 2 pounds (450 to 900 g). With the exception of plastic bannetons, they cannot be washed and therefore must be cleaned with a dry brush. Keep in a dry area to prevent them from molding.

Plastic Dough Scraper

Usually made of flexible plastic you can hold directly in your hand, a dough scraper works a lot like a silicone spatula to help scrape the bottom of the bowl clean. It's also useful to scrape dough off your hands.

CLEAN AS YOU GO

Cleaning as you go can make the difference between a fun, chill baking experience and one that ends in an overwhelming heap of dough-crusted bowls and tools. Unless you are making something highly time-sensitive, like pastry cream or caramel, it is always worth it to pause and take a few minutes to clean. Here are a few rules to keep in mind:

Always start with a clean kitchen and an empty sink. Removing distractions and clutter will allow you to focus fully on the recipe at hand.

Keep all your dirties in one place. Whether it's a corner of the counter or a stack in the sink, don't let your workspace become cluttered. As soon as you're done with a dirty bowl or utensil, move it to the designated spot until you have a minute to wash up.

Stay soaking. As soon as you transfer a sticky preferment or wet dough from one bowl to another, fill the dirty bowl with warm water and soap. It'll make cleaning much easier and prevent you from struggling to scrape off cemented bits later on.

FLATBREADS

If you're new to bread making, flatbreads are a great place to start. In the same way that pancakes are a lower-stakes entry point to whole-grain baking than, say, croissants, flatbreads are easier, faster, and more forgiving than sourdoughs and other more complex yeasted breads.

Flatbreads can be made with or without yeast. Take tortillas, for example, the ultimate form of bread from Mexico to Panamá. Tortillas can be part of pretty much every meal and are made with nixtamalized cornmeal or wheat flour. Even when made with wheat flour, they never contain yeast or any natural leaveners. Lavash, the popular Armenian bread that is available in Middle Eastern markets, bakeries, and restaurants across the country, can be risen with minimal amounts of yeast or with a lump of prefermented dough (commonly called "old dough"). Other flatbreads, such as pita, contain yeast and ferment pretty much like other doughs. The final dough is then divided and flattened into individual disks that need to be proofed before baking. Even when the breads themselves are meant to remain flat, this fermentation process, along with the whole-grain flour, makes them more digestible and flavorful, with a soft and pliable texture.

MULTIGRAIN CRACKERS

MAKES 8 CRACKERS

1¼ cups (160 g) whole-grain hard white wheat flour, such as Starr or Edison
½ cup (65 g) whole-grain spelt flour
½ cup (65 g) whole-grain or dark rye flour
2 teaspoons (10 g) fine sea salt
¾ cup plus 1 tablespoon (190 ml) water
1 tablespoon honey
5 tablespoons (75 ml) olive oil
Coarse sea salt, such as Maldon, for sprinkling

Crackers are a classic multigrain destination for good reason. Without the structural concerns that inform bread and pastry making, you can really up the grain ante. They're an ideal bake for experimenting with different flour blends, too. You can taste more nuanced notes when there are only a few ingredients at play. Olive oil provides richness and ensures the crackers aren't too hard or dry, while honey brings subtle warmth and tenderness. Throw these on a cheese board to impress your guests, or pair them with hummus or your favorite creamy dip for a light, fiber-packed lunch. Rolling crackers with a rolling pin requires a certain degree of perseverance. You shouldn't give up until they are as thin as you can get them. I've always felt that using a rolling pin is a form of athleticism, especially when working with firm doughs. You must stand squarely in front of the work table, leaning forward as you roll so that your upper body weight helps flatten the dough. I aim for the thickness of cardstock, which is $\frac{1}{16}$ inch (1.5 mm), more or less. Here's a tip: To save yourself the workout, you can use a hand-crank pasta machine if you have one. Not all doughs are suited to being rolled through the pasta machine, but this one certainly is.

1. Combine all the flours and the fine salt in a medium bowl. Using your hands, make a well in the center of the dry ingredients. Add the water and honey and mix by hand until a uniform dough forms. Transfer to a floured surface and knead into a ball. Flatten into a disk and wrap tightly with plastic. Refrigerate for 1 hour.

2. Place two oven racks in the middle positions and preheat the oven to 350°F (175°C). Using a pastry brush, coat two rimmed baking sheets lightly with olive oil.

3. Divide the chilled dough in 2 equal portions. Using a rolling pin, roll each into a 16-by-8-inch (40.5 by 20 cm) rectangle on a floured surface. Cut into 8-by-4-inch (20 by 10 cm) rectangles with a pastry wheel cutter. You should end up with 8 rectangles.

continues

4. Carefully transfer the crackers to the prepared baking sheets. Once the dough rectangles are on the sheets, you may want to use your hands to stretch them a bit more to cover the length of the sheet. Note that the crackers can be close together since they will shrink a bit as they bake.

5. Using a skewer or a fork, poke holes over the surface of each cracker (the holes will prevent the crackers from developing air pockets). Brush each cracker with olive oil and sprinkle with coarse salt.

6. Bake the crackers for 12 minutes. Then rotate the baking sheets and switch their positions and bake for another 12 minutes, until the crackers are golden brown and crispy. Let them cool completely. The crackers will keep for up to 1 week in an airtight container or ziplock bag at room temperature.

ZA'ATAR FLATBREADS

MAKES 8 FLATBREADS

1 tablespoon instant yeast

1 cup (240 ml) lukewarm (98–105°F/37–41°C) water

2½ cups (325 g) whole-grain hard white or red wheat flour, such as Starr or Red Fife

½ cup (120 ml) plain yogurt

¼ cup (60 ml) olive oil, plus extra for brushing

2 teaspoons (10 g) fine sea salt

1 tablespoon za'atar

Za'atar—a Middle Eastern spice blend that typically includes fragrant herbs, nutty sesame seeds, and tangy sumac—provides flavor and a bit of texture to these flatbreads. The dough also includes yogurt, which adds fat, acid, and moisture, all of which make for more tender bread. Plain whole-milk yogurt and Greek yogurt both fit the bill. The yogurt also encourages browning. The dough's structure should be strong, so a higher-gluten flour, such as hard white or red wheat, is my go-to. These flatbreads are multipurpose and can be eaten as a snack or as part of any meal. My favorite way to enjoy them is with a Middle Eastern breakfast of feta, herbs, and sliced tomatoes and cucumbers.

1. Sprinkle the yeast over the lukewarm water in a small bowl. Stir with a spoon to help it dissolve, then let it sit for 5 minutes.

2. In the bowl of a stand mixer fitted with the dough hook attachment, combine the flour, yogurt, olive oil, salt, and dissolved yeast mixture on low speed until it comes together, about 2 minutes, scraping the sides of the bowl with a silicone spatula if necessary. Increase the speed to medium and mix to further develop the gluten in the dough, about 2 more minutes. Transfer the dough to a floured surface and knead into a ball.

3. Place the dough in a bowl lightly coated with nonstick spray, cover with a kitchen towel or plastic wrap, and let it rise until doubled, 1½ to 2 hours.

4. Transfer the dough to a floured surface and flatten gently with your hand. Divide the dough into 8 portions (about 90 g/ 3¼ ounces each). Roll each portion into a ball. Cover with a kitchen towel and let rest for 20 minutes. This resting period will allow the gluten in the dough to relax, making rolling the flatbreads a lot easier.

continues

5. Place two oven racks in the middle positions and preheat the oven to 400°F (205°C). Brush two rimmed baking sheets generously with olive oil.

6. Using a rolling pin, flatten each dough portion into a round 6 inches (15 cm) in diameter, dusting the work surface with flour as necessary. Transfer the rolled flatbreads to the prepared baking sheets, spacing them at least 2 inches (5 cm) apart. Brush lightly with olive oil and sprinkle with za'atar.

7. Bake for 6 minutes. Then rotate the baking sheets and switch their positions in the oven and bake for another 6 minutes, or until puffy and just golden.

8. Remove the flatbreads from the oven and stack them on a plate lined with a linen napkin. Cover the flatbreads with another linen napkin and let them rest for at least 10 minutes. The steam emitted by the warm flatbreads will keep them soft and supple. The flatbreads can be used right away or stored in a ziplock bag in the refrigerator for up to 3 days. They can also be wrapped tightly in plastic and frozen for up to 2 weeks.

HOW TO READ BREAD DOUGH

If you've made the same bread recipe more than once, you've likely noticed that the dough can behave differently each time. Baking bread regularly teaches us how to "read" our dough—to recognize what it needs beyond what the recipe says. While following a recipe is essential, developing your bread baker's intuition allows you to make minimal adjustments that improve the final result. Even a shelf-stable ingredient like flour can vary greatly from batch to batch, affecting the dough's texture and behavior. Trust your instincts and experience: Add a bit of extra flour if the dough feels too loose and sticky, or a splash of water if it seems too dry or too stiff. In time, you'll learn to feel your way to better bread.

SWISS CHARD, FETA, AND EGG PIDE

MAKES 4 PIDES

FOR THE DOUGH

1 teaspoon instant yeast

1 cup (240 ml) lukewarm (98–105°F/37–41°C) water

1 cup (130 g) whole-grain hard red wheat flour, such as Turkey Red or Red Fife

¾ cup (105 g) all-purpose flour

2 teaspoons (10 g) fine sea salt

FOR THE FILLING

3 tablespoons olive oil, plus extra for brushing

½ shallot, thinly sliced

2 garlic cloves, minced

1 bunch Swiss chard (stems and leaves), roughly chopped

Kosher salt to taste

Pinch of chili flakes

½ cup (120 ml) Greek yogurt

5 large eggs

¾ cup (80 g) crumbled feta

Originating in Turkey, pides are round or oblong flatbreads topped with anything from spiced ground meat to tender veggies and salty cheese. First you flatten the dough into an oval with a rolling pin, then you fill it with toppings. To finish, the borders are folded inward. The shaping is not only aesthetically pleasing, it also serves a function: Creating a pizza-like border along the edge of the oval keeps the ingredients from spilling. It takes a bit of playing around to get it right, but by your second pide, you'll get the hang of it. Adding a bit of all-purpose flour makes this dough malleable and easy to work with. Red wheat imparts great flavor. I like a robust variety that will come through, especially since the dish hails from wheat's ancestral home.

Inspired by the classic pairing of greens and eggs, this version incorporates garlicky Swiss chard, crumbled feta, and runny, golden egg yolk. Think of them as personal-size breakfast pizzas; one per person is ideal. The dough comes together easily, then hangs out in the fridge overnight. By morning, the pides are quick to assemble and bake, making them an excellent option for a weekend breakfast. It's a fun activity to make pides according to everyone's taste and enjoy them as soon as they come out of the oven. Or make them in advance; they reheat very well. They can also be enjoyed for lunch or dinner, or even as appetizers for a casual party.

1. To make the dough, sprinkle the yeast over the lukewarm water in a small bowl. Stir with a spoon to help it dissolve, then let it activate for 5 minutes.

continues

2. Mix the flours and fine salt in a medium bowl. Using your hands, make a well in the center of the dry ingredients. Pour the dissolved yeast mixture into the well and mix by hand until a rough dough forms. Turn the dough onto a lightly floured surface and knead for 1 to 2 minutes, dusting with additional flour if necessary until it comes together in a uniform ball.

3. Transfer the dough to an oiled bowl, cover with a kitchen towel or plastic wrap, and let it rise until doubled, 1½ to 2 hours. Rub the dough with olive oil and put in a ziplock bag. Refrigerate overnight, or for up to 2 days.

4. The next morning, place an oven rack in the lowest position and preheat the oven to 450°F (230°C). Lightly brush two rimmed baking sheets with olive oil.

5. In a medium sauté pan, heat the olive oil over medium-low heat. Cook the shallot and garlic until softened, 1 to 2 minutes. Add the chard and cook until tender, stirring occasionally, about 5 minutes. Season with kosher salt and chili flakes to taste, then transfer to a plate to cool completely.

6. In a small bowl, combine the yogurt with 1 egg and a pinch of kosher salt.

7. Divide the dough into 4 equal portions (about 120 g/4¼ ounces each) and knead each into a ball on a lightly floured surface. Let them sit on the kitchen counter for 20 minutes. This resting time will allow the gluten in the dough to relax, making rolling the pides a lot easier. Use your fingertips to pat each dough ball into a disk, then use a rolling pin to flatten into a 10-by-5-inch (25.5 by 12.5 cm) oval. Transfer the ovals to the prepared baking sheets, two per sheet.

8. Spread 2 tablespoons of the yogurt mixture in the center of each oval, leaving a 1-inch (2.5 cm) border uncovered. Top each with equal amounts of the chard, then sprinkle with the feta. Using your fingertips, roll the edges of each oval inward to form a thick border encasing the filling. Crack an egg in the middle of each pide, drizzle with 1 teaspoon olive oil, and season with kosher salt. Using a pastry brush, varnish the border of each pide with olive oil.

9. Bake until the dough is golden and the egg in the center is fully set, 10 to 12 minutes. Remove from the oven and serve immediately.

HEIRLOOM MASA TORTILLAS

MAKES EIGHT 5-INCH (13 CM) TORTILLAS

EQUIPMENT: tortilla press; comal, cast-iron pan, or electric griddle

1¼ cups (155 g) masa harina
1¼ to 1½ cups (300 to 360 ml) water at 90°F (32°C)
1 teaspoon fine sea salt

Few things beat a homemade tortilla. They're a simple and delicious whole-grain staple with unlimited applications, from stuffing or filling to dunking in soup to eating hot off the comal, when their nutty, toasty flavor is at its best. The difference between a forgettable tortilla and a sublime one lies, quite literally, in the hands of the tortilla maker. Here in Los Angeles, tacos are memorable not only for the tasty fillings but because of the tortilla quality. The ones made at beloved eateries like Guisados and HomeState are a topic of conversation among tortilla connoisseurs. If you've never made tortillas before, the idea might seem a bit intimidating, but the process is easy. Your first ones might look a bit wonky, but rest assured that after a few tries, you'll get the hang of things. They require minimal equipment and only three ingredients: masa, water, and salt.

They can be made ahead of time and stored in a ziplock bag, then frozen or refrigerated. They reheat easily in a toaster oven, skillet, or microwave.

1. Cut sixteen 8-inch (20 cm) squares of parchment paper.

2. Put the masa harina in a mixing bowl and add the water gradually, mixing until it forms a uniform dough. If the masa is too stiff, add a couple more tablespoons of water. Similarly, if the masa is too loose, add a bit more masa until the mixture is soft and workable—similar to play dough. Add the salt and mix to incorporate.

3. Cover and let it rest for 20 minutes to allow the masa to hydrate.

4. Divide the masa into 8 equal portions (about 50 g/2 ounces each). Shape each portion into a ball.

5. Line a tortilla press with a parchment square, place a ball of masa in the center, top with another parchment square, and flatten with the press into a tortilla about 5 inches (13 cm) in diameter. Keep the tortilla between the paper squares. Repeat with the remaining masa balls.

6. Heat a comal or cast-iron pan over medium heat. (Alternatively, heat an electric griddle to medium.)

7. Peel the top layer of parchment from a tortilla and place the tortilla directly on the hot surface. Quickly peel off the other parchment layer. Cook for about 2 minutes. When the surface looks dry around the edges, flip and continue to cook on the other side for 1 minute. It's also effective to flip the tortilla a few times to ensure both sides cook evenly. The tortilla may puff during the cooking process but will deflate as it cools, so don't fret. It's actually a sign that it was rolled sufficiently thin.

8. Transfer the cooked tortilla to a plate lined with a linen napkin and cover with another linen napkin. If necessary, wipe the comal with paper towels before cooking the next tortilla. You can stack the tortillas, making sure to cover the stack with the linen napkin so they remain warm and steamy—this important step will keep your tortillas soft and pliable. Enjoy fresh or store in the refrigerator wrapped in plastic. Reheat briefly in a pan, toaster oven, or microwave before serving.

HYBRID TORTILLAS

MAKES EIGHT 6-INCH (15 CM) TORTILLAS

EQUIPMENT: tortilla press; comal, cast-iron pan, or electric griddle

1¼ cups (155 g) masa harina
¾ cup (100 g) whole-grain all-purpose wheat flour, such as Sonora or Frederick
1 tablespoon fine cornmeal
2 tablespoons unsalted butter, solid coconut oil, or vegetable shortening
1 teaspoon fine sea salt
Pinch of baking powder
1 to 1¼ cups (240 to 300 ml) water at 90°F (32°C)

As much as I love corn tortillas, these hybrid tortillas—made with both heirloom masa and whole wheat flour—are my favorite to make because they're a bit more forgiving. They're more flexible, have a bit more spring to them, and don't dry out as fast. Note that the suggested 6-inch (15 cm) diameter is a guideline; you can make them as large (or small) as desired. Use like any other tortilla. They make a great taco.

1. Cut sixteen 8-inch (20 cm) squares of parchment paper.

2. Combine the masa harina, flour, cornmeal, butter, salt, and baking soda in a mixing bowl. Add the water gradually, mixing by hand until a uniform dough forms. If the masa is too stiff, add a couple more tablespoons of water. If the masa is too loose, add a bit more masa until the mixture is soft and workable—similar to play dough. Add the salt and mix to incorporate.

3. Cover and let it rest for 20 minutes to allow the masa to hydrate.

4. Divide the masa into 8 equal portions (65 g/2¼ ounces) each. Shape each portion into a ball.

5. Line a tortilla press with a parchment square, place a ball of masa in the center, top with another parchment square, and flatten with the press into a tortilla about 6 inches (15 cm) in diameter. Keep the tortilla between the parchment squares. Repeat with the remaining masa balls.

6. Heat a comal or cast-iron pan over medium heat. (Alternatively, heat an electric griddle to medium.)

7. Peel the top layer of parchment from a tortilla and place the tortilla directly on the hot surface. Quickly peel off the other parchment layer. Cook for about 2 minutes. When the surface looks dry around the edges, flip, and continue to cook on the other side for 1 minute. It's also effective to flip the tortilla a few times to ensure both sides cook evenly.

8. Transfer the cooked tortilla to a plate lined with a linen napkin and cover with another linen napkin. If necessary, wipe the comal with paper towels before cooking the next tortilla. You can stack the tortillas, making sure to cover the stack with the linen napkin so they remain warm and steamy—this important step will keep your tortillas soft and pliable. Enjoy fresh or store in the refrigerator wrapped in plastic. Reheat briefly in a pan, toaster oven, or microwave before serving.

MASA AND OTHER NIXTAMALIZED FOODS

In the United States—specifically California and other Southwestern states—nixtamalized foods are everywhere. Tortillas, tamales, pupusas, empanadas, sopes, pozole, and more can be seen in food stands, farmers' markets, restaurant menus, and grocery stores, where they're understood and appreciated by people from diverse backgrounds.

Nixtamalization is an ancient Mesoamerican process that involves soaking and cooking corn in an alkaline solution, traditionally wood ash or crushed limestone. These calcium oxide–rich substances react with the maize, softening it and coaxing out essential vitamins and minerals, like niacin, calcium, and iron.

If you were to pulverize dried maize kernels, you'd get a stiff, hard-to-digest cornmeal. Grind nixtamalized corn and you're left with a fine, nutritious, and highly digestible substance. This is masa: the epitome of nutritious, whole-grain fare. The discovery of nixtamalization transformed tough, starchy dent corn into a versatile staple, one that fueled entire societies and allowed pre-Columbian empires to thrive.

The masa-making process has six main steps: washing, cooking, steeping, rinsing, milling, and cooking again. Stop after rinsing but before milling and you're left with soft, saturated kernels, called hominy, the main ingredient in pozole. Nixtamalized corn that's dehydrated to become shelf-stable is masa harina. (That's a bit of a misnomer, though—masa harina translates to "dough flour." "Nixtamalized corn flour" would be a more accurate name. In Spanish, we refer to masa harina simply as "masa.")

Masa harina lines the shelves of many conventional supermarkets and can also be ordered online (see page 325). Never try replacing it with cornmeal, which is coarser and not nixtamalized and thus will behave differently when cooked.

TORTILLAS ALIÑADAS

MAKES EIGHT 6-INCH (15 CM) TORTILLAS

EQUIPMENT: tortilla press; comal, cast-iron pan, or electric griddle

2 cups (250 g) masa harina
1¼ to 1½ cups (295 to 355 ml) water at 90°F (32°C)
1 teaspoon fine sea salt
½ cup (50 g) grated cotija
½ cup (30 g) shredded mozzarella
⅓ cup (75 g) sour cream, plus extra for serving
¼ cup (55 g/½ stick/2 ounces) unsalted butter at room temperature
Vegetable oil as needed to cook the tortillas

FOR SERVING
Sour cream, avocado slices, refried beans, and/or pickled vegetables

Tortillas aliñadas is what Costa Ricans call a large enriched corn tortilla served with trimmings that transform it into a meal. This tortilla starts like a regular corn tortilla, with heirloom masa. The masa is combined with cheese, sour cream, and butter, making it rich and flavorful. The tortilla can be served simply with natilla—a sour cream similar to Mexican crema—or spruced up with refried beans, sliced avocado, shredded cabbage salad, or vegetable escabeche. My favorite tortillas aliñadas are served at El Churrasco. The legendary Costa Rican restaurant is conveniently located in the foothills of the Poás Volcano National Park, home to an active volcano with one of the largest craters in the world and a turquoise sulfur lagoon. Their tortillas are equally popular among locals and tourists, and you can always find tortilla fans making the trek from all over the country. If you happen to visit the Poás volcano (which you should do very early in the morning) only to realize the skies won't be clear enough to see the crater in all its glory (sadly, it happens more often than not), don't be totally disappointed. Know there's a tortilla aliñada waiting for you at the foot of the mountain. The tortilla is larger than a regular tortilla, 10 to 12 inches (25.5 to 30 cm) in diameter, and is definitely more than enough breakfast for one. For sensible eaters, I like to make them smaller, as I do here.

1. Cut sixteen 8-inch (20 cm) squares of parchment paper.

2. In a mixing bowl, combine the masa harina and salt. Using your hands, make a well in the center of the dry ingredients. Pour the water into the well and mix by hand until a uniform dough forms. Add the cheeses, sour cream, and butter and continue mixing by hand until well incorporated.

continues

3. Cover and let it rest for 20 minutes to allow the masa to hydrate.

4. Divide the masa into 8 equal portions (about 100 g/3½ ounces each). Shape each portion into a ball.

5. Line a tortilla press with a parchment square, place a ball of masa in the center, top with another parchment square, and flatten with the press into a tortilla about 6 inches (15 cm) in diameter. Keep the tortilla between the parchment squares. Repeat with the remaining masa balls.

6. Heat a comal or cast-iron skillet over medium heat and drizzle with vegetable oil. (Alternatively, heat an electric griddle to medium.)

7. Peel the top layer of parchment from a tortilla and place the tortilla directly on the hot surface. Quickly peel off the other parchment square. When the tortilla starts to turn golden, about 3 minutes, flip and continue to cook on the other side, about 3 minutes more.

8. Transfer the cooked tortilla to a plate and serve immediately with your favorite toppings.

YEASTED BREADS

For the most part, breads baked with commercial yeast can be made in less time than sourdough, and allow for the sort of consistency that's harder to nail down with wild yeast cultures. There are multiple ways to enhance and highlight ferment-y flavors when working with commercial yeast. A personal favorite is poolish—a preferment made with a small quantity of yeast, plus equal parts flour and water. Allowed to ferment overnight, the mixture develops tangy notes as well as a few other bread-enhancing qualities (for the poolish 411, see the recipe for Khorasan Baguettes on page 209). But for enriched breads, which get flavor from dairy, eggs, sweeteners, and other seasonings, I tend to add the yeast straight up (dissolved in milk or water for even dispersal, then incorporated into the dough).

At the bakery and at home, we store yeast in an airtight container in the fridge. If you're concerned that your yeast might be weak or near the end of its life, it's always best to do a trial run before embarking on a time-consuming recipe. Just combine ½ cup warm water with 1 teaspoon sugar and 2 teaspoons instant yeast. After a few minutes, the yeast should look foamy and smell bready. If it doesn't, it's time for some new yeast.

KHORASAN BAGUETTES

MAKES 4 BAGUETTES

EQUIPMENT: instant-read thermometer, roasting pan for steam bath, bread lame

FOR THE POOLISH
- ½ cup plus 2 tablespoons (150 ml) room-temperature (68–77°F/20–25°C) water
- 1 cup (125 g) whole-grain Khorasan wheat flour
- ⅛ teaspoon instant yeast

FOR THE BAGUETTE DOUGH
- 1 teaspoon instant yeast
- 1⅓ cups (315 ml) lukewarm (98–105°F/37–41°C) water
- 1 cup (130 g) whole-grain hard white or red wheat flour, such as Starr or Red Fife
- 1½ cups (190 g) whole-grain Khorasan wheat flour
- 1 cup (135 g) bread flour, plus extra for dusting
- 2 teaspoons (10 g) fine sea salt

At Friends & Family, baguettes have become an optimal vehicle for trying new grains. Anytime we want to check on a new flour's flavor or performance, we add it to our trusty baguette recipe. We've made some incredibly delicious baguettes as a result. My preference is for those made with darker wheats or blends of wheat and rye, but the rest of the crew likes to keep baguettes on the lighter side. This recipe is hands down their most beloved version. It relies on a preferment made entirely from whole-grain Khorasan wheat (see My Favorite Flours, page 313). The magical mixture is poolish—a baking staple combining flour and water, plus a small amount of instant yeast. After a few hours, the loose batter becomes bubbly and pleasantly acidic. Giving the Khorasan a jump start on fermentation allows its flavor and aroma to shine, so the finished bread is more complex. Poolish also aids the dough's extensibility, allowing it to stretch without tearing (think of a balloon being inflated), yielding a more open crumb.

I recommend making the poolish the day before you plan to bake, then refrigerating it overnight. About an hour before you mix the dough, bring the poolish to room temperature. The recipe takes about 3 hours from there, so mix the dough in the early afternoon if you want fresh baguettes for dinner, or in the morning if you'd like them ready for lunch. If you want baguettes for breakfast, you can mix the day before, ferment, shape, refrigerate overnight, and bake them in the morning.

I've found that four is a solid number of baguettes to make at once. If the overall mass is any smaller, the dough won't ferment as nicely. Also, a decent amount of time and technique goes into preparing baguettes. With a yield of four, you can enjoy one or two immediately, then pop any leftovers in the freezer. Plus, when learning, it's nice to have four to shape and score—more practice opportunities!

continues

1. To make the poolish, combine the water, flour, and yeast in a mixing bowl and stir until the mixture resembles a thick pancake batter. Cover tightly with plastic wrap and let it ferment at room temperature for 3 to 4 hours, until the poolish is bubbly and has increased in volume. At this point the poolish can be refrigerated for up to 2 days.

2. When ready to mix the baguette dough, remove the poolish from the refrigerator and let it sit at room temperature for 1 hour.

3. Sprinkle the yeast over the lukewarm water in a small bowl. Stir with a spoon to help it dissolve, then let it activate for 5 minutes.

4. In the bowl of a stand mixer fitted with the dough hook attachment, combine the flours and salt with the dissolved yeast mixture and the tempered poolish and mix on low speed until the ingredients form a ball, about 2 minutes, scraping the sides of the bowl with a silicone spatula if necessary. Increase the speed to medium and mix for another 2 minutes to develop the dough further.

5. Transfer to a lightly floured surface and knead into a ball. The dough should be somewhat firm but pliable, and shouldn't stick to your hands. Transfer to a bowl lightly coated with nonstick spray and let it ferment at room temperature for 1½ to 2 hours, until the dough doubles in volume.

6. Put the bowl of fermented dough in the refrigerator and chill for 30 minutes. This step will make shaping the baguettes a lot easier.

7. Turn the dough onto a floured surface. Using a bench knife, divide into 4 equal pieces (about 265 g/9¼ ounces each). Shape each portion into a loose rectangle, resisting punching the dough as much as possible. Let the dough rectangles rest on the work surface for 10 minutes. This waiting period will allow the gluten in the dough to relax.

8. Place two oven racks in the middle positions and preheat the oven to 450°F (230°C). Place an empty roasting pan at the bottom of the oven. Coat two rimmed baking sheets lightly with nonstick spray.

9. Working with one rectangle at a time, flatten each portion with your fingertips into a 3-by-4-inch (8 by 10 cm) rectangle. Roll the rectangle from top to bottom into a tight cylinder (as you would a jelly roll), trying to create as much tension as possible. Using both hands, roll the cylinder into a rope 12 to 15 inches (30 to 40 cm) long (or about the length of your baking sheet) with tapered ends. Transfer the finished baguettes to the prepared baking sheets. You should be able to place two baguettes per tray, 4 inches (10 cm) apart. Let the baguettes proof for 20 minutes, uncovered, at room temperature.

10. Sprinkle the tops of the baguettes lightly with flour. Using a lame, score 3 or 4 diagonal slits, 1 inch (2.5 cm) apart, along the length of each baguette. Right before baking, carefully pour 2 cups water into the hot roasting pan in the oven. Immediately put the sheets in the oven and bake for 10 minutes. Avoid opening the oven during the first 10 minutes to prevent the steam from dissipating. Then rotate the sheets and switch their positions in the oven. At this point, you do want the steam to escape the oven so the baguettes can develop a crispy crust.

11. Bake for another 10 to 15 minutes, or until the baguettes turn amber brown. Enjoy the baguettes the day they're prepared or wrap in plastic and freeze for up to 2 weeks. Freshen the thawed baguettes by reheating in a 350°F (175°C) oven for a few minutes.

HOW TO CREATE STEAM IN YOUR OVEN

Before I worked with steam injection ovens at the bakery, I couldn't be bothered with all the DIY advice out there. But after seeing the difference a little steam makes in breads and croissants, I knew I would have to give it a go. The effect is not unlike what happens when you bake bread in a Dutch oven: Moisture emanating from a highly hydrated loaf is captured by the lid, allowing the surface of the bread to remain soft, moist, and able to expand as much as possible before the crust begins to set. Steam also makes your crust shinier and pleasantly chewier. The simplest and safest method to create steam inside your oven is to place a roasting pan at the bottom of the oven while it's preheating. Once the oven and roasting pan are hot, quickly pour 2 cups of water into the roasting pan, put your breads on the bottom or middle rack, and close the oven door. Timing is crucial: You must add the water right before the bread goes in to make the most of the initial burst of steam. Be careful! The water will hiss and splatter when it hits the hot pan. The steam is most impactful during the first 10 minutes of baking, so you must keep the door shut during this stage; after that you can let the water run dry while the bread finishes baking. To break down your steam setup after baking, turn off the oven and let the roasting pan cool completely, then remove from the oven. Use this method to bake Khorasan Baguettes (page 209), Rosemary Sandwich Loaf (page 212), Durum Ciabatta (page 214), Benched Sourdough Rolls (page 248), Apple Levain (page 250), and Chocolate-Cherry Pan Loaf (page 273). If you're up for it, I would even recommend steaming croissants.

ROSEMARY SANDWICH LOAF

MAKES 1 LOAF

EQUIPMENT: instant-read thermometer, 8½-by-4½-inch (22 by 11 cm) loaf pan, roasting pan for steam bath

FOR THE POOLISH

⅓ cup (80 ml) room-temperature (68–77°F/ 20–25°C) water

½ cup (65 g) whole-grain hard white or red wheat flour, such as Starr or Red Fife

Pinch of instant yeast

FOR THE DOUGH

1 teaspoon instant yeast

1 cup (240 ml) room-temperature (68–77°F/ 20–25°C) water

1¼ cups (165 g) whole-grain hard white or red wheat flour, such as Starr or Red Fife

1¼ cups (170 g) bread flour, plus extra for dusting

2 teaspoons (10 g) fine sea salt

2 tablespoons olive oil, plus extra for brushing

1 tablespoon coarsely chopped fresh rosemary

Like the Khorasan Baguettes (page 209), this recipe relies on poolish, the powerhouse preferment that has been adding complexity and extensibility to breads since the nineteenth century. To keep your baking timeline reasonable, mix the poolish the day before you plan to bake and refrigerate it overnight. Let the mixture come to room temperature, then proceed with the recipe.

Choose a high-gluten whole-grain wheat flour for this bread. Rosemary is an assertive flavor and will stand out even when combined with strong-tasting wheats. The recipe also includes bread flour, which helps the loaf to be more expansive. I recommend baking this bread in a loaf pan. It will make shaping a lot easier, and the bread will yield perfect sandwich slices.

For a quick, delicious breakfast, smear softened butter over a thick slice of rosemary bread, then top with prosciutto. At the height of summer, use your freshly baked loaf to make an old-school tomato sandwich: Cut substantial slices of tomato, season generously with olive oil and sea salt, coat 2 slices of rosemary bread with thick mayo, and sandwich the tomato slices between them.

1. To make the poolish, combine the water, flour, and yeast in a mixing bowl and stir until the mixture resembles a thick pancake batter. Cover tightly with plastic wrap and let it ferment at room temperature for 3 to 4 hours, until the poolish is bubbly and has increased in volume. At this point, the poolish can be refrigerated for up to 2 days.

2. When ready to mix the dough, remove the poolish from the refrigerator and let it sit at room temperature for 1 hour.

3. Sprinkle the yeast over the lukewarm water in a small bowl. Stir with a spoon to help it dissolve, then let it activate for 5 minutes.

4. In a mixing bowl, combine the flours, salt, and olive oil with the dissolved yeast mixture and the tempered poolish and mix by hand until the ingredients come together in a dough. Mix in the chopped rosemary.

5. Transfer to a floured surface and knead for 2 minutes to further develop the structure of the dough. The dough should be somewhat firm yet pliable. Transfer to a bowl lightly coated with nonstick spray and let it ferment at room temperature until doubled, 1½ to 2 hours.

6. Brush an 8½-by-4½-inch (22 by 11 cm) loaf pan with olive oil.

7. Turn the dough onto a floured surface and gently flatten it into a rough 8-inch (20 cm) square. With both hands, roll the dough away from you to form a thick log (as you would a jelly roll). Place the cylinder, seam side down, in the prepared loaf pan and brush generously with olive oil. Cover loosely with a kitchen towel and proof for 1½ to 2 hours at room temperature.

8. Place an oven rack in the middle position and preheat the oven to 375°F (190°C). Put an empty roasting pan at the bottom of the oven.

9. Right before baking, carefully pour 2 cups water into the hot roasting pan in the oven. Immediately put the pan in the oven and bake for 20 minutes. Avoid opening the oven during this period to prevent the steam from dissipating. Then rotate the pan and bake for another 10 to 15 minutes, until the top of the loaf is light golden brown and an instant-read thermometer inserted in the center reaches 200°F (93°C).

10. Remove the loaf from the oven and transfer to a cooling rack. Let it rest for at least 1 hour before cutting into it. Store the baked loaf in a paper bag at room temperature for 2 days. Or wrap in plastic and freeze for up to 2 weeks. Freshen the thawed loaf by reheating in a 350°F (175°C) oven for a few minutes.

DURUM CIABATTA

MAKES 1 CIABATTA

EQUIPMENT: instant-read thermometer, roasting pan for steam bath

FOR THE POOLISH
- ½ cup plus 2 tablespoons (150 ml) room-temperature (68–77°F/20–25°C) water
- 1 cup (130 g) whole-grain hard white or red wheat flour, such as Starr or Red Fife
- ⅛ teaspoon instant yeast

FOR THE CIABATTA DOUGH
- ¾ teaspoon instant yeast
- 1 cup (240 ml) lukewarm (98–105°F/37–41°C) water
- ¾ cup (100 g) whole-grain hard white or red wheat flour, such as Starr or Red Fife
- ½ cup (70 g) whole-grain durum wheat flour
- ¾ cup (100 g) bread flour, plus extra for dusting
- 2 teaspoons (10 g) fine sea salt

Ciabatta is a fairly new invention. In the 1980s, Arnaldo Cavallari, a baker and miller in northeastern Italy, set out to create a sandwich bread fit to compete with baguettes—the skinny French loaves had taken the Italian market by storm. He was committed to using organic, locally grown wheat and a high-hydration dough. After trial and error, he landed on the crisp, open-crumbed ciabatta we know and love. Ciabatta is an excellent sandwich bread—Italian cold-cut sandwiches come to mind—but it's also a great table bread ideal for dipping into hearty stews or sopping the last bit of sauce on a plate.

To keep the timeline manageable, I suggest making the poolish the day before you plan to bake, then refrigerating it. Let it come to room temperature for about an hour before mixing the dough. Because this dough is wet and batter-like, your mixer's paddle attachment is a more effective mixing tool than the dough hook. A bit of bread flour in combination with the whole wheat makes working with this loose dough much easier.

1. To make the poolish, combine the water, flour, and yeast in a mixing bowl and stir until the mixture resembles a thick pancake batter. Cover tightly with plastic wrap and let it ferment at room temperature for 3 to 4 hours, until the poolish is bubbly and has increased in volume. At this point the poolish can be refrigerated for up to 2 days.

2. When ready to mix the ciabatta dough, remove the poolish from the refrigerator and let it sit at room temperature for 1 hour.

3. Sprinkle the yeast over the lukewarm water in a small bowl. Stir with a spoon to help it dissolve, then let it activate for 5 minutes.

4. In the bowl of a stand mixer fitted with the paddle attachment, combine the flours and salt with the dissolved yeast mixture and tempered poolish and mix on low speed until the ingredients come together in a loose and slack dough, 1 minute. Increase the speed to medium and mix for another 2 minutes, then increase the speed to high and mix for another 2 minutes to develop the dough further. Transfer to a medium bowl lightly coated with nonstick spray and cover with a kitchen towel or plastic wrap. Let sit at room temperature for 30 minutes.

5. Moisten your hands with water and dig under the front end of the dough, stretch it out, and fold it back on top of the dough. Dig under the back end of the dough and repeat the same stretch-and-fold motion. Do the same on each of the sides. Finally, turn the dough over and tuck it into a ball. This process is known as stretching and folding and helps strengthen the dough. After each series of stretching and folding, the dough should feel significantly stronger.

6. Cover the dough and let it rest for 30 minutes. Then stretch and fold a second time, just as you did before. Let it rest for another 30 minutes, then stretch and fold one last time, for a total of three times. Let the dough ferment for 30 minutes after the last fold.

7. Place an oven rack in the middle position and preheat the oven to 450°F (230°C). Place an empty roasting pan at the bottom of the oven. Sprinkle a rimmed baking sheet with durum flour.

8. Turn the dough onto a generously floured surface. Loosely stretch the dough into a 12-by-8-inch (30 by 20 cm) rectangle; resist punching the dough to avoid releasing the gases produced during the fermentation process. Fold the dough in thirds, as if you were folding a business letter to insert in an envelope, and, using both hands, transfer carefully to the prepared baking sheet. Let the ciabatta rise at room temperature for 30 minutes.

9. Right before baking, carefully pour 2 cups water into the hot roasting pan in the oven. Immediately put the sheet in the oven and bake for 12 minutes. Avoid opening the oven during the first 12 minutes to prevent the steam from dissipating. Then rotate the sheet and bake for another 10 minutes, or until the ciabatta is a rich mahogany brown.

10. Remove from the oven and transfer to a cooling rack. Let the ciabatta rest for at least 1 hour before cutting into it. Store the ciabatta, tightly wrapped in plastic, at room temperature for up to 2 days or in the freezer for up to 2 weeks. Freshen the thawed ciabatta by reheating in a 350°F (175°C) oven for a few minutes.

MILK AND HONEY BRIOCHE

MAKES 1 LOAF

EQUIPMENT: instant-read thermometer, 8½-by-4½-inch (22 by 11 cm) loaf pan

- ½ cup (120 ml) lukewarm (98–105°F/37–41°C) whole milk
- ¼ cup (60 ml) honey
- ¾ teaspoon instant yeast
- 2⅓ cups (305 g) whole-grain hard white wheat flour, such as Starr or Edison, plus extra for dusting
- 2 large eggs at room temperature plus 1 large beaten egg for brushing
- 11 tablespoons (155 g/5½ ounces) unsalted butter at room temperature, cut into 1-inch (2.5 cm) cubes
- 2 teaspoons (10 g) fine sea salt

Brioche will be forever imbued with an air of decadence and indulgence. After all, brioche was once a symbol of the type of foods royalty feasted on while the common man starved. With a butter content that can match that of the flour by weight, depending on the recipe, it is best saved for special occasions that justify the splurge in calories and butter dollars.

Traditionally, brioche is hydrated with eggs and a bit of water, and lightly sweetened with a small amount of sugar. When we developed this recipe at Friends & Family, we leaned on milk and honey to highlight the elegant, warm cereal flavor of the heirloom wheat flours we like to use to make enriched doughs.

Brioche is an ideal bread to make solely with whole wheat flour. Remember, whole-grain wheat flour loves butter, and brioche contains the highest butter quantity in the bread kingdom. With its naturally high fiber content, whole wheat performs quite well in enriched doughs. All that bran acts like a sponge, swelling with fat content and retaining moisture. I like to make brioche with hard white wheat because it gives the brioche a creamy white hue. However, hard reds work just as well, and since they tend to have a strong, full-bodied flavor profile, they make for a very flavorful brioche. So pick your wheat depending on what you plan to do with your brioche dough. If pairing with soft herbs, stone fruits, or summer berries, opt for a hard white, and if pairing with chocolate, cured meats, or nuts, use hard red. Just make sure that it's high in gluten.

Brioche will last for several days and makes delicious morning toasts, pain perdu or French toast, and sandwiches. The dough itself can be used for all kinds of preparations, such as Cinnamon-Raisin Brioche (page 221), Brioche Jam Buns (page 223), and Brioche à la Crème (page 227).

1. Combine the lukewarm milk and honey in a small bowl and sprinkle the yeast over them. Stir with a spoon to help it dissolve, then let it activate for 5 minutes.

continues

2. In the bowl of a stand mixer fitted with the dough hook attachment, combine the flour with the eggs and the dissolved yeast mixture. Mix on low speed for 2 minutes, or until the ingredients come together in a dough. Turn off the mixer and let the dough sit for 20 minutes. This resting period will allow the flour to hydrate, properly building strength and extensibility in the process.

3. Add the butter in three batches, mixing on medium speed for 2 minutes after each addition. Take care to scrape the bottom and sides of the bowl with a silicone spatula occasionally to ensure the butter is fully incorporated. Once all the butter is in, add the salt and mix for 2 more minutes. Increase the speed to high and mix for 1 minute to develop the dough's structure further. At this point, the brioche dough will be quite sticky.

4. Transfer the dough to a generously floured working surface, dust additional flour on top of the dough, and knead gently into a ball. Coat a medium bowl with nonstick spray and place the dough in it. Cover with a kitchen towel or plastic wrap and let it rise until doubled, 1½ to 2 hours.

5. Punch the dough in the middle with your fist to release the gases built up during fermentation, cover once again, and refrigerate for 2 hours or, even better, overnight.

6. The next day, remove the dough from the refrigerator and let it sit at room temperature for 1 hour. Cut a 12-by-7-inch (30 by 15 cm) rectangle of parchment paper. Lightly coat an 8½-by-4½-inch (22 by 11 cm) loaf pan with nonstick spray, line with the parchment paper rectangle, and fold the excess paper outward to the sides. This paper sling will make the step of unmolding the brioche much easier.

7. Working on a floured surface, divide the dough into 2 equal portions (about 375 g/ 13¼ ounces each). Shape each portion into a ball. Put the balls side by side in the loaf pan.

8. Cover loosely with a kitchen towel and proof at warm room temperature for 3 to 4 hours, until the dough is puffy and soft to the touch and has risen to the point that it fills the pan. You can also test if your dough is properly proofed by pressing it lightly with a moistened finger. If the dough bounces back, it needs to proof longer; if your finger leaves an indentation, the dough is ready to be baked.

9. Place an oven rack in the middle position and preheat the oven to 350°F (175°C).

10. Brush the top of the loaf with the beaten egg and bake for 20 minutes. Then rotate the pan and bake for another 20 minutes, until the top of the brioche is deep mahogany brown and an instant-read thermometer inserted in the center reaches 200°F (93°C).

11. Remove the loaf from the oven. Let it rest for 20 to 30 minutes, or until cool enough to handle, then use the paper sling to pull the brioche from the mold, transfer to a cooling rack, and let it sit for 1 hour, until it reaches room temperature.

12. The brioche can be enjoyed immediately or saved for later. Wrap tightly with plastic and store at room temperature for up to 2 days, in the refrigerator for up to 1 week, or in the freezer for up to 1 month.

FOR BRIOCHE SUCCESS

I would place brioche as intermediate on the difficulty scale because it requires full attention from the baker at several critical points.

First, although many traditional recipes skip this, I hydrate the flour with the liquid ingredients (milk, honey, and eggs) and let it sit before mixing in the butter, which contributes greatly to the development of the dough. Think of this step as a cheater's autolyse—a popular bread-making technique in which we mix flour and water, then let it rest for about 20 minutes to help gluten development and build strength in the dough.

Second, bear in mind that the temperature of the butter will dictate the rhythm of the recipe. To mix it in, it's essential to use room-temperature butter. Equally important is taking your time when incorporating it, adding a bit at a time. It may be tempting to rush the process of incorporating the butter, but be patient. It takes a while for the dough to absorb all the fat. As much as I like to believe that brioche can be made by hand, it is quite difficult to incorporate such a large amount of butter efficiently. A stand mixer is a must.

Lastly, after fermenting and before baking, you must refrigerate the dough until firm, a step best accomplished by chilling overnight. (So yes, take note: This recipe requires 2 days.) The next morning, allow the dough to come to temperature so that it's pliable enough to shape. Be sure to dust your work surface with the same flour you used in the dough. The mixture is soft and sticky, so the flour on your countertop will get picked up by the dough.

CINNAMON-RAISIN BRIOCHE

MAKES 1 LOAF

EQUIPMENT: instant-read thermometer, 8½-by-4½-inch (22 by 11 cm) loaf pan

1 batch Milk and Honey Brioche dough (page 217), chilled overnight
3 tablespoons packed dark brown sugar
1 tablespoon ground cinnamon
Pinch of kosher salt
All-purpose flour for dusting
1 large egg, beaten
½ cup (70 g) golden raisins (optional)

Most of the cinnamon-raisin bread recipes I've tried overpromise and underdeliver. That's because their characteristic cinnamon swirl causes the bread to gap or collapse. The secret lies in ensuring the swirl ingredients pack a cinnamony punch without compromising the integrity of the loaf. It's more a feat of engineering than anything else.

For this variation, I recommend making the dough with a hard red flour. Its assertive flavor is a worthy match for the intensity of cinnamon and sugar. The raisins add great texture and delicious chew, but they also bring a slight tartness. For maximum cinnamon flavor, I make a concentrated blend of cinnamon and dark brown sugar, sprinkle it over the surface of the stretched-out brioche dough, then scatter on a few golden raisins and roll into a log as if I were making cinnamon rolls.

The most effective way to ensure the sugar sticks to the dough is to brush the surface with beaten egg. To avoid drama, make sure to stick to the indicated amount of cinnamon sugar, even if it's tempting to add more, and roll your log as tightly as you can to prevent uncoiling. The stuffed log is baked in a loaf pan, seam side down, to keep all its parts in their place.

Enjoy the brioche an hour after pulling it out of the oven. Resist breaking into the loaf sooner—slicing it early could tragically smash down the bread. It will keep for a couple of days at room temperature, and longer in the refrigerator or freezer. Older bread still makes for delicious toast—and French toast!

1. Pull the brioche dough from the refrigerator and let it come to room temperature on the kitchen counter for 1 hour.

2. In a small bowl combine the brown sugar, cinnamon, and salt.

3. Cut a 12-by-7-inch (30 by 15 cm) rectangle of parchment paper. Lightly coat an 8½-by-4½-inch (22 by 11 cm) loaf pan with nonstick spray, line with the parchment paper rectangle, and fold the excess paper outward to the sides. This paper sling will make the step of unmolding the loaf much easier.

continues

4. Roll the brioche dough into an 8-by-16-inch (20 by 40.5 cm) rectangle on a lightly floured surface. Orient the dough rectangle so that the shorter ends are parallel to your shoulders. Brush the brioche with a thin layer of the beaten egg all the way to the edges with a pastry brush. Reserve the leftover beaten egg to brush the loaf prior to baking.

5. Cover with the cinnamon sugar, using the palm of your hand to spread it gently and evenly over the entire surface. Sprinkle with the raisins, if using.

6. With both hands, roll the dough away from you to form a log (as you would a jelly roll). Rock the log back and forth to tighten it and elongate it a bit. Gently tuck the edges and transfer to the prepared loaf pan.

7. Cover loosely with a kitchen towel or plastic wrap and proof at warm room temperature for 3 to 4 hours, until the loaf is puffy and soft to the touch, or until it no longer bounces back when you gently press with a moistened index finger.

8. Place an oven rack in the middle position and preheat the oven to 350°F (175°C).

9. Gently brush the top of the proofed loaf with the remaining beaten egg. Bake for 20 minutes. Then rotate the loaf pan and bake for another 25 minutes, until the top is golden and an instant-read thermometer inserted in the center registers 200°F (93°C).

10. Remove from the oven. Let it rest for 30 minutes, then remove from the pan, transfer to a cooling rack, and wait at least 1 hour before slicing. The brioche can be enjoyed immediately or saved for later. Wrap tightly with plastic and store at room temperature for up to 2 days, in the refrigerator for up to 1 week, or in the freezer for up to 1 month.

BRIOCHE JAM BUNS

MAKES 9 BUNS

- 1 batch Milk and Honey Brioche dough (page 217), chilled overnight
- 3 tablespoons whole-grain all-purpose or hard red wheat flour, such as Sonora or Red Fife, plus extra for dusting
- 3 tablespoons sugar
- 2 tablespoons cold unsalted butter, cut into ½-inch (1.25 cm) cubes
- 1 large egg, beaten
- ¾ cup (180 ml) any flavor store-bought or homemade jam (page 76) or marmalade (page 177)

We don't make these regularly at the bakery, but when we do, it's because we have a special jam we want to highlight. To celebrate our favorite fruits, we throw four festivals throughout the year. The first one is strawberry themed, followed by cherry, then peach. We save apples, pears, and quinces for the last festival of the year, Spice Fest, which is right around the holidays. Our festivals are a one-day affair. We come up with a small menu of six or seven pastries featuring the fruit of the season, then bake truckloads of them. It's a great creative outlet for us bakers, and our customers love them, too. Peach Fest is so huge we've had to turn it into a two-day festival instead of just one. No matter the festival, you can count on us making these brioche buns and filling them with the fruit of the moment.

The buns are very easy to prepare and always look enticing. Think buttery brioche, jam center, and streusel topping, which adds more texture and also prevents the jam from burning. Because the buns are smaller, they can potentially proof fast, so keep a watchful eye. You can use the flavor of your jam as a cue for what wheat variety to use, but it really doesn't matter in this recipe. The jam will hold its own because it is deposited right in the center of the bun, rather than spread throughout. Any jam works, but these are particularly delicious with Cara Cara Orange Marmalade (page 177).

1. Pull the brioche dough from the refrigerator and let it come to room temperature on the kitchen counter for 1 hour. Line two rimmed baking sheets with parchment paper.

2. Transfer the brioche to a lightly floured surface. Divide the dough into 9 equal portions (about 85 g/3 ounces each) and roll each into a ball. Arrange the buns on the prepared sheets, spacing them at least 3 inches (7.5 cm) apart.

3. Let them rise at room temperature for 1 hour, or until they no longer bounce back when you press them gently with a moistened finger.

continues

4. In the meantime, make the streusel. Combine the flour and sugar in a medium bowl. Quickly cut the cold butter cubes into the dry ingredients by pinching the butter with your fingertips—imagine you're snapping your fingers—until the mixture resembles a coarse meal with crumbs the size of a pea. Refrigerate the streusel until ready to use.

5. Place two oven racks in the middle positions and preheat the oven to 350°F (175°C).

6. Brush the buns with the beaten egg. Insert your index finger in the center of each bun and move it in a circular motion, pressing all the way down to create a crater. Fill the crater with 2 tablespoons jam or marmalade. Top each bun with the streusel, making sure to cover the jam center.

7. Bake for 12 minutes. Rotate the sheets, switch their positions in the oven, and bake for another 12 minutes, until the streusel is golden brown.

8. Remove from the oven. Let the buns cool completely before serving. Store in an airtight container at room temperature for up to 1 day.

STREUSEL

If you ever visit our bakery, Friends & Family, you'll soon realize that I'm obsessed with crumble toppings. Streusel is the type I make most often. Its name comes from old German and means "something strewn." We use it in all the traditional ways, like sprinkled over coffee cakes and muffins, as well as in not-so-traditional ways, like atop cookies or yeasted pastries that need a little pizzazz. It comes together easily by progressively pinching pieces of butter into flour and sugar until the mixture resembles small rocks and pebbles. Whenever I'm showing this technique to a new baker, I tell them to think of kitty litter (a gross but effective example). Keep in mind that it is easy to overmix—if you take it too far, you'll wind up with cookie dough. For guaranteed streusel success, I recommend chilling your ingredients prior to mixing. This will prevent the butter from warming up too fast. If you can feel the streusel melting in your hands, be sure to take a pause, refrigerate for 30 minutes, then resume streusel making. If you're a streusel lover like me, make extra and freeze it. Just sprinkle it on a tray and put it in the freezer. Once it is rock solid, consolidate into a ziplock bag. You'll have streusel to sprinkle on a whim whenever your heart desires!

BRIOCHE À LA CRÈME

MAKES ONE 10-INCH (25.5 CM) TART

1 batch Milk and Honey Brioche dough (page 217), chilled overnight
All-purpose flour for dusting
1 cup (240 ml) sour cream
1 large egg plus 1 large beaten egg for brushing
¼ cup (50 g) sugar, plus extra for sprinkling
Candied Kumquats (page 229), golden raisins, or prunes to garnish (optional)

This cream-filled tart-like creation was developed by Nancy Silverton as the base of a very famous dessert at Campanile. It was a tough pickup for me as a young dessert plater: You had to warm up your brioche tart in the oven while simultaneously poaching fruit that would turn to mush if you didn't pay close attention. The warm brioche went on the plate first, sauced generously with the poached fruit. The final touch was a cold, fluffy sabayon, which would begin to melt as soon as it hit the hot fruit. All this while screaming for a runner to take the dessert to the table *stat*. Whenever possible, I would save a leftover slice to take home and have for breakfast, which is how I know that it makes a great morning pastry. To this day, whenever I run into an old Campanile regular, they ask if I still make their beloved brioche dessert. Now they can make it themselves.

In this tart, the brioche is the crust. Because it is free-form and no mold is required, make sure to construct a nice border that will hold the creamy center in. You can top the tart with dried fruit or candied citrus peel. I love Candied Kumquats (page 229) for this.

I recommend a neutral hard white wheat flour for the brioche dough so you can really appreciate the subtly tangy cream filling. You'll need only half a batch of the brioche dough recipe; I suggest reserving the other half to make a half batch of Brioche Jam Buns (page 223).

1. Line a rimmed baking sheet with parchment paper.

2. Transfer the refrigerated brioche to a lightly floured surface and divide into 2 equal portions (about 360 g/13 ounces each). Put one portion back in the refrigerator to use for another project. Let the remaining portion come to room temperature on the kitchen counter for 1 hour. (Refrigerated brioche dough must be used within a day. You can also freeze the dough for up to 3 days; after that, it begins to deteriorate. To thaw the frozen dough, let it sit at room temperature for 2 to 3 hours and use as desired.)

3. To form the brioche, round the remaining portion into a ball. Using a rolling pin, flatten the dough into a 12-inch (30 cm) circle. Transfer to the prepared baking sheet.

continues

4. Use your fingertips to dimple the middle until completely flat, leaving a 2-inch (5 cm) thick border untouched—the rolled brioche will resemble a pizza. To make a decorative border, place your thumb on the edge, fold the dough over your thumb, and press where the edge connects with the circle to secure. Repeat to form a ropelike pattern all around the edge. The thick border will prevent the filling from spilling over.

5. Let it rise at room temperature for 1 hour, until it no longer bounces back when you press gently with a moistened finger.

6. Place an oven rack in the middle position and preheat the oven to 350°F (175°C).

7. While the brioche is proofing, prepare the cream. In a small bowl, whisk together the sour cream, egg, and sugar.

8. Dimple the proofed brioche one more time, brush the edges with the beaten egg, pour the cream in the center, and decorate with the candied kumquats or your preferred dried fruit (if using). Sprinkle generously with sugar.

9. Bake for 12 minutes. Then rotate the sheet and bake until the brioche is golden brown and the cream has set, about 12 minutes.

10. Remove from the oven and transfer to a cooling rack. Let cool for at least 15 minutes. Slice and serve while still warm or at room temperature. The brioche à la crème is best the day it is baked.

CANDIED KUMQUATS

MAKES 1 QUART/LITER

2 pounds (910 g) kumquats, stems removed
3½ cups (700 g) sugar
½ vanilla bean

1. Fill a medium pot halfway with water and bring to a boil over high heat. Carefully drop the kumquats into the boiling water and blanch for 1 minute. Drain the kumquats in a colander and discard the blanching water. Repeat two more times with fresh boiling water. Set the blanched kumquats aside.

2. Put the sugar in another pot and add 4 cups (about 1 liter) fresh water. Split the vanilla bean lengthwise with a paring knife and scrape the pulp with the back of the knife. Put the pod and pulp in the pot. Bring the mixture to a boil over high heat.

3. Lower the heat to low, add the blanched kumquats, and bring the candying syrup to a simmer. Cut a parchment paper circle a bit larger than the circumference of the pot and place it over the kumquats, just touching the syrup, to keep the kumquats submerged. Allow the kumquats to simmer in their syrup for 90 minutes, or until the skin of the kumquats is translucent and can be pierced with your fingernail. Let cool completely.

4. Transfer the candied kumquats and their syrup to a glass container. Cover and let stand at room temperature overnight. The next day, place them in the refrigerator, where they will keep indefinitely.

POTATO NIGELLA BUNS

MAKES 12 BUNS

EQUIPMENT: instant-read thermometer

1 large russet potato (170 to 225 g/6 to 8 ounces), peeled and cut into 2-inch (5 cm) chunks

1 cup (240 ml) whole milk

1¼ teaspoons active yeast

¼ cup (60 ml) olive oil

1 large egg plus 1 large beaten egg for brushing

1¾ cups (230 g) whole-grain hard white or red wheat flour, such as Starr or Red Fife

1 cup (140 g) all-purpose flour, plus extra for dusting

2 tablespoons sugar

1 tablespoon kosher salt

1 tablespoon nigella seeds

This is a simple yet terrific bun. The potato provides body and suppleness, while a sprinkle of nigella seeds adds deep, savory flavor. I use hard white or red wheat flour, matched with a good helping of all-purpose flour, which makes the buns a bit loftier. A harder variety of wheat gives the dough ample strength, which is critical if you're using the bun to make a sandwich or a burger that has to hold its own. The potato will balance the strong flour, keeping the buns moist and tender. It also brings starch content without additional gluten. Be sure to cook the potato in plenty of water until very soft, then mash well.

At the bakery and at home, I employ a little trick to make these buns extra soft. As soon as they are out of the oven, I cover them loosely with a kitchen towel. My go-to type for this job is a thin flour-sack tea towel. As the buns cool, the towel helps them retain moisture, keeping them soft and squishy for even longer.

These buns are the base of Friends & Family's popular eggwich: pillowy buns filled with scrambled eggs, breakfast sausage, arugula, and maple mayo. If you prefer, you can ask for bacon instead of sausage, and vegetarians can opt for avocado. Beyond breakfast, the buns make great burger and fried chicken sandwich bases, another Friends & Family favorite. Shape them slightly more elongated for a superb lobster roll, or a bit smaller for tasty dinner rolls.

1. Put the potato chunks in a small saucepan and cover with water. Bring to a boil and cook for 25 to 30 minutes, until the potato is very tender when poked with a fork. Drain, transfer to a bowl, and mash with the back of a fork while still warm. Let the mash cool completely before using. (You can make the mash up to 2 days ahead and store in an airtight container in the refrigerator.)

2. Warm the milk in a small saucepan until lukewarm (98–105°F/37–41°C), transfer to the bowl of a stand mixer fitted with the paddle attachment, and sprinkle the yeast on top. Stir with a spoon to help it dissolve, then let it activate for 5 minutes.

3. Add 1 cup (140 g) of the mashed potato, the oil, egg, flours, sugar, and salt and mix on low speed until the ingredients come together, about 2 minutes. Increase the speed to medium and mix for another 2 minutes, or until the dough looks smooth and uniform. Transfer the dough to a floured surface and knead briefly into a ball. Lightly coat a medium bowl with nonstick spray and place the dough in it. Cover with a kitchen towel or plastic wrap and let the dough rise at room temperature until doubled, 1½ to 2 hours.

4. Line two rimmed baking sheets with parchment paper. Turn the risen dough onto a lightly floured surface. Divide the dough into 12 equal portions (about 85 g/3 ounces each) and roll each one into a ball. Place the buns at least 2 inches (5 cm) apart on the prepared baking sheets. Let them rise at room temperature for 30 to 45 minutes, until they no longer bounce back when you press them gently with a moistened index finger.

5. Place two oven racks in the middle positions and preheat the oven to 350°F (175°C).

6. Gently brush the tops of the buns with the beaten egg and sprinkle generously with the nigella seeds. Bake for 15 minutes. Then rotate the baking sheets, switch their positions, and bake for another 15 minutes, until the buns are golden.

7. Remove from the oven and cover with a tea towel until completely cool. The buns will keep in an airtight container at room temperature for up to 2 days. They can also be frozen for up to 2 weeks. Freshen the thawed buns by reheating in a 350°F (175°C) oven for a few minutes.

FINNISH MALT BREAD

MAKES 1 LOAF

EQUIPMENT: instant-read thermometer, 8½-by-4½-inch (22 by 11 cm) loaf pan

- 1½ cups (355 ml) buttermilk
- 2 teaspoons instant yeast
- ½ cup (120 ml) malt syrup
- 2½ cups (320 g) whole-grain hard red wheat flour, such as Turkey Red or Red Fife
- ½ cup (65 g) whole-grain or dark rye flour
- ¾ cup (75 g) old-fashioned rolled oats, plus extra for sprinkling
- 1 teaspoon fine sea salt

I ran into this recipe while searching for what to do with a bottle of sugarcane syrup from Sweden. In Scandinavian baking, it's common to find breads, cakes, or cookies made with dark syrups derived from unrefined beet or cane sugar to add color and sweetness. The syrups are affordable and widely available in Scandinavia but hard to find outside Europe. When I ran out of my bottle of syrup, I settled for malt syrup. Also known as malt extract, malt syrup can be used as a sweetener and flavor enhancer in place of honey, molasses, or in this case, sugarcane syrup.

This dough incorporates hard red wheat, dark rye, and rolled oats. The addition of buttermilk simulates the acidity of sourdough, balances the intensity of the malt, and keeps the bread moist for longer. The bran-rich flours and the thick oats will absorb most of the liquid, baking into a loaf that is almost cake-like.

The batter-like dough comes together easily, mixed in a bowl with a wooden spoon or a silicone spatula and requires no shaping—just put it in the pan.

This loaf pairs nicely with traditional Scandinavian ingredients like cured salmon, pickled herring, and marinated beets, and it's the star of Clark Street Bakery's Nordic Breakfast Plate (page 234).

1. Cut a 12-by-7-inch (30 by 18 cm) rectangle of parchment paper. Lightly coat an 8½-by-4½-inch (22 by 11 cm) loaf pan with nonstick spray, line with the parchment paper rectangle, and fold the excess paper outward to the sides. This paper sling will make the step of unmolding the loaf much easier.

2. Put the buttermilk in a small saucepan and warm over low heat until an instant-read thermometer reaches 100°F (38°C). Transfer to a bowl, then sprinkle the yeast over the buttermilk. Stir with a spoon to help the yeast dissolve, then let it activate for 5 minutes. Add the syrup and stir to combine.

3. In a mixing bowl, combine the flours, oats, and salt. Pour in the dissolved yeast mixture and mix with a wooden spoon or silicone spatula until well combined. The dough should be very sticky.

4. Transfer the dough to the prepared loaf pan. Use a spatula to smooth out the top, cover with a kitchen towel or plastic wrap, and let it rise for 1½ to 2 hours, until the dough has doubled in volume and you're able to see a few cracks on top.

5. Place an oven rack in the middle position and preheat the oven to 350°F (175°C).

6. Sprinkle the top of the loaf decoratively with a handful of oats and bake for 45 minutes. Then rotate the pan and bake for another 15 minutes, until the top of the loaf is dark brown and an instant-read thermometer inserted in the center reaches 208°F (98°C).

7. Remove the loaf from the oven. Let it rest for 20 to 30 minutes, until cool enough to handle. Use the paper sling to pull the loaf from the mold, transfer to a cooling rack, and let it sit for 1 hour, or until it reaches room temperature.

8. The loaf can be enjoyed immediately or saved for later. Store the loaf wrapped with plastic at room temperature for up to 2 days, in the refrigerator for up to 1 week, or in the freezer for up to 1 month.

CLARK STREET BAKERY'S NORDIC BREAKFAST PLATE

SERVES 1

1 to 2 thin slices smoked ham

1 to 2 thin slices Havarti

2 to 3 thin lengthwise slices Persian cucumber

2 thin slices Finnish Malt Bread (page 232) or your preferred whole-grain bread

1 to 2 tablespoons unsalted butter at room temperature

1 tablespoon jam

1 soft- or hard-boiled egg

Coarse sea salt

When my friend Zack Hall opened Clark Street Bakery in Echo Park, this plate stood out on his menu the way simple yet pertinent things do. As is often the case with the less-is-more approach, the quality of the ingredients is vital, but it won't be necessary to spend a pretty penny to get your hands on some. Sliced bread is the main character on the plate, and I favor a dark Scandi-inspired bread such as the Finnish Malt Bread (page 232), but any fresh, rustic bread will do.

1. Choose a beautiful plate that you love. Then take a minute to arrange the makings of your breakfast in an appealing fashion. Think of it as an exercise in mindfulness in which you are present and in the moment while selecting the foods that will nourish you through the day.

2. Arrange the sliced ham, cheese, and cucumber slightly overlapping in the center of the plate. Place the bread slices on the edge of the plate. Put the butter and jam in small cups or ramekins to include on the plate or leave on the side. Lastly, add the egg. If you're having a soft-boiled egg, put it in an egg cup and peel a portion of eggshell off the top large enough to insert a small spoon; season with a pinch of salt. For a hard-boiled egg, peel, cut in half lengthwise, and sprinkle with a touch of salt. Enjoy right away.

DARK RYE ROLLS

MAKES 8 ROLLS

EQUIPMENT: instant-read thermometer

1 teaspoon anise seeds
1 teaspoon fennel seeds
1 teaspoon dried cardamom seeds
Peel of 1 orange
1¼ cups (300 ml) water
2 tablespoons molasses
¼ cup packed (55 g) dark brown sugar
1¼ teaspoons instant yeast
1½ cups (190 g) whole-grain or dark rye flour, plus extra for dusting
1¾ cups (230 g) whole-grain hard white or red wheat flour, such as Starr or Red Fife
1 tablespoon kosher salt
1 large egg, beaten
2 tablespoons unsalted butter at room temperature

This recipe is a mishmash of the many enriched, slightly sweet Nordic rye bread recipes I've played with over the years. I like to keep these rolls entirely whole grain, combining dark rye with hard wheat. Molasses, brown sugar, egg, and butter counter the strength of the wheat and density of the rye, softening the dough to make supple, tender rolls. The mixing method is very simple, but you'll have to make a stovetop infusion to extract the intense flavors and aromas of the cardamom, anise, fennel, and orange. Think of it as making a spice tea. The rolls are similar in texture and flavor to limpa, a traditional Swedish yeasted bread that is sweet, dense, and spiced.

The rolls get an old-world finish from a dusting of rye flour. One of these rolls slathered with butter and jam is absolutely perfect for breakfast, but I also enjoy making a sweet-savory sandwich with ham, cheddar, and, to honor its Scandi origins, a bit of lingonberry jam. Try making these rolls around the holidays if you're hosting overnight guests. Waking up to the heady aroma of the rolls baking in the morning takes the hygge factor to the nth degree. These flavors are very evocative of fall and winter and get along well with foods traditionally eaten during this time of year. Their dark brown color gives them an elegant charm and, arranged in a bread basket, they'll elevate any holiday tablescape.

1. Using a mortar and pestle, crush the anise, fennel, and cardamom seeds into a coarse powder. Put in a small saucepan. Add the orange peel and water and bring to a boil over medium heat, then immediately remove from the heat. Cover with a lid and let the aromatics steep in the water for at least 2 hours or overnight. Strain through a fine-mesh sieve into a small saucepan, add the molasses and brown sugar, stir to dissolve, and set aside. Discard the spices.

continues

2. When you're ready to mix the bread, warm up the steeped water over medium heat until lukewarm (98–105°F/37–41°C). Transfer to a small bowl, then sprinkle the yeast over the liquid. Stir with a spoon to help the yeast dissolve, then let it activate for 5 minutes.

3. In the bowl of a stand mixer fitted with the dough hook attachment, combine the flours and salt with the egg, butter, and dissolved yeast mixture. Mix on low speed until the dough comes together, about 2 minutes, scraping the sides of the bowl with a silicone spatula as necessary. Increase the speed to medium and mix for 2 more minutes to further develop the dough. It will feel somewhat sticky.

4. Transfer to a floured surface and knead briefly into a ball. Place in a medium bowl lightly coated with nonstick spray. Cover with a kitchen towel or plastic wrap and let the dough rise at room temperature until doubled, 1½ to 2 hours.

5. Place an oven rack in the middle position and preheat the oven to 350°F (175°C). Line a rimmed baking sheet with parchment paper.

6. Turn the risen dough onto a lightly floured surface. Divide the dough into 8 equal portions (about 100 g/3.5 ounces each) and roll each into a ball, using additional flour if necessary. Transfer the rolls to the prepared sheet, placing them 2 inches (5 cm) apart. Let them rise at room temperature for 1 hour, or until they no longer bounce back when you press them gently with a moistened index finger.

7. Dust the tops of the buns lightly with rye flour and bake for 12 minutes. Then rotate the baking sheet and bake for another 12 minutes.

8. Remove from the oven and serve while still warm or at room temperature. The rolls will keep in an airtight container for up to 2 days at room temperature or in the freezer for up to 1 month; reheat the thawed rolls in a 350°F (175°C) oven for a few minutes to regain their soft texture.

SOURDOUGH BREADS

The magic of sourdough is undeniable: a humble mixture of flour and water that, when looked after properly, can leaven a proud, tall loaf with a cavernous crumb and chewy, flavorful crust. This sorcery requires patience, though, and adequate foresight. Sourdough bread making is a multiday process, so you'll have to plan these bakes in advance. Think of it as a habit or discipline that you practice somewhat frequently. In fact, most successful home sourdough bakers I know bake bread every 2 to 3 weeks.

All sourdough baking starts with a well-maintained starter (see page 240), which takes at least 1 week to create. With sourdough starter in hand, you can move on to my recipe for Basic Sourdough Bread (page 244), which is the point of departure I recommend if you're new to the game.

Before you begin, read the detailed step-by-step recipe from start to finish. Notice that the steps will be scheduled over two to three days to help you plan ahead. From there, the world is your sourdough oyster—think savory Pumpkin Spelt Bread (page 254), umami-packed Caramelized Onion, Comté, and Nigella Boule (page 263), or the easy-peasy method for turning any proofed loaf into a batch of crowd-pleasing Benched Sourdough Rolls (page 248).

MAKE YOUR OWN SOURDOUGH STARTER

EQUIPMENT: digital scale, instant-read thermometer, 1-quart/liter glass jar with a lid

A sourdough starter is a culture of yeasts and bacteria that allows bread dough to be leavened naturally without the help of conventional yeast or any other artificial leaveners. This is my tried-and-true method for developing a starter in 8 days. You will need a small amount of rye flour to get the culture going. Whole-grain rye is a great tool because it encourages the propagation of yeasts and lactobacilli. After that, you can feed your starter with any whole-grain wheat flour. Since a good portion of your starter will be discarded, I recommend using a run-of-the-mill flour (pun intended!)—that is, one that doesn't cost too much or isn't hard to come by, yet is of good quality and nutritious.

Technique-wise, mixing a sourdough starter couldn't be simpler. I recommend a wide-mouth glass jar—Weck jars (see page 325) are my preferred brand—for holding the starter and a wooden spoon to stir it. It requires no more than combining water and flour to form a batter. Be diligent so that the starter is fed at set times (think breakfast and dinner) and keep it in a spot with a constant room temperature. I do insist on using a scale when feeding a starter since inaccuracy in the amounts of water, flour, and culture can easily throw off the balance.

At Friends & Family, we start a sourdough culture every year. As is common practice in the industry, we like to give it a proper name. Over the years, we have brought to life Aretha, Simone, Bjørk, Jolene, Esther, and most recently, Rose Marie. I'm never impressed by an older starter or its poetic origin story. It's healthy to work with a young starter, and using a starter that has been maintained for years (some claim, decades) doesn't necessarily make better bread and doesn't make you a better baker. A sourdough starter is, at its most basic, a culture of yeast and bacteria that go about their day metabolizing carbohydrates and producing carbon dioxide and ethanol as a result. It's an ecosystem that is directly affected by what you put in it as much as by the surrounding environment.

In the throes of a busy bakery, a starter is put to the test on a daily basis. The room temperature, which greatly impacts the rate of fermentation, can fluctuate between 67°F and 95°F (19°C to 35°C). Then there's the feeding schedule. Even in a well-run operation, it's easy to miss a feeding by a few hours or even a day. With all the commotion, it isn't uncommon for the starter to lose its equilibrium. The first sign that our starter is a little off is overly sour bread. A closer look will show that the crumb is a bit stickier and the hole structure is a bit tighter. We may also notice a peculiar acceleration or slowing down of the rising time. Any of these changes give us the cue that it's time to get a new starter going.

You should keep a sourdough starter only if you bake sourdough bread often. Home bakers who bake bread every 2 to 3 weeks keep their starter in the refrigerator, pulling it out 2 days before they bake again. This 2-day window, in which the starter is fed diligently, is enough time to let the starter regain its strength and get ready to make bread again. If you don't have the wherewithal to make your own, you'd be surprised how willing your local bakery may be to share some of theirs. By now, descendants of Friends & Family starters are baking bread all over Los Angeles. I hope they're making us proud.

DAY 1

Combine 125 g whole-grain wheat or dark rye flour with 180 g room-temperature (68–77°F/20–25°C) water in a 1-quart/liter glass container. Mix thoroughly until no flour streaks remain. Cover and store at room temperature.

DAY 2

Combine the culture from Day 1 with 130 g whole-grain wheat flour and 130 g room-temperature (68–77°F/20–25°C) water. Cover and store at room temperature.

DAY 3

Measure out 115 g culture from Day 2 and combine it with 130 g whole-grain wheat flour and 130 g room-temperature (68–77°F/20–25°C) water. Cover and store at room temperature. Discard the rest of the Day 2 culture.

DAY 4

Measure out 115 g culture from Day 3 and combine it with 130 g whole-grain wheat flour and 130 g room-temperature (68–77°F/20–25°C) water. Cover and store at room temperature. Discard the rest of the Day 3 culture.

DAYS 5, 6, AND 7

Start feeding the starter twice a day. Feedings should be 8 to 12 hours apart—think of them as breakfast and dinner. Always use a scale when feeding your starter at this stage. For each feeding, combine 30 g culture with 150 g whole-grain wheat flour and 150 g room-temperature (68–77°F/20–25°C) water. Cover and store at room temperature. Discard the remaining culture.

DAY 8

Your starter is fully ripe and ready to use on the morning of Day 8. The surface should be bubbly, almost frothy, with a pleasantly sour smell. To use, measure out the amount you need for your desired recipe, then feed the remaining starter per the instructions for Day 5 and discard the excess as usual. This excess is what we call sourdough starter discard, and can be used in Don't Wait Sourdough Discard Pancakes (page 100). Have you named your starter yet?

WHAT COULD POSSIBLY GO WRONG?

Starters are pretty resilient and it's hard to kill one. However, they're creatures of habit and thrive on consistency: consistent feedings, consistent quality of ingredients, and consistent room temperature. Paying attention to the following factors will help you keep your new baking buddy in top form.

WATER QUALITY AND TEMPERATURE: If the tap water in your region is highly chlorinated, consider using filtered water since chlorine can hinder growth. I've always used Los Angeles tap water—which is known for its high content of dissolved minerals—to feed my starters without any noticeable consequences. The way I see it, if it's good enough for me to drink, it's good enough for my starter. If you're unsure about water quality in your area, a public report from your utility company or municipality should be available online. More crucial is water temperature, which will have a direct effect on the rate of fermentation of your starter. Room-temperature (68–77°F/20–25°C) water is ideal, but if you want to accelerate the process, you can use warmer water—just make sure that it never exceeds 100°F (38°C). The microorganisms in the starter can die when their environment reaches 120°F (49°C).

FEEDING SCHEDULE: I recommend feedings at 12-hour intervals, once in the morning and once at night. But you should establish feeding times that work for you and your lifestyle. Always weigh the ingredients. Eyeballing will almost always throw off the percentage of inoculation (percentage of active starter mixed with the fresh flour and water), potentially causing your starter to lose its balance. If you forget to feed your starter for a day or two, resume feedings as soon as you realize it. Avoid baking with it for a day or two, until it has regained its full strength.

RETARDING YOUR STARTER: Refrigerating your starter will retard its activity level by slowing down its metabolic rate. If you bake bread less frequently than once a week, I recommend refrigerating in between bakes. In my experience, a starter can withstand 2 weeks unfed in the refrigerator without deteriorating. To do so, refrigerate the starter once it's ripe on the day you used it last, shortly after taking what you needed for your recipe. This is a smart way to save flour, time, and effort. A couple of days before you want to bake again, resume feeding twice a day per the instructions for Day 5, storing it at room temperature. I like to give my starter 2 days of regular feedings at room temperature for it to regain its activity level. Then you can bake with it as usual.

GET TO KNOW YOUR STARTER: Every starter is a unique ecosystem with its own composition, and in time you will get to know your starter's smell, appearance, and consistency. Becoming familiar with it will help you assess if it's having any difficulties. I find that when my starter is healthy it tends to have a strong buttermilk-y smell, a brownish-grayish color, and a yogurt-like consistency. During the winter months, when the ambient temperature in the bakeshop can be as low as 65°F (18°C), it can get a little sluggish, taking a long time to become ripe. If that's the case, I feed it with warmer water and throw a little bit of rye flour into the maintenance flour. Then I let it rise in a warmer spot. It needs a little comfort, just like we do. In the warmer months, when the starter rises much faster, we run the risk of letting it get too sour. To prevent this, we feed three times a day instead of two, always using colder water. This keeps our needy summer starter in balance.

DON'T IGNORE THE PINK STUFF: A common but not harmful phenomenon is a dark watery layer atop the starter; it looks almost as if the starter has separated. This can happen when your starter has been underfed. Simply drain the watery part and resume feeding twice a day. However, a definitive sign that your starter is beyond saving is the presence of mold, such as white spores, greenish gunk, or a pink film on the surface. All these visual cues, along with an off smell, mean you should discard it. Keeping your starter jar clean will help prevent unnecessary contamination. Swap glass jars often, especially if you see crusty buildup forming close to the mouth of the jar.

A NOTE ABOUT SALT

Fine sea salt is commonly used in bread making because it dissolves quickly and therefore can be easily incorporated into the dough. Avoid using coarse salt; its large granules can affect the crumb of the bread because they rip into the gluten strands. Salt will inhibit rapid fermentation, helping the dough rise at a slower pace and thus producing a more flavorful bread. Always adhere to the amounts called for in the recipe. Besides retarding fermentation and adding flavor and preserving qualities, salt will toughen the dough slightly, contributing to its texture. Without salt, bread dough would run amok, resulting in an overfermented, sour, and sloppy mess

BASIC SOURDOUGH BREAD

MAKES 1 LOAF

EQUIPMENT: instant-read thermometer, 8-inch (20 cm) round or oval banneton, bread lame, 4½-quart/liter Dutch oven with lid

TO FEED THE STARTER

1 tablespoon (13 g) sourdough starter (see page 240)
7 tablespoons (50 g) whole-grain hard red wheat flour, such as Turkey Red or Red Fife
3 tablespoons plus 1 teaspoon (50 ml) room-temperature (68–77°F/20–25°C) water

FOR THE DOUGH

4 cups (520 g) whole-grain hard red wheat flour, such as Turkey Red or Red Fife, plus extra for dusting
1¾ cups plus 2 tablespoons (450 ml) lukewarm (98–105°F/37–41°C) water
1 tablespoon honey
2 teaspoons (10 g) fine sea salt
Rice flour for dusting the banneton

This straightforward loaf is the ideal starting point if you're new to whole-grain sourdough. It's a great canvas for learning about flours, and also a great setting for customizing to your liking with different grains and mix-ins, once you have a handle on the base recipe. At Friends & Family, making a tester sourdough with a batch of new flour is a common R&D project. Sometimes we're exploring a new wheat; other times we want to see how a new crop of a known wheat is holding up. As a rule, we use only hard wheat varieties for our sourdough bread, sometimes combined with refined bread flour and sometimes on their own. We aren't concerned with the broader white or red category. We just want to make sure it's high in gluten (see My Favorite Flours, page 313). Bakers seeking a milder sourdough loaf with a lighter texture can opt for the variation on page 246, where I substitute half the volume of the whole-grain flour with refined bread flour.

And yes, take notes! I recommend keeping a log of your flour selection, room and water temperatures, and rising times. There's definitely a learning curve, and observation will be your best teacher. Your first loaf may not be all that you want it to be, but it is only a matter of time before your loaves look and taste better.

Sourdough bread has natural preservatives built in and thus lasts a long time. Because the bread is so hydrated, it doesn't dry out nearly as fast as conventional bread, even if kept on the kitchen counter for a couple of days. If you live in an area with high humidity, store it in the refrigerator to prevent it from molding. Or keep it in the freezer, where it can last up to 2 weeks or even longer. At home, I keep slices of sourdough in a ziplock bag in the freezer, and pull on demand to put directly in the toaster oven for a quick breakfast. Even after all these years of toasting frozen bread, it feels quite luxurious to have access to such good toast with such little effort.

PREP DAY

1. The day before you'd like to bake the bread, feed the starter by combining it with the flour and water in a clean glass jar. Cover and let it ferment at room temperature for 6 to 8 hours, until it has increased in volume and formed bubbles on the surface.

2. When the starter is ready, hydrate (autolyse) the flour: In a medium bowl, combine the flours with the lukewarm water to attain a wet, sticky dough. Cover and let rest for 1 hour. (This resting phase, in which the flour is allowed to hydrate, is known as the autolyse. Autolysing the flour promotes elasticity as well as enzymatic activity, contributing to gluten development in the dough.)

3. In the bowl of a stand mixer fitted with the dough hook attachment, mix the autolysed flour with the fed sourdough starter on medium speed for 2 minutes. If necessary, stop the mixer and scrape the sides of the bowl with a silicone spatula to promote even mixing. Add the honey and mix for another 2 minutes at medium speed. Add the salt and mix for another 2 minutes. Transfer the dough to a medium bowl and cover with a kitchen towel or plastic wrap. Let sit at room temperature for 30 minutes.

4. Moisten your hands with water and dig under the front end of the dough, stretch it out, and fold it back on top of the dough. Dig under the back end of the dough and repeat the same stretch-and-fold motion. Do the same on each of the sides. Finally, turn the dough over and tuck it into a ball. This process is known as stretching and folding and helps strengthen the dough. After each series of stretching and folding, the dough should feel significantly stronger. Cover the dough and let it rest for 30 minutes.

5. Stretch and fold a second time, just as you did before. Let it rest for another 30 minutes, then stretch and fold one last time, for a total of three times. Cover the dough and let it ferment for 1½ hours more, for a total of 3 hours from mixing to shaping.

6. To shape into a loaf, transfer the dough to a floured surface. Gently flatten the dough into a rough square and bring all four corners to the center. Pinch the corners together with your fingertips. Now you have a much smaller dough square. Repeat one more time, bringing all four corners to the center and pinching them together to create more tension. Invert the boule on the work surface and, using your hands, gently rotate the boule against the surface to tighten it further and seal the bottom where the corners connect. Flour an 8-inch (20 cm) banneton generously with rice flour and place the boule inside with the seam side up. Refrigerate uncovered overnight.

continues

BAKING DAY

1. Remove the dough from the refrigerator 1 hour prior to baking and let it sit at room temperature. At this point, the loaf should be proofed all the way. It will be noticeably puffy and larger in size. It will also jiggle a bit if you shake it gently, and bounce back slowly if you press it with a moistened index finger. If the loaf still seems tight after the 1-hour rest, you can let it sit out for another 30 minutes to 1 hour.

2. Place an oven rack in the lowest position and place a lidded 4½-quart/liter Dutch oven on the rack. Preheat the oven to 450°F (230°C) for 30 minutes.

3. Cut a piece of parchment paper a few inches wider than the boule. Invert the banneton on the parchment paper to release the bread. Using a lame or a sharp paring knife, cut a crosshatch (#) about ½ inch (1.25 cm) deep on the surface of the boule. These cuts will serve as steam release vents and open zippers when the bread expands in the oven.

4. Using oven mitts, carefully put the hot Dutch oven on a heatproof surface and remove the lid. Lift the parchment paper by the sides to transfer the bread and parchment to the Dutch oven. Put the lid back on and place the Dutch oven back in the oven. Bake for 30 minutes (the lid helps retain enough steam inside the pot, allowing the surface of the bread to remain supple and expand).

5. Remove the lid and bake for another 15 to 20 minutes (removing the lid will help the bread's exterior caramelize and bake into a chewy crust). The bread is ready when the crust is a dark mahogany brown and an instant-read thermometer inserted in the center reaches between 200° and 208°F (93° and 98°C).

6. Using oven mitts, carefully remove the Dutch oven from the oven. Gently invert it over a cooling rack to release the bread. Let cool completely before slicing. The bread will keep in a paper bag at room temperature for up to 2 days. Or wrap it with plastic and freeze for up to 2 weeks. Freshen the thawed loaf by reheating in a 350°F (175°C) oven for a few minutes.

VARIATION

For a lighter sourdough, replace the flour amount for the dough with 2 cups (260 g) whole-grain hard red wheat flour, such as Turkey Red or Red Fife, plus 2 cups (270 g) bread flour.

BENCHED SOURDOUGH ROLLS

MAKES 8 ROLLS

EQUIPMENT: 8-inch (20 cm) round or oval banneton, roasting pan for steam bath, bench knife, bread lame

1 batch Basic Sourdough Bread dough (page 244), shaped into a boule, put in a banneton, and refrigerated overnight

All-purpose or bread flour for dusting

When describing bread rolls, "benched" simply means that a bench knife is used to portion them. It's as simple as turning a proofed, refrigerated loaf out onto your work surface and chopping it into roll-size portions. I call for Basic Sourdough Bread (page 244) here, but the technique is universal: You can make benched rolls with any dough.

I learned how to do this as we learn most things these days, by watching a video on Instagram. One of my favorite bread accounts (Daniel Larsson, @danlarn, a pretty serious sourdough baker based in Sweden) was inverting a perfectly shaped and proofed boule onto a cutting board and cutting it into rolls with a large bench knife. I couldn't wait to try it myself. It was surprisingly easy but made perfect sense. A loaf that has been properly shaped is built to hold structure and not just bake into a lump; therefore, the rolls are also well structured and will hold their shape. The look of a benched roll is also very cool with its sharp edges. Skilled slashers will delight at decorating each individual roll with their favorite bread lame.

If you're making a sourdough recipe to be cut into rolls, tailor your flour selection to what you want to do with the rolls. You can keep them whole-grain if you'd like to have a roll every morning for breakfast with butter and jam. But you could also make a lighter roll, following the variation on page 246, if you'd like to turn the rolls into sandwiches for school lunches. Kids especially love rolls decorated with crunchy seeds; see the variation for Seeded Benched Sourdough Rolls that follows.

1. Place an oven rack in the middle position and preheat the oven to 450°F (230°C). Place an empty roasting pan at the bottom of the oven. Line a rimmed baking sheet with parchment paper.

2. Turn the banneton with the loaf inside onto a well-floured cutting board. Use a bench knife to cut the loaf in half. Separate the halves and then cut each half into 4 wedges similar in size. Use the bench knife to transfer each wedge to the prepared sheet, placing them 2 inches (5 cm) apart. Let the rolls rest at room temperature for 10 minutes.

3. Using a lame or a sharp paring knife, cut a 2-inch (5 cm) slit about ¼ inch (6 mm) deep on the surface of each roll. These cuts will serve as steam release vents and open zippers when the bread expands in the oven.

4. Right before baking, carefully pour 2 cups water into the hot roasting pan in the oven to generate steam. Immediately put the sheet in the oven and bake for 10 minutes. Avoid opening the oven during this stage to prevent the steam from dissipating. Then rotate the sheet and bake for another 10 minutes, or until the tops of the rolls are golden.

5. Remove from the oven. Transfer the rolls to a cooling rack and let sit for at least 1 hour before enjoying. The rolls will keep in a paper bag at room temperature for up to 2 days. Or wrap them with plastic and freeze for up to 2 weeks. Freshen the thawed rolls by reheating in a 350°F (175°C) oven for a few minutes.

VARIATION

Seeded Benched Sourdough Rolls

Seeding benched rolls is very easy. Sesame, poppy, sunflower, or pumpkin seeds can transform the rolls into beautiful and flavorful little breads. Make 1 batch of dough for Basic Sourdough Bread (page 244) and shape into a boule. Brush the surface of the boule with water. Sprinkle generously with ¾ cup (120 g) raw pumpkin seeds (pepitas), making sure the entire surface is covered. Place in a round or oval banneton seed side down. The seeds will prevent the dough from sticking to the banneton, so it isn't necessary to flour the banneton. Refrigerate overnight. The next morning, cut and bake following the instructions above.

APPLE LEVAIN

MAKES 1 PAN LOAF

EQUIPMENT: instant-read thermometer, 8½-by-4½-inch (22 by 11 cm) loaf pan, roasting pan for steam bath, bread lame

TO FEED THE STARTER

1 tablespoon (13 g) sourdough starter (see page 240)

7 tablespoons (50 g) whole-grain hard red wheat flour, such as Turkey Red or Red Fife

3 tablespoons plus 1 teaspoon (50 ml) room-temperature (68–77°F/20–25°C) water

FOR THE APPLE PUREE

1 small apple, peeled, cored, and cut into ½-inch (1.25 cm) cubes

½ cup (120 ml) water

1 cinnamon stick

1 teaspoon ground cinnamon

FOR THE DOUGH

4 cups (520 g) whole-grain hard red wheat flour, plus extra for dusting

1½ cups (360 ml) lukewarm (98–105°F/37–41°C) water

2 teaspoons (10 g) fine sea salt

This loaf is made exclusively with hard red wheat. It pairs wonderfully with the cinnamon-scented apple puree, which I add for warm, subtle spicing as well as moisture, lending the bread impressive staying power. Robust varieties such as Red Fife or Turkey Red that have an intense wheaty flavor are best. These are the kinds of flours that require a high level of hydration, which the apple puree takes care of. The apple also adds a source of sugar, helping the loaf brown very nicely. If you're trying to convince people who are not too keen on the flavor and texture that bran imparts to 100 percent whole wheat breads, this is a great place to start. I like to use a loaf pan here, which makes the bread easy to shape, bake, and keep.

This is not a sweet bread. It's a sourdough loaf with subtle undertones of roasted apple that can be enjoyed just like any other sourdough. A toasted slice with a bit of apple butter makes a perfect breakfast, and it makes the best grilled cheese, such as the Apple and Roquefort Grilled Cheese Sandwich (page 252).

PREP DAY

1. The day before you'd like to bake the bread, feed the starter by combining it with the flour and the water in a clean glass jar. Cover and let it ferment at room temperature for 6 to 8 hours, until it has increased in volume and formed bubbles on the surface.

2. Put the apple pieces in a small saucepan and add the water and cinnamon stick. Cover and cook over low heat for 15 minutes, or until the apple is fork-tender. Remove the cinnamon stick and transfer the apple mixture to a blender. Add the ground cinnamon while the apple is still warm and puree. You should end up with ⅓ cup (75 g) apple puree.

3. When the starter is ready, hydrate (autolyse) the flour: In a medium bowl, combine the flour for the dough with the lukewarm water and apple puree. Cover and let rest for 1 hour. (This resting phase, in which the flour is allowed to hydrate, is known as the autolyse. Autolysing the flour promotes elasticity as well as enzymatic activity, contributing to gluten development in the dough.)

4. In the bowl of a stand mixer fitted with the dough hook attachment, mix the autolysed flour with the fed sourdough starter on medium speed for 2 minutes. If necessary, stop the mixer and scrape the sides of the bowl with a silicone spatula to promote even mixing. Add the salt and mix for another 2 minutes at medium speed. Transfer the dough to a medium bowl and cover with a kitchen towel or plastic wrap. Let sit at room temperature for 30 minutes.

5. Moisten your hands with water and dig under the front end of the dough, stretch it out, and fold it back on top of the dough. Dig under the back end of the dough and repeat the same stretch-and-fold motion. Do the same on each of the sides. Finally, turn the dough over and tuck it into a ball. This process is known as stretching and folding and helps strengthen the dough. After each series of stretching and folding, the dough should feel significantly stronger. Cover the dough and let it rest for 30 minutes.

6. Stretch and fold a second time, just as you did before. Let it rest for another 30 minutes, then stretch and fold one last time, for a total of three times. Cover the dough and let it ferment for 1½ hours more, for a total of 3 hours from mixing to shaping.

7. Lightly coat an 8½-by-4½-inch (22 by 11 cm) loaf pan with nonstick spray. To shape the dough into a pan loaf, transfer the dough to a floured surface. Gently flatten the dough into a rough rectangle and roll into a cylinder (as you would a jelly roll). Place the cylinder seam side down in the prepared pan. Refrigerate uncovered overnight.

BAKING DAY

1. Remove the dough from the refrigerator 1 hour prior to baking and let it sit at room temperature. At this point, the loaf should be proofed all the way. It will be noticeably puffy and larger in size. It will also jiggle a bit if you shake it gently, and bounce back slowly if you press it with a moistened index finger. If the loaf still seems tight after the 1-hour rest, you can let it sit out for another 30 minutes to 1 hour.

2. Place an empty roasting pan at the bottom of the oven. Place an oven rack in the middle position and preheat the oven to 450°F (230°C).

continues

3. Use a lame or a sharp paring knife to cut a slit about ½-inch (1.25 cm) deep along the length of the loaf. Right before baking, carefully pour 2 cups water into the hot roasting pan in the oven to generate steam. Immediately put the pan in the oven and bake for 20 minutes. Avoid opening the oven at this stage to prevent the steam from dissipating. Then rotate the pan and bake for another 20 minutes or until the top of the loaf is a rich golden brown and an instant-read thermometer inserted in the center reaches between 200° and 208°F (93° and 98°C).

4. Remove the pan from the oven and place on a cooling rack. Let it sit for at least 1 hour before unmolding and enjoying it. The bread will keep in a paper bag at room temperature for up to 2 days. Or wrap it with plastic and freeze for up to 2 weeks. Freshen the thawed loaf by reheating in a 350°F (175°C) oven for a few minutes.

> **APPLE AND ROQUEFORT GRILLED CHEESE SANDWICH**
>
> Make the ultimate grilled cheese with crunchy apple and crumbled Roquefort. Spread two slices of apple levain with apple butter, then fill with sliced Comté and crumbled Roquefort (or your preferred blue cheese) and thin slices of apple. Melt a bit of butter in a sauté pan and pan-fry the sandwich on both sides until the cheese is melty. Cut in half on a diagonal and serve immediately.

PUMPKIN SPELT BREAD

MAKES 1 LOAF

EQUIPMENT: instant-read thermometer, 8-inch (20 cm) round or oval banneton, 4½-quart/liter Dutch oven with lid, bread lame

TO FEED THE STARTER

1 tablespoon (13 g) sourdough starter (see page 240)

7 tablespoons (50 g) whole-grain hard white wheat flour, such as Starr or Edison

3 tablespoons plus 1 teaspoon (50 ml) room-temperature (68–77°F/20–25°C) water

FOR THE DOUGH

2 teaspoons cumin seeds

3¼ cups (420 g) whole-grain hard white wheat flour, such as Starr or Edison, plus extra for dusting

¾ cup (100 g) whole-grain spelt flour

1½ cups (360 ml) lukewarm (98–105°F/37–41°C) water

⅓ cup (75 g) Pumpkin Puree (page 90) or canned

¼ cup (40 g) raw pumpkin seeds (pepitas)

2 teaspoons (10 g) fine sea salt

Rice flour for dusting the banneton

A fresh loaf of pumpkin bread is a delicious seasonal contribution to the breakfast table, to be served with butter or cream cheese. It can also be the base for a vegetarian sandwich such as the Open-Face Carrot Sandwich (page 257). Cumin keeps the flavor profile savory, away from the trendy pumpkin spice. It may be tempting to speed things up by using preground cumin, but fight the urge! Toasting whole seeds and then blitzing them guarantees a bold, complex flavor.

Canned pumpkin works well, but I encourage you to roast your own (see page 90). The puree brings beautiful color and plenty of moisture to the bread for a creamier texture. Besides butternut and honeynut, I recommend kabocha or kuri squash. They tend to be smallish but also pleasantly dense, with a starchier feel than other varieties. A small squash—even the most manageable varieties like butternut or honeynut—will likely yield more puree than what you need for this bread. You can save any extra in the freezer for future use, or make it part of your dinner.

PREP DAY

1. The day before you'd like to bake the bread, feed the starter by combining it with the flour and water in a clean glass jar. Cover and let it ferment at room temperature for 6 to 8 hours, until it has increased in volume and formed bubbles on the surface.

2. Toast the cumin seeds in a small skillet over medium-low heat until they begin releasing their aroma; this will be quick, about 1 minute. Make sure to swirl the skillet nonstop, which will prevent the seeds from burning. Remove from the heat and let the seeds cool, then pound them to a powder with a mortar and pestle or grind in a spice grinder.

3. When the starter is ready, hydrate (autolyse) the flour: In a medium bowl, combine the flours for the dough with the lukewarm water and pumpkin puree. Cover and let rest for 1 hour. (This resting phase, in which the flour is allowed to hydrate, is known as the autolyse. Autolysing the flour promotes elasticity as well as enzymatic activity, contributing to gluten development in the dough.)

4. Soak the pumpkin seeds in cold water for 5 minutes. Drain and set aside.

5. In the bowl of a stand mixer fitted with the dough hook attachment, mix the autolysed flour with the fed sourdough starter on medium speed for 2 minutes. If necessary, stop the mixer and scrape the sides of the bowl with a silicone spatula to promote even mixing. Add the salt and cumin and mix for another 2 minutes. Add the soaked pumpkin seeds and mix at low speed just to combine. Transfer the dough to a medium bowl and cover with a kitchen towel or plastic wrap. Let sit at room temperature for 30 minutes.

6. Moisten your hands with water and dig under the front end of the dough, stretch it out, and fold it back on top of the dough. Dig under the back end of the dough and repeat the same stretch-and-fold motion. Do the same on each of the sides. Finally, turn the dough over and tuck it into a ball. This process is known as stretching and folding and helps strengthen the dough. After each series of stretching and folding, the dough should feel significantly stronger. Cover the dough and let it rest for 30 minutes.

7. Stretch and fold a second time, just as you did before. Let it rest for another 30 minutes, then stretch and fold one last time, for a total of three times. Cover the dough and let it ferment for 1½ hours more, for a total of 3 hours from mixing to shaping.

8. To shape into a loaf, transfer the dough to a floured surface. Gently flatten the dough into a rough square and bring all four corners to the center. Pinch the corners together with your fingertips. Now you have a much smaller dough square. Repeat one more time, bringing all four corners to the center and pinching them together to create more tension. Invert the boule on the work surface and, using your hands, gently rotate the boule against the surface to tighten it further and seal the bottom where the corners connect. Flour an 8-inch (20 cm) banneton generously with rice flour and place the boule inside with the seam side up. Refrigerate uncovered overnight.

BAKING DAY

1. Remove the dough from the refrigerator 1 hour prior to baking and let it sit at room temperature. At this point, the loaf should be proofed all the way. It will be noticeably puffy and larger in size. It will also jiggle a bit if you shake it gently, and bounce back

continues

slowly if you press it with a moistened index finger. If the loaf still seems tight after the 1-hour rest, you can let it sit out for another 30 minutes to 1 hour.

2. Place an oven rack in the lowest position and place a 4½-quart/liter lidded Dutch oven on the rack. Preheat the oven to 450°F (230°C) for 30 minutes.

3. Cut a piece of parchment paper a few inches wider than the boule. Invert the banneton on the parchment paper to release the bread. Using a lame or a sharp paring knife, cut an X about ½ inch (1.25 cm) deep on the surface of the boule. These cuts will serve as steam release vents and open zippers when the bread expands in the oven.

4. Using oven mitts, carefully put the hot Dutch oven on a heatproof surface and remove the lid. Lift the parchment paper by the sides to transfer the bread and parchment to the Dutch oven. Put the lid back on and place the Dutch oven back in the oven. Bake for 30 minutes (the lid helps retain enough steam inside the pot, allowing the surface of the bread to remain supple and expand).

5. Remove the lid and bake for another 15 to 20 minutes (removing the lid will help the bread's exterior caramelize and bake into a chewy crust). The bread is ready when the crust is dark brown and an instant-read thermometer inserted in the center reaches between 200° and 208°F (93° and 98°C).

6. Using oven mitts, carefully remove the Dutch oven from the oven. Gently invert it over a cooling rack to release the bread. Let cool completely before slicing. The bread will keep in a paper bag at room temperature for up to 2 days. Or wrap it with plastic and freeze for up to 2 weeks. Freshen the thawed loaf by reheating in a 350°F (175°C) oven for a few minutes.

OPEN-FACE CARROT SANDWICH

MAKES 4 SANDWICHES

FOR THE PEPITA PESTO
3 tablespoons raw pumpkin seeds (pepitas)
½ cup (20 g) chopped fresh flat-leaf parsley
½ cup (30 g) chopped fresh cilantro
1 garlic clove, peeled and crushed
½ cup (120 ml) olive oil, or as needed
1 tablespoon lemon juice
1 teaspoon kosher salt

FOR THE ROASTED CARROTS
1 teaspoon coriander seeds
20 small young carrots, stems trimmed
2 tablespoons olive oil
Kosher salt to taste

FOR THE SANDWICHES
4 slices Pumpkin Spelt Bread (page 254)
Olive oil for brushing
⅓ cup (50 g) crumbled feta (optional)

FOR THE BITTER GREENS
2 handfuls mixed bitter greens, such as arugula, frisée, dandelion, or mustard greens
1 teaspoon harissa
1 tablespoon sherry vinegar
3 tablespoons olive oil
Kosher salt to taste

This chic vegetarian sandwich is so packed with flavor and texture that no one will miss the meat. I serve it as a tartine, or open-face sandwich, which is very pretty and easier to eat. Use slender, sweet young carrots, preferably from the farmers' market—the more colorful, the better. Roasted with coriander, the carrots complement the cumin-spiked Pumpkin Spelt Bread (page 254) wonderfully. A pepita pesto provides crunch and earthy, herbal flavor. The recipe makes a bit more pepita pesto than you need, but it keeps for up to 3 days in the fridge and is great over roasted vegetables or pan-fried fish, or as a garnish for creamy butternut squash or carrot soup. Salty feta and bitter greens tossed with smoky harissa bring everything together.

1. Place an oven rack in the middle position and preheat the oven to 350°F (175°C).

2. To start the pepita pesto, scatter the pumpkin seeds on a rimmed baking sheet. Toast in the oven until they puff in the center, about 8 minutes. Remove from the oven and leave the oven on. Let the pumpkin seeds cool completely.

3. Meanwhile, prepare the carrots. Toast the coriander in a small skillet over medium-low heat until the seeds begin releasing their aroma; this will be quick, about 1 minute. Make sure to swirl the skillet nonstop to prevent the seeds from burning. Let the seeds cool, then pound them to a powder with a mortar and pestle or grind in a spice grinder.

continues

4. Put the carrots on a rimmed baking sheet, drizzle with the olive oil, and season with the ground coriander and salt. Rub with your hands to make sure the carrots are well coated with oil and spices. Roast in the oven until tender, 25 to 30 minutes, depending on the size of your carrots. Remove from the oven and leave the oven on.

5. While the carrots are roasting, finish the pesto. Combine the toasted pumpkin seeds, parsley, cilantro, garlic, olive oil, and lemon juice in a food processor and blitz to a chunky puree. You may need to stop every so often to scrape the sides of the bowl and help the herbs puree evenly. Season with the salt and pulse to combine.

6. Using a pastry brush, coat one side of the bread slices with olive oil. Transfer to a rimmed baking sheet and toast until golden but not all the way crispy.

7. Dress the bitter greens next. Place the greens in a bowl. Whisk the harissa and vinegar together in a separate bowl. Add the olive oil in a steady stream while whisking vigorously until the dressing emulsifies. Season with salt. Toss the greens with 2 to 3 tablespoons of the dressing—all the leaves should be nicely coated but not drenched.

8. To assemble, drizzle the toasted bread slices generously with the pepita pesto, pile a few carrots on top of each slice, and top with a generous amount of bitter greens. Garnish with the crumbled feta, if using. Serve immediately.

DILL, CHIVE, AND BLACK PEPPER LOAF

MAKES 1 LOAF

EQUIPMENT: instant-read thermometer, 8-inch (20 cm) round or oval banneton, 4½-quart/liter Dutch oven with lid, bread lame

TO FEED THE STARTER

1 tablespoon (13 g) sourdough starter (see page 240)

7 tablespoons (50 g) whole-grain hard red wheat flour, such as Turkey Red or Red Fife

3 tablespoons plus 1 teaspoon (50 ml) room-temperature (68–77°F/20–25°C) water

FOR THE DOUGH

4 cups (520 g) whole-grain hard red wheat flour, such as Turkey Red or Red Fife, plus extra for dusting

1¾ cups plus 2 tablespoons (450 ml) lukewarm (98–105°F/37–41°C) water

1 tablespoon honey

2 teaspoons (10 g) fine sea salt

1 teaspoon cracked black pepper

¼ cup (15 g) minced fresh chives

¼ cup (15 g) minced fresh dill

Rice flour for dusting the banneton

When we first made this loaf, we thought it would scream herbs, but the feedback we received was more about how surprising the touch of black pepper was. Black pepper has the ability to inject baked goods with its sharp, woodsy aroma. Like salt, it can enhance other flavors while adding depth. In this loaf, it's a perfect background for the herbs, which hit the palate second but provide a fresh allure. All this to say, even if the amounts of black pepper, chives, and dill sound like a lot, sticking to them is nonnegotiable if you want to experience the full alchemy of this well-balanced trio. Since this is an intensely flavored loaf, it's a good idea to be bold with your flour. Choose a hard red wheat such as Red Fife or Turkey Red without fear that it will dull the herb flavor. You could use a whiter wheat but only if that's what you have on hand or you generally like more neutral flours.

Mixing the dough in the stand mixer is easy enough. Once you add the herbs at the end of the mixing process, though, they might be hard to incorporate. If that's the case, feel free to use your hands to work them in.

This bread is unapologetically savory and makes a great accompaniment to an egg with a runny yolk, whether fried or soft-boiled. It makes an ideal tuna salad sandwich, and it's also a great stand-in for a bagel, so everything you would put on a bagel can go here. Later in the day, for predinner or late-night snacks, try it freshly baked or toasted with cheeses that already have a bite, such as sharp cheddar, aged Gouda, salty fontina, or even a creamy blue like English Stilton or Spanish Valdeón. Should you have leftovers, this loaf makes for particularly tasty croutons.

PREP DAY

1. The day before you'd like to bake the bread, feed the starter by combining it with the flour and water in a clean glass jar. Cover and let it ferment at room temperature for 6 to 8 hours, until it has increased in volume and formed bubbles on the surface.

2. When the starter is ready, hydrate (autolyse) the flour: In a medium bowl, combine the flours with the lukewarm water to attain a wet, sticky dough. Cover and let rest for 1 hour. (This resting phase, in which the flour is allowed to hydrate, is known as the autolyse. Autolysing the flour promotes elasticity as well as enzymatic activity, contributing to gluten development in the dough.)

3. In the bowl of a stand mixer fitted with the dough hook attachment, mix the autolysed flour with the fed sourdough starter on medium speed for 2 minutes. If necessary, stop the mixer and scrape the sides of the bowl with a silicone spatula to promote even mixing. Add the honey and mix for another 2 minutes at medium speed. Add the salt and mix for another 2 minutes. Add the black pepper and minced herbs at low speed just to combine. Transfer the dough to a medium bowl and cover with a kitchen towel or plastic wrap. Let sit at room temperature for 30 minutes.

4. Moisten your hands with water and dig under the front end of the dough, stretch it out, and fold it back on top of the dough. Dig under the back end of the dough and repeat the same stretch-and-fold motion. Do the same on each of the sides. Finally, turn the dough over and tuck it into a ball. This process is known as stretching and folding and helps strengthen the dough. After each series of stretching and folding, the dough should feel significantly stronger. Cover the dough and let it rest for 30 minutes.

5. Stretch and fold a second time, just as you did before. Let it rest for another 30 minutes, then stretch and fold one last time, for a total of three times. Let the dough ferment for 1½ hours more, for a total of 3 hours from mixing to shaping.

6. To shape into a loaf, transfer the dough to a floured surface. Gently flatten the dough into a rough square and bring all four corners to the center. Pinch the corners together with your fingertips. Now you have a much smaller dough square. Repeat one more time, bringing all four corners to the center and pinching them together to create more tension. Invert the boule on the work surface and, using your hands, gently rotate the boule against the surface to tighten it further and seal the bottom where the corners connect. Flour an 8-inch (20 cm) banneton generously with rice flour and place the boule inside with the seam side up. Refrigerate uncovered overnight.

continues

BAKING DAY

1. Remove the dough from the refrigerator 1 hour prior to baking and let it sit at room temperature. At this point, the loaf should be proofed all the way. It will be noticeably puffy and larger in size. It will also jiggle a bit if you shake it gently, and bounce back slowly if you press it with a moistened index finger. If the loaf still seems tight after the 1-hour rest, you can let it sit out for another 30 minutes to 1 hour.

2. Place an oven rack in the lower position and place a lidded 4½-quart/liter Dutch oven on the rack. Preheat the oven to 450°F (230°C) for 30 minutes.

3. Cut a piece of parchment paper a few inches wider than the boule. Invert the banneton on the parchment paper to release the bread. Using a lame or a sharp paring knife, cut an X about ½ inch (1.25 cm) deep on the surface of the boule. These cuts will serve as steam release vents and open zippers when the bread expands in the oven.

4. Using oven mitts, carefully put the hot Dutch oven on a heatproof surface and remove the lid. Lift the parchment paper by the sides to transfer the bread and parchment to the Dutch oven. Put the lid back on and place the Dutch oven back in the oven. Bake for 30 minutes (the lid helps retain enough steam inside the pot, allowing the surface of the bread to remain supple and expand).

5. Remove the lid and bake for another 15 to 20 minutes (removing the lid will help the bread's exterior caramelize and bake into a chewy crust). The bread is ready when the crust is dark brown and an instant-read thermometer inserted in the center reaches between 200° and 208°F (93° and 98°C).

6. Using oven mitts, carefully remove the Dutch oven from the oven. Gently invert it over a cooling rack to release the bread. Let cool completely before slicing. The bread will keep in a paper bag at room temperature for up to 2 days. Or wrap it with plastic and freeze for up to 2 weeks. Freshen the thawed loaf by reheating in a 350°F (175°C) oven for a few minutes.

CARAMELIZED ONION, COMTÉ, AND NIGELLA BOULE

MAKES 1 BOULE

EQUIPMENT: instant-read thermometer, 8-inch (20 cm) round or oval banneton, 4½-quart/liter Dutch oven with lid, bread lame

TO FEED THE STARTER

1 tablespoon (13 g) sourdough starter (see page 240)

7 tablespoons (50 g) whole-grain hard red wheat flour, such as Turkey Red or Red Fife

3 tablespoons plus 1 teaspoon (50 ml) room-temperature (68–77°F/20–25°C) water

FOR THE DOUGH

4 cups (520 g) whole-grain hard red wheat flour, such as Turkey Red or Red Fife, plus extra for dusting

1¾ cups plus 2 tablespoons (450 ml) lukewarm (98–105°F/37–41°C) water

1 tablespoon honey

2 teaspoons (10 g) fine sea salt

1 tablespoon nigella seeds

1 batch Caramelized Onions (page 162)

1 cup (100 g) grated Comté

Rice flour for dusting the banneton

By now, you've probably picked up on my affinity for alliums. Onions, chives, leeks, scallions—you name it. In this loaf, I've doubled down on oniony goodness. The crumb is peppered with nigella seeds, which have a smoky, allium-rich flavor (in fact, folks often mistake them for onion seeds). Then, I match the dough with an umami-packed mixture of caramelized onions and nutty Comté cheese. Just like in French onion soup, which loosely inspired this bread, the recipe's success lies in the balance of sweet caramelized onions and rich, salty Comté. Sweet onion varieties such as Maui or Walla Walla are almost always recommended for caramelizing, but regular yellow onions also work well. So that the caramelized onions pack a punch and don't get lost in the loaf, I parbake the bread, then top it with the onion and grated Comté mixture before putting it back in to finish baking. That way, the bread can fully rise without being weighed down by the fatty melting cheese, and the already cooked caramelized onions aren't at risk of becoming too dark. I've made this loaf with Rouge de Bordeaux, Glenn, and Yecora Rojo (see My Favorite Flours, page 313)—all strong, forward-tasting wheats that match the sweet intensity of the caramelized onions.

continues

PREP DAY

1. The day before you'd like to bake the bread, feed the starter by combining it with the flour and water in a clean glass jar. Cover and let it ferment at room temperature for 6 to 8 hours, until it has increased in volume and formed bubbles on the surface.

2. When the starter is ready, hydrate (autolyse) the flour: In a medium bowl, combine the flour for the dough with at least 1½ cups (355 ml) of the lukewarm water, adding more as needed to attain a wet, sticky dough. Cover and let rest for 1 hour. (This resting phase, in which the flour is allowed to hydrate, is known as the autolyse. Autolysing the flour promotes elasticity as well as enzymatic activity, contributing to gluten development in the dough.)

3. In the bowl of a stand mixer fitted with the dough hook attachment, mix the autolysed flour with the fed sourdough starter on medium speed for 2 minutes. If necessary, stop the mixer and scrape the sides of the bowl with a silicone spatula to promote even mixing. Add the honey and mix for another 2 minutes at medium speed. Add the salt and mix for another 2 minutes. Add the nigella seeds and mix at low speed just to combine. Transfer the dough to a medium bowl and cover with a kitchen towel or plastic wrap. Let sit at room temperature for 30 minutes.

4. Moisten your hands with water and dig under the front end of the dough, stretch it out, and fold it back on top of the dough. Dig under the back end of the dough and repeat the same stretch-and-fold motion. Do the same on each of the sides. Finally, turn the dough over and tuck it into a ball. This process is known as stretching and folding and helps strengthen the dough. After each series of stretching and folding, the dough should feel significantly stronger. Cover the dough and let it rest for 30 minutes.

5. Stretch and fold a second time, just as you did before. Let it rest for another 30 minutes, then stretch and fold one last time, for a total of three times. Let the dough ferment for 1½ hours more, for a total of 3 hours from mixing to shaping.

6. To shape into a loaf, transfer the dough to a floured surface. Gently flatten the dough into a rough square and bring all four corners to the center. Pinch the corners together with your fingertips. Now you have a much smaller dough square. Repeat one more time, bringing all four corners to the center and pinching them together to create more tension. Invert the boule on the work surface and, using your hands, gently rotate the boule against the surface to tighten it further and seal the bottom where the corners connect. Flour an 8-inch (20 cm) banneton generously with rice flour and place the boule inside with the seam side up. Refrigerate uncovered overnight.

BAKING DAY

1. Remove the dough from the refrigerator 1 hour prior to baking and let it sit at room temperature. At this point, the loaf should be proofed all the way. It will be noticeably puffy and larger in size. It will also jiggle a bit if you shake it gently, and bounce back slowly if you press it with a moistened index finger. If the loaf still seems tight after the 1-hour rest, you can let it sit out for another 30 minutes to 1 hour.

2. Place an oven rack in the lower position and place a lidded 4½-quart/liter Dutch oven on the rack. Preheat the oven to 450°F (230°C) for 30 minutes.

3. Cut a piece of parchment paper a few inches wider than the boule. Invert the banneton on the parchment paper to release the bread. Using a lame or a sharp paring knife, cut an X about ½ inch (1.25 cm) deep on the surface of the boule. These cuts will serve as steam release vents and open zippers when the bread expands in the oven.

4. Using oven mitts, carefully put the hot Dutch oven on a heatproof surface and remove the lid. Lift the parchment paper by the sides to transfer the bread and parchment to the Dutch oven. Put the lid back on and place the Dutch oven back in the oven. Bake for 20 minutes (the lid helps retain enough steam inside the pot, allowing the surface of the bread to remain supple and expand).

5. Combine the caramelized onions and grated Comté in a small bowl.

6. Remove the lid and arrange the onion-Comté mixture in the center of the boule; right where you scored the X previously. Bake for another 15 to 20 minutes (removing the lid will help the bread's exterior caramelize and bake into a chewy crust). The bread is ready when the cheese is golden, the crust is dark brown, and an instant-read thermometer inserted in the center reaches between 200° and 208°F (93° and 98°C).

7. Using oven mitts, carefully remove the Dutch oven from the oven. Carefully, transfer the warm loaf to a cooling rack. Let cool completely before slicing. Wrap any leftovers with plastic and store in the refrigerator for up to 1 week or in the freezer for up to 2 weeks. Freshen the thawed loaf by reheating in a 350°F (175°C) oven for a few minutes.

SPROUTED GRAIN LOAF

MAKES 1 LOAF

EQUIPMENT: instant-read thermometer, 8-inch (20 cm) oval banneton, 4½-quart/liter Dutch oven with lid, bread lame

TO FEED THE STARTER

1 tablespoon (13 g) sourdough starter (see page 240)

7 tablespoons (50 g) whole-grain hard red wheat flour, such as Turkey Red or Red Fife

3 tablespoons plus 1 teaspoon (50 ml) room-temperature (68–77°F/20–25°C) water

FOR THE DOUGH

4¼ cups (550 g) whole-grain hard red wheat flour, such as Turkey Red or Red Fife

1¾ cups (415 ml) lukewarm (98–105°F/37–41°C) water

2 teaspoons (10 g) fine sea salt

Rice flour for dusting the banneton

FOR THE SEED MIX

¼ cup (40 g) raw pumpkin seeds (pepitas)

3 tablespoons (30 g) sunflower seeds

1 tablespoon flax seeds

FOR THE SPROUTED WHEAT

¾ cups (145 g) wheat berries

If I were allowed to bake only one recipe for the rest of my life, this would be it. Made with strong red wheat and studded with sprouted wheat berries and seeds, this hearty loaf is an institution at Friends & Family. Originally, I used a compact mash of already sprouted wheat sold by Central Milling, but in time we decided to sprout our own grains. Because the goal was a tight structure filled with many tasty and textured elements, it wasn't particularly hard to create. I just had to watch the hydration levels, given that many of the ingredients were very thirsty. With all that strong flour, the loaf is also very easy to shape and always expands nicely in the oven.

This is the place for your most offensive flour. The boldest of the bold. The coarsest of the coarse. Red wheats are at home here, and if you mill your own grain at home, this is the ideal recipe to use it in. I've made this loaf with many different flours, and I find it interesting how the taste of each specific wheat gives the loaf a personal twist. To the flour and sprouted wheat, I add a mix of sunflower, pumpkin, and flax seeds.

Before you start, it's important to map out the recipe over a few days since you'll need to sprout your wheat berries, a process that can take 2 to 3 days. Sprouting berries involves soaking them in water for a few minutes over a few days until they germinate and a little tail protrudes from them. Before mixing them into the dough, blitz them into smaller pieces in the food processor.

If you don't feel ready to go full hippie yet and would like an easier introduction to this style of bread, make the variation on page 269 for a lighter Sprouted Grain Loaf with a bit more mass appeal. Made with a blend of whole-grain wheat flour and refined bread flour, it produces a softer and less dense bread without losing the hippie effect brought by the seed mix and the sprouted wheat kernels.

Like other sourdough breads, this keeps for many days and can be refrigerated or frozen. It makes the absolute best avocado toast (Californians' favorite breakfast) and PB&J. I often have it toasted with butter and orange marmalade or, when I'm watching my sugar intake, a spoonful of hummus. For the full hippie experience, make the Friends & Family Famous Hippie Sandwich on Sprouted Wheat Bread (page 271), which hits the spot any time of day.

PREP DAYS

1. Start the process of sprouting the wheat berries 3 days before making the bread. Soak the berries in water for 5 minutes. Drain and transfer to a glass container with a lid. Let sit overnight on the kitchen counter. Repeat the same process for two consecutive days. When the berries start to germinate—they'll have an incipient stem protruding from within. By the time the berries have germinated, you should end up with 1½ cups (200 g) sprouted berries. Pulse the sprouted grains in the food processor to chop them into smaller pieces. Refrigerate until ready to use.

2. The day before you'd like to bake the bread, feed the starter by combining it with the flour and water in a clean glass jar. Cover and let it ferment at room temperature for 6 to 8 hours, until it has increased in volume and formed bubbles on the surface.

3. When the starter is ready, hydrate (autolyse) the flour: In a medium bowl, combine the flour for the dough and the water. Cover and let rest for 1 hour. (This resting phase, in which the flour is allowed to hydrate, is known as the autolyse. Autolysing the flour promotes elasticity as well as enzymatic activity, contributing to gluten development in the dough.)

4. Soak the pumpkin, sunflower, and flax seeds in water for 5 minutes. Drain and combine with the chopped sprouted wheat berries.

5. In the bowl of a stand mixer fitted with the dough hook attachment, mix the autolysed flour with the fed sourdough starter on medium speed for 2 minutes. If necessary, stop the mixer and scrape the sides of the bowl with a silicone spatula to promote even mixing. Add the salt and mix for another 2 minutes at medium speed. Add the soaked seeds and berries mixture and mix just to incorporate. Transfer the dough to a medium bowl and cover with a kitchen towel or plastic wrap. Let sit at room temperature for 30 minutes.

6. Moisten your hands with water and dig under the front end of the dough, stretch it out, and fold it back on top of the dough. Dig under the back end of the dough and repeat the same stretch-and-fold motion. Do the same on each of the sides. Finally, turn the dough over and

continues

tuck it into a ball. This process is known as stretching and folding and helps strengthen the dough. After each series of stretching and folding, the dough should feel significantly stronger. Cover the dough and let it rest for 30 minutes.

7. Stretch and fold a second time, just as you did before. Let it rest for another 30 minutes, then stretch and fold one last time, for a total of three times. Let the dough ferment for 1½ hours more, for a total of 3 hours from mixing to shaping.

8. To shape into a loaf, transfer the dough to a floured surface. Gently flatten the dough into a rough square and bring all four corners to the center. Pinch the corners together with your fingertips. Now you have a much smaller dough square. Repeat one more time, bringing all four corners to the center and pinching them together to create more tension. Invert the boule on the work surface and, using your hands, gently rotate the boule against the surface to tighten it further and seal the bottom where the corners connect. Flour an 8-inch (20 cm) banneton generously with rice flour and place the boule inside with the seam side up. Refrigerate uncovered overnight.

BAKING DAY

1. Remove the dough from the refrigerator 1 hour prior to baking and let it sit at room temperature. At this point, the loaf should be proofed all the way. It will be noticeably puffy and larger in size. It will also jiggle a bit if you shake it gently, and bounce back slowly if you press it with a moistened index finger. If the loaf still seems tight after the 1-hour rest, you can let it sit out for another 30 minutes to 1 hour.

2. Place an oven rack in the lowest position and place a lidded 4½-quart/liter Dutch oven on the rack. Preheat the oven to 450°F (230°C) for 30 minutes.

3. Cut a piece of parchment paper a few inches wider than the loaf. Invert the banneton on the parchment paper to release the bread. Using a lame or a sharp paring knife, cut a slit lengthwise about ½ inch (1.25 cm) deep on the surface of the loaf. This cut will serve as a steam release vent and open zipper when the bread expands in the oven.

4. Using oven mitts, carefully put the hot Dutch oven on a heatproof surface and remove the lid. Lift the parchment paper by the sides to transfer the bread and parchment to the Dutch oven. Put the lid back on and place the Dutch oven back in the oven. Bake for 30 minutes (the lid helps retain enough steam inside the pot, allowing the surface of the bread to remain supple and expand).

5. Remove the lid and bake for another 15 to 20 minutes (removing the lid will help the bread's exterior caramelize and bake into a chewy crust). The bread is ready when the crust is dark brown and an instant-read thermometer inserted in the center reaches between 200°F and 208°F (93°C and 98°C).

6. Using oven mitts, carefully remove the Dutch oven from the oven. Gently invert it over a cooling rack to release the bread. Let cool completely before slicing. The bread will keep in a paper bag at room temperature for up to 2 days. Or wrap it with plastic and freeze for up to 2 weeks. Freshen the thawed loaf by reheating it in a 350°F (175°C) oven for a few minutes.

VARIATION

For a less dense Sprouted Grain Loaf, replace the flour amount for the dough with 2¼ cups (290 g) whole-grain hard red wheat flour, such as Turkey Red or Red Fife, plus 2 cups (270 g) bread flour.

FRIENDS & FAMILY FAMOUS HIPPIE SANDWICH

MAKES 2 SANDWICHES

FOR THE PEA MASH
2 tablespoons olive oil
1 small shallot, thinly sliced
1 cup (140 g) frozen peas (no need to thaw)
Kosher salt to taste
Finely grated lemon zest and lemon juice to taste

FOR THE HERB DRESSING
1 small garlic clove, peeled and crushed
Kosher salt to taste
2 tablespoons minced fresh chives
2 tablespoons minced fresh dill
¼ cup (10 g) minced fresh flat-leaf parsley
¼ cup (10 g) roughly chopped fresh basil
1 tablespoon minced shallot
Juice of ½ lemon
¼ cup (60 ml) extra virgin olive oil

TO ASSEMBLE THE SANDWICH
4 slices Sprouted Grain Loaf (page 266)
4 butter lettuce leaves
2 radishes, thinly sliced
1 Persian cucumber, sliced lengthwise into thin slivers
4 ounces (112 g) feta, sliced into ½-inch (1.25 cm) slabs
1 medium Hass avocado, peeled, pitted, and thinly sliced, seasoned with salt and a squeeze of lemon juice
½ heaping cup (70 g) sunflower sprouts

This cult-favorite sandwich has been on the Friends & Family menu since we opened, and it has developed quite a following over the years. It's a dream for vegetarians, though regulars with a bit of insider information know to order the Dirty Hippie, which is a Hippie plus bacon. Months before we even wrote our first menu, my husband, Daniel Mattern—Friends & Family's chef, co-founder, mastermind, and jack-of-all-trades—wanted to include an old-school veggie sandwich. The kind with super-seedy whole-grain bread and lots of green fillings, reminiscent of California's 1960s and '70s organic food movement. The bread came first, and from there, the Hippie was born. I would've been happy with a bunch of crunchy veggies and some cheese, but Dan wouldn't stop tinkering until he achieved the perfect balance of fresh green vegetables, creamy avocado, salty feta, and zesty herb dressing. The rest is history. The recipe for the herb dressing makes a bit more than you need, but it won't be hard to come up with ways to use it all up. It keeps for up to 3 days in the fridge and is great over chicken, fish, and roasted potatoes; tossed with butter lettuces; or as a dairy-free dip for crudités.

continues

1. Start with the pea mash. Heat the olive oil in a medium sauté pan over medium heat. Add the shallot and sauté until soft and translucent, about 2 minutes. Add the frozen peas and cook for 2 to 3 minutes, until soft. Season lightly with salt. Transfer to the bowl of the food processor while still warm. Add the lemon zest and juice and blitz until a uniform paste forms. Taste and add more salt if necessary. Transfer to a bowl and let the pea mash cool completely.

2. To make the herb dressing, pound the garlic in a mortar and pestle with a pinch of salt to make a paste. Add the herbs little by little and pound to a paste. Transfer to a small bowl, add the shallot and lemon juice, and whisk to combine. Add the olive oil in a steady, slow stream while whisking vigorously. Season with salt to taste.

3. To assemble a sandwich, spread 2 to 3 tablespoons pea mash on each slice of bread. Lay 2 lettuce leaves slightly overlapping on the bottom bread slice, then top with a layer of radishes, followed by a few slivers of cucumber. Follow with the sliced feta, then fan the avocado slices over the width of the sandwich. Top with a hefty handful of sprouts and drizzle generously with the herb dressing. Finish with the remaining slice of bread (pea mash facing down). Repeat to make the remaining sandwich. Cut each sandwich in half and serve immediately.

CHOCOLATE-CHERRY PAN LOAF

MAKES 1 PAN LOAF

EQUIPMENT: instant-read thermometer, 8½-by-4½-inch (22 by 11 cm) loaf pan, roasting pan for steam bath, bread lame

TO FEED THE STARTER

- 1 tablespoon (13 g) sourdough starter (see page 240)
- 7 tablespoons (50 g) whole-grain hard red wheat flour, such as Turkey Red or Red Fife
- 3 tablespoons plus 1 teaspoon (50 ml) room-temperature (68–77°F/20–25°C) water

FOR THE DOUGH

- 3 cups (390 g) whole-grain hard red wheat flour, such as Turkey Red or Red Fife, plus extra for dusting
- 1 cup (125 g) whole-grain or dark rye flour
- 1¾ cups plus 2 tablespoons (450 ml) lukewarm (98–105°F/37–41°C) water
- ½ cup (80 g) dried cherries
- 1 tablespoon honey
- 2 teaspoons (10 g) fine sea salt
- Heaping ½ cup (100 g) coarsely chopped bittersweet (65–80%) chocolate

Sweet-tart cherries, nutty rye, and earthy, bittersweet chocolate are a match made in baking heaven. Their flavors complement one another wonderfully, whether in cereal, scones, or sourdough bread. For the flour mix, I blend one part dark rye flour with three parts hard red wheat. The red wheat gives the bread structure, and rye contributes flavor and a pleasant density to the loaf. Rye flour makes this a slightly acidic dough, providing a nice stage for the tart dried cherries. The loaf is hydrated at the same rate as many of the sourdough recipes included in this chapter, but don't expect an airy, lofty loaf—it will remain a little tight and dense, which works well with the mix-ins, not unlike a fruit and nut bread. I bake this dough in a loaf pan to prevent the chocolate in the dough from burning.

The loaf banks on the sober side of chocolate, highlighting its bitter, tobacco-like depth, rather than its sweet side. When sourcing dried cherries, it is worth looking for the good stuff at well-stocked grocery stores or nature marts. I prefer the plump sweet ones often labeled "dark sweet cherries," which come from sweeter varieties such as Bing or Lapins. If you enjoy a really puckery cherry, opt for tart dried cherries. They're generally sour cherry varieties such as Montmorency and Balaton.

PREP DAY

1. The day before you'd like to bake the bread, feed the starter by combining it with the flour and water in a clean glass jar. Cover and let it ferment at room temperature for 6 to 8 hours, until it has increased in volume and formed bubbles on the surface.

2. When the starter is ready, hydrate (autolyse) the flour: In a medium bowl, combine the flours for the dough with the

continues

lukewarm water. Cover and let rest for 1 hour. (This resting phase, in which the flour is allowed to hydrate, is known as the autolyse. Autolysing the flour promotes elasticity as well as enzymatic activity, contributing to gluten development in the dough.)

3. Soak the dried cherries in cold water for 5 minutes. Drain and set aside.

4. In the bowl of a stand mixer fitted with the dough hook attachment, mix the autolysed flour with the fed sourdough starter on medium speed for 2 minutes. If necessary, stop the mixer and scrape the sides of the bowl with a silicone spatula to promote even mixing. Add the honey and mix for another 2 minutes at medium speed. Add the salt and mix for another 2 minutes. Add the soaked cherries and chocolate and mix at low speed just to combine. Transfer the dough to a medium bowl and cover with a kitchen towel or plastic wrap. Let the dough sit at room temperature for 30 minutes.

5. Moisten your hands with water and dig under the front end of the dough, stretch it out, and fold it back on top of the dough. Dig under the back end of the dough and repeat the same stretch-and-fold motion. Do the same on each of the sides. Finally, turn the dough over and tuck it into a ball. This process is known as stretching and folding and helps strengthen the dough. After each series of stretching and folding, the dough should feel significantly stronger. Cover the dough and let it rest for 30 minutes.

6. Stretch and fold a second time, just as you did before. Let it rest for another 30 minutes, then stretch and fold one last time, for a total of three times. Let the dough ferment for 1½ hours more, for a total of 3 hours from mixing to shaping.

7. Lightly coat an 8½-by-4½-inch (22 by 11 cm) loaf pan with nonstick spray. To shape the dough into a pan loaf, transfer the dough to a floured surface. Gently flatten the dough into a rough rectangle and roll into a cylinder (as you would a jelly roll). Place the cylinder seam side down in the prepared pan. Refrigerate uncovered overnight.

BAKING DAY

1. Remove the dough from the refrigerator 1 hour prior to baking and let it sit at room temperature. At this point, the loaf should be proofed all the way. It will be noticeably puffy and larger in size. It will also jiggle a bit if you shake it gently, and bounce back slowly if you press it with a moistened index finger. If the loaf still seems tight after the 1-hour rest, you can let it sit out for another 30 minutes to 1 hour.

2. Place an empty roasting pan at the bottom of the oven. Place an oven rack in the middle position and preheat the oven to 450°F (230°C).

3. Use a lame or a sharp paring knife to cut a slit about ½ inch (1.25 cm) deep along the length of the loaf.

4. Right before baking, carefully pour 2 cups of tap water into the hot roasting pan to generate steam. Immediately put the pan in the oven and bake for 30 minutes, or until the loaf turns dark fudge brown. Avoid opening the oven halfway to prevent the steam from dissipating.

5. Remove the pan from the oven and place on a cooling rack. Let it sit for at least 1 hour before enjoying. The bread will keep in a paper bag at room temperature for up to 2 days. Or wrap it with plastic and freeze for up to 2 weeks. Freshen the thawed loaf by reheating in a 350°F (175°C) oven for a few minutes.

> **VARIATION**
> You could also use dehydrated pears instead of cherries, which pair well with both rye and chocolate. I love the pear version for breakfast served with a chunk of Brie and a sliced Bartlett pear next to a cup of dark coffee.

CHAPTER 7

ANYTIME WHOLE-GRAIN BAKES

Recipes

Build-Your-Own Granola   280
Midnight Cookies   283
Rye Shortcrust   285
Heart Tarts   287
Fig-Strawberry Pillows   289
Cornelés   291
Spiced Vegan Teacake   294
Apricot Crostata   295
Chocolate Chiffon Cake   298
Coconut Layer Cake with White Chocolate Buttercream   301
Sour Cream Pie Dough   304
Cherry Cutout Pie   305
Perfect Quiche   308

If you've made it this far, you're well-versed in whole-grain magic. Think of this as a bonus chapter, here to remind you that the textures, flavors, and aromas whole grains bring to morning bakes can be employed across the board.

Apt to be made and enjoyed anytime, the following recipes are some of my trustiest standbys. You'll find some of my greatest hits: customizable granola (plus a thorough primer to match), a decadent late-night cookie, a fruity tart, a chocolate cake, an elaborate layer cake, a killer fruit pie, a tender quick bread, a few bite-size confections, and a workhorse recipe for the perfect quiche.

I've also included four fundamental pastry formulas, which I think every well-rounded baker should know: shortcrust, pasta frolla, pie dough, and pâte brisée. These are the building blocks of many other bakes, sweet and savory. Dive into them at your leisure, giving yourself the freedom to improvise and make the recipes your own.

And while we're at it, let's make sure your kitchen is ready for the task. The right molds and pans will make baking smoother and yield ideal results. Throughout this chapter, I've included exact dimensions so each batch fits the pan perfectly. I favor coated nonstick pans because they're durable and easy to clean. If you're stocking up, shop for a couple of cake pans, a springform, a loaf pan, and, my personal favorite, a Bundt pan. Any well-loved heirloom or flea-market find also deserves a place in your kitchen. Just remember to grease them generously, wash gently, and dry thoroughly so they keep serving you for years to come.

With a varied palette of whole-grain flours, there isn't a cake, cookie, or tart that can't be made better. Outside of having fun with the following bakes, I hope you remember that a similar approach can be taken with any recipe. Try adding some cornmeal to your favorite yellow cake, or throw a bit of buckwheat into your tried-and-true cookies. The sky's the limit! Bake whatever makes you happy. And maybe it goes without saying, but don't forget to save a slice (or two) for breakfast.

OPPOSITE:
Granola is endlessly customizable. Just mix and match your preferred ingredients to make it your own.

BUILD-YOUR-OWN GRANOLA

MAKES 6 CUPS (1.4 L)

Mixing and matching ingredients to create the granola of your dreams is simple—you just have to stick to a few basic principles. Start with the ratios outlined below and pick flakes, dried fruits, nuts, and seeds that please your personal granola palate. Every ingredient serves a purpose. The flakes (thin grain kernels that have been steamed and rolled) are our base: They add nutrition, texture, and a clean slate on which to build a flavorful cereal. Oat flakes are common because they hold up well during baking and complement other ingredients nicely, but there are other flake varieties to add and experiment with for flavor and texture. Dried fruits contribute overall sweetness, acidity, and diverse flavors while amping up the granola's energy-giving properties. Nuts add crunch, healthy fats, and flavor. Try to choose a varied selection of large and small seeds, which makes for a more interesting bite.

Oil is crucial here; it helps the granola roast evenly and stay dry all the way through, extending its shelf life as a result. Most of the liquid you add will evaporate during the roasting process, so it's important to hydrate the ingredients properly prior to roasting. It's this slow process of dehydrating in the oven that makes a crisp, toasty granola. I stay away from refined sugar but think granola should be at least slightly sweetened. The dried fruits added at the end will do their part, but I might also include applesauce, maple syrup, honey, or golden syrup.

Notice that I prefer liquid sweeteners over turbinado, date, or coconut sugar. This is because their sweetness is more nuanced and they don't need to be dissolved, so they blend easily into the cereal. The granola toasting technique is quite simple, but you do need to be patient. As tempting as it may be to crank up the oven and be done with it, you must bake the granola low and slow for 45 minutes to 1 hour, stirring with love and care every 15 minutes.

To create your own granola blend, choose ingredients from the listed categories, sticking with the indicated quantities. As long as you work within the ratios given, any flavor combination is possible. As far as method goes, it's the same regardless of ingredient choice; the only variant is baking time. I've included some of my favorite mixtures for inspiration on page 282.

Here is the formula:

1½ cups (160 g) flakes (barley, rye, oats)

¾ cup (100 g) nuts

½ cup (70 g) large seeds (sunflower, pumpkin)

¼ cup (35 g) small seeds (sesame, black sesame, flax)

2 tablespoons (15 g) drying agent (almond flour, dry milk)

2 teaspoons ground warm spices (optional)

½ teaspoon kosher salt

½ cup (120 ml) sweetener (honey, maple syrup, agave nectar, golden syrup, barley syrup, brown rice syrup)

¼ cup (60 ml) vegetable oil

¼ cup (60 ml) liquid (applesauce, pureed banana, egg white, whole milk, water)

1 teaspoon vanilla or almond extract (optional)

1 cup (150 g) dried fruits (raisins, currants, blueberries; chopped apricot, pear, dates) or chopped dark or bittersweet chocolate

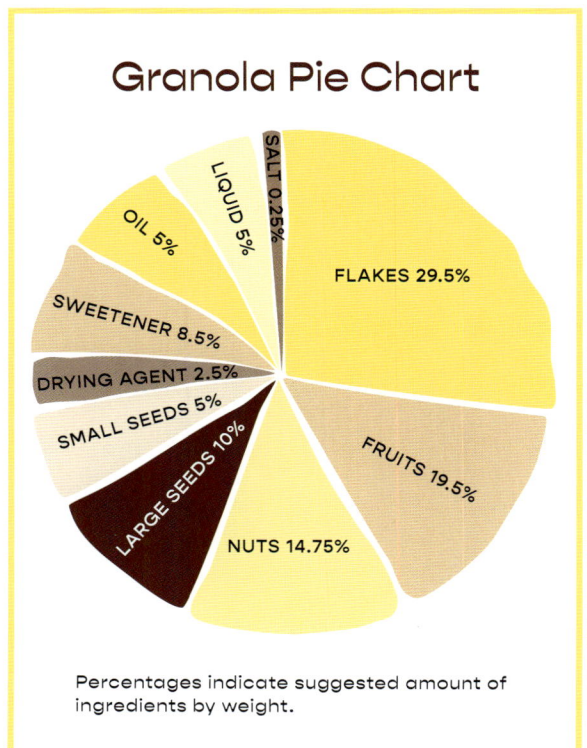

Percentages indicate suggested amount of ingredients by weight.

GRANOLA IN 5 EASY STEPS:

1. Place an oven rack in the middle position and preheat the oven to 325°F (160°C). Coat a roasting pan lightly with nonstick spray.

2. Combine the flakes, nuts, seeds, drying agent, spices (if using), and salt in a large bowl. Toss with both hands to blend.

3. Heat the sweetener, oil, liquid, and extract (if using) in a small saucepan over low heat until lukewarm (98–105°F/37–41°C). Pour over the dry ingredients. Using a silicone spatula or wooden spoon, stir until all the dry ingredients are well coated. Transfer to the prepared roasting pan.

4. Toast in the oven for 45 minutes, stirring every 15 minutes so the granola toasts evenly.

5. Spread the granola on a rimmed baking sheet lined with parchment paper and let it cool completely, 20 to 30 minutes. Combine with your choice of dried fruits or chocolate and store in an airtight container at room temperature for up to 2 weeks.

WINNING GRANOLA COMBINATIONS

- Barley flakes + walnuts + pumpkin seeds + applesauce + dried apples + warm spices (ground cinnamon, nutmeg, cloves, allspice, cardamom)
- Barley flakes + pecans + sunflower seeds + dark honey + ginger + dried cranberries
- Rye flakes + almonds + black and white sesame seeds + orange zest and juice + cinnamon + dates
- Rye flakes + almonds + dried cherries + dark chocolate chunks + coconut flakes + golden syrup + ground cloves
- Rolled oats + macadamia nuts + dried apricots + dried blueberries + coconut flakes + ground cardamom
- Rolled oats + cashews + banana puree + dehydrated banana + dates + ground allspice

MIDNIGHT COOKIES

MAKES 16 COOKIES

- ½ cup (60 g) whole-grain or dark rye flour
- 1 cup (130 g) whole-grain all-purpose wheat flour, such as Sonora or Frederick
- ⅓ cup (35 g) Dutch-processed cocoa powder
- ½ teaspoon baking powder
- ½ teaspoon baking soda
- ½ teaspoon kosher salt
- ½ cup (112 g/1 stick/4 ounces) unsalted butter, melted and cooled slightly
- ½ cup (100 g) granulated sugar
- ½ cup packed (110 g) dark brown sugar
- 1 large egg
- 1 teaspoon vanilla extract
- ½ cup (90 g) bittersweet (65–80%) chocolate chunks
- ½ cup (70 g) chopped chocolate-covered mint candies, such as After Eight mints, Junior Mints, or York Peppermint Patties

While unlocking the bakery at 3 a.m., it's not uncommon to run into late-night barflies walking the streets of Thai Town. We've occasionally struck up a conversation, and more than once, someone has asked me for a warm cookie. Some folks have even suggested that if we were to sell fresh-baked cookies to tipsy passersby, we wouldn't need to open the rest of the day. Well, in that alternate universe, these are the cookies I would make. I call them Midnight Cookies because they're the kind of indulgence I'd bake for a middle-of-the-night snack attack if I weren't an adult with lots of responsibilities. They come together more easily than other chocolate chip cookies because you don't need a mixer. The best part is that you can bake them immediately after mixing, unlike traditional chocolate chip cookies, which spread too much in the oven if you don't refrigerate them first.

The dough, made with Dutch-processed cocoa, is super decadent on its own, but even more so with chocolate chips, which you can buy at the store or chop yourself from bittersweet chocolate bars. I also add chopped chocolate-covered mint candies like After Eight mints, Junior Mints, or York Peppermint Patties. This add-in takes the cookie into adult territory, but I see no reason to hold back. If mint and chocolate is not your favorite combo, you could throw in milk chocolate or white chocolate chips. Or opt for different add-ins altogether—perhaps toffee bits, mini pretzels, peanut butter chips, coconut flakes, chocolate-covered espresso beans, or dehydrated bananas. The point is to break the rules, so you do you.

Don't be shocked to see rye flour in the ingredient list. Rye, as you'll notice by glossing through this recipe repertoire, is one of my favorite flours to mix with chocolate. If you'd like to prep ahead, the cookie dough or the rolled cookies can be refrigerated for 3 to 4 days, or frozen for up to 2 weeks. If making them straight from the refrigerator or from frozen, just add a minute or two to the baking time.

continues

1. Place two oven racks in the middle positions and preheat the oven to 350°F (175°C). Line two rimmed baking sheets with parchment paper.

2. Whisk together the flours, cocoa powder, baking powder, baking soda, and salt in a mixing bowl.

3. In a separate bowl, combine the melted butter with the sugars and stir with a silicone spatula until just combined. Add the egg and vanilla and stir until smooth. Add the dry ingredients in two additions, making sure the first is fully incorporated before adding the remainder. Fold the chocolate chunks and mint candies into the batter until evenly distributed. The dough should be soft but not sticky.

4. Divide the dough into 16 equal portions (about 45 g/1½ ounces each) and round each portion with your hands. Place the cookies on the prepared baking sheets, 2 inches (5 cm) apart to prevent the cookies from touching as they bake. Bake for 8 minutes. Then rotate the sheets, switch their positions, and bake for another 8 minutes, until the cookie edges look matte but the centers are still a little shiny and gooey.

5. Let the cookies cool completely on the baking sheets or enjoy while still warm. The cookies will keep in an airtight container at room temperature for up to 2 days.

RYE SHORTCRUST

**MAKES ENOUGH FOR 5 TO 6 HEART TARTS (PAGE 287)
OR 24 FIG-STRAWBERRY PILLOWS (PAGE 289)**

- ¾ cup (170 g/1½ sticks/6 ounces) cold unsalted butter, cut into ½-inch (1.25 cm) cubes
- 1 cup plus 2 tablespoons (160 g) all-purpose flour, plus extra for dusting
- ¾ cup (100 g) whole-grain or dark rye flour
- ½ cup (100 g) sugar
- ¾ teaspoon kosher salt
- 1 tablespoon plus 1 teaspoon vanilla extract
- ¼ cup (60 ml) iced water

This versatile shortcrust is the base for our jam-filled heart tarts and fig-strawberry "pillows." The dough is flexible and easy to work with, and it bakes up wonderfully tender. It is more like a sandy cookie dough than piecrust and can be used to make many filled pastries other than tarts.

Here's an example of how flour rules don't always apply. Rye, which is a low-gluten, deeply earthy, and naturally sour flour, is considered one of the harshest grains out there. It represents vast regions of the world that experience extreme weather and short growing seasons. One would be correct to associate rye more with the dense breads of Scandinavia than with dainty, delicate pastries, yet this shortcrust shows how rye can deliver quiet elegance, beautiful texture, and stunning flavor. The combination of rye and fig in the Fig-Strawberry Pillows (page 289) is truly mind-blowing, but even more cheerful ingredients, like the raspberry jam used to make the Heart Tarts, are compatible with the proud, heavy-hitting rye.

This recipe is most successful made with dark rye and refined all-purpose flour, which adds flexibility to the dough. The raw pastry has a beautiful light charcoal color, and once the pastry is baked it turns a rich golden brown.

1. In the bowl of a stand mixer fitted with the paddle attachment, mix the butter, flours, sugar, and salt on low speed until a coarse meal forms, about 5 minutes.

2. Combine the vanilla and ice water and add. Mix until a uniform dough comes together. Turn onto a lightly floured surface and knead briefly. Pat down into a disk and follow the rolling and cutting instructions for your desired shape, or wrap tightly with plastic and refrigerate for up to 2 days. It also freezes well for up to 2 weeks.

HEART TARTS

MAKES 5 TO 6 HEART TARTS

EQUIPMENT: fluted pastry wheel cutter, heart-shaped cookie cutter

1 batch Rye Shortcrust (page 285)
All-purpose flour for dusting
½ cup (120 ml) Raspberry Jam (page 76) or store-bought
1 large egg, beaten
Granulated sugar for sprinkling

These whimsical handheld tarts are a Friends & Family staple. When I first made them, I was trying to rip off a Pop-Tart and ended up with something so much better, no sprinkles required. They are called heart tarts because a heart-shaped cutout reveals the fragrant berry jam tucked inside. The rye shortcrust is ideal here because of its pleasantly crumbly texture and melt-in-your-mouth effect. The recipe makes five tarts, but if you roll every bit of dough scrap you will end up with six. The pastry must be rolled quite thin before cutting it into squares, since you will end up building a sandwich. To cut the squares neatly, I recommend using a ruler and a pastry cutter—a fluted pastry cutter will make a lovely edge. If a heart motif is not your vibe, you could choose another shape—a star or even a plain circle comes to mind—just make sure to have an opening for steam to escape, preventing the seams from opening while baking.

The tarts can be assembled in advance and baked frozen. Don't skip the beaten egg varnish and sugar sprinkle right before baking. It gives the tarts a luscious, caramelized look. Raspberry jam is my favorite filling because it packs concentrated berry flavor, ensuring each bite of pastry has the right jam quotient. I always recommend making your own jam, but if you must use store-bought jam, choose a thick jam made from whole fruit and not just fruit juice. Although Pop-Tarts are considered a breakfast food, I wouldn't shy away from serving these as a dessert, slightly warm with a scoop of ice cream.

1. Place an oven rack in the middle position and preheat the oven to 350°F (175°C). Line a rimmed baking sheet with parchment paper.

2. Divide the dough into 2 equal portions. Place each dough portion between two sheets of parchment paper and flatten roughly into a 10-inch (25.5 cm) square with a rolling pin. The rolled dough should be no thicker than ¼ inch (6 mm). Refrigerate for at least 30 minutes.

continues

3. Peel off the top parchment sheet from one dough square and dust lightly with flour. Invert the dough on a work surface and peel off the other sheet of parchment. Cut out four 4-inch (10 cm) squares. Repeat with the other dough square. Gather the scraps and repeat the steps of rolling and cutting to get four additional 4-inch (10 cm) squares. Using a heart-shaped cookie cutter, cut out a heart in the center of half of the squares; these will be the tops of the heart tarts.

4. Fill a pastry bag with the raspberry jam and pipe a 2-inch (5 cm) jam square in the center of each bottom, making sure to leave a 1-inch (2.5 cm) border. Paint the border with a pastry brush dipped in water, then fit the top squares directly on top. Gently press the border with your fingers, then trim ⅛ to ¼ inch (3 to 6 mm) off the edges with the pastry wheel cutter. Use an offset spatula to transfer the heart tarts to the prepared baking sheet, spacing them at least 1 inch (2.5 cm) apart.

5. Brush each tart with beaten egg and sprinkle generously with sugar. Bake the heart tarts for 20 minutes. Then rotate the sheet and bake for another 10 to 15 minutes, until the heart tarts are golden brown. If you like, you can sprinkle the heart cutouts with sugar and bake for 10 to 12 minutes on a separate baking sheet. Remove from the oven and let cool completely before enjoying. Store leftovers in an airtight container for up to 3 days.

FIG-STRAWBERRY PILLOWS

MAKES 24 COOKIES

EQUIPMENT: plain pastry wheel cutter

¾ cup (150 g) sugar
½ cup (120 ml) water
½ vanilla bean
2 cups (300 g) fresh hulled and quartered strawberries
1 heaping cup (250 g) ripe Black Mission figs, roughly chopped
1 batch Rye Shortcrust (page 285)
All-purpose flour for dusting
1 large egg, beaten
Granulated sugar for sprinkling

These cookies may strike you as similar to a Fig Newton—and they are! Though often billed as a cookie, this American lunch box staple, made famous by Nabisco, is more like a soft cake with a sweet fig filling. My version employs rye shortcrust, taking it into crisp cookie territory. The result is a more texture-rich Fig Newton that I like to call a pillow. They aren't overly sweet, and the lovely, crumbly crust gives way to a soft, yielding center with pleasant pops of fig seeds throughout. I prefer filling them with homemade fig-strawberry jam over pureed dehydrated figs. The jam is easy to prepare at the height of summer when figs and strawberries are in season. I love combining the two in this jam—figs bring a lovely consistency and honey-like sweetness, while strawberries add their pleasant rosy tang.

You can use store-bought fig jam, but you'll have to make sure it's truly thick or it will ooze out of the pillows during baking.

They may seem tricky to produce, but after your first row of pillows, you'll have it down. Busy bakers can prepare them in advance: I recommend shaping, cutting, and freezing the pillows ahead of time, then baking them from frozen. Brushed with beaten egg and sprinkled with sugar, the pillows take on an attractive sheen. They should bake to a deep golden brown. This may take longer than you'd expect, but it's necessary because you want the dough to remain crispy while encasing all that soft, moist filling.

1. Put the sugar in a medium saucepan. Add the water to moisten the sugar, but do not stir. Split the vanilla bean lengthwise with a paring knife, scrape out the sticky pulp with the back of the knife, and put both pulp and pod in the pot. Cook over high heat until the mixture comes to a boil. Lower the heat to medium and reduce the mixture to a thick syrup, 3 to 5 minutes.

2. Add the strawberries and figs and cook for 12 to 15 minutes while stirring vigorously with a wooden spoon. (Stirring is crucial because it breaks down the fruit while preventing overcaramelization,

continues

which may cause the jam to stick to the bottom of the pot.) To test the jam's readiness, chill a small plate in the freezer, spoon a bit of jam onto it, and run your finger through the jam. If your finger leaves a trace on the plate, the jam is ready. Transfer to a heatproof container and let it cool completely. Remove the vanilla bean and discard. Pulse the jam in a food processor until it forms a paste. Transfer to a pastry bag.

3. Place the dough between two sheets of parchment paper and flatten with a rolling pin into a rough 16-by-9-inch (40.5 by 23 cm) rectangle. The rolled dough should be no thicker than ¼ inch (6 mm). Refrigerate for at least 30 minutes.

4. Peel off the top parchment sheet, dust lightly with flour, invert the dough on a work surface, and peel off the other sheet of parchment. Cut into three 16-by-3-inch (40.5 by 7.5 cm) rectangles with a pastry wheel cutter or paring knife.

5. Pipe the jam lengthwise down the middle of each rectangle, leaving 2 inches (5 cm) of dough uncovered at the top and bottom edges. Fold the long edges of each rectangle inward so they meet in the center and gently pinch them together to form a 1½-inch (3.8 cm) thick log that is 16 inches (40.5 cm) long. Invert each filled log onto a rimmed baking sheet so that the seam is facing down and refrigerate for 30 minutes.

6. Place two oven racks in the middle positions and preheat the oven to 350°F (175°C). Line two rimmed baking sheets with parchment paper. Coat lightly with nonstick spray.

7. Using a chef's knife, cut each log into 8 pieces, each 2 inches (5cm) long. Arrange the pillows on the prepared baking sheets, placing them 2 inches (5 cm) apart. Brush each pillow with beaten egg and sprinkle generously with sugar. Bake the pillows for 20 minutes. Then rotate the sheets, switch their positions, and bake for another 10 to 15 minutes, until the pillows are golden. Remove the pillows from the oven and let cool completely before enjoying. Store leftovers in an airtight container for up to 2 days.

CORNELÉS

MAKES 10 CORNELÉS

EQUIPMENT: instant-read thermometer, eight 2-inch (5 cm) canelé molds

- 2 cups (480 ml) whole milk
- 2 tablespoons unsalted butter
- ½ vanilla bean
- 2 large eggs
- 2 large egg yolks
- 1 teaspoon vanilla extract
- 2 tablespoons dark rum
- 1¼ cups (250 g) sugar
- ¾ cup plus 2 tablespoons (110 g) whole-grain all-purpose wheat flour, such as Sonora or Frederick
- 3 tablespoons (30 g) fine yellow cornmeal
- 5 tablespoons (70 g/2½ ounces) ghee
- ½ cup (70 g) food-grade beeswax pellets

No, cornelé is not a typo, and it's all Ari's fault. In a past life, before moving on to write full-time, my co-writer Ari Smolin was a baker at Friends & Family. A lover of portmanteaus, she'd take any opportunity to smash two words into one. Case in point: corn plus canelé equals cornelé. The name stuck and we can't go back!

Canelés are small fluted French pastries with a soft custardy center and a thick, caramelized crust. They're baked in an ad hoc fluted copper tin and are believed to have originated in the convents of Bordeaux during the late Middle Ages. My version is 100 percent whole grain, combining cornmeal with soft whole-grain flour. The high dairy and egg content ensures a luscious pudding-like center. Traditionally, canelé molds are made nonstick by a beeswax coating. The beeswax is warmed in a double boiler until pourable, then a small amount is added to each mold to coat its interior. I use a blend of beeswax and ghee, Indian clarified butter. Cutting the beeswax with butter prevents the canelé coating from becoming too waxy, while adding some buttery flavor. I also prefer clarified butter because it does not include the milk solids typically present in butter, which can cause the canelés to stick. The wax and ghee mixture keeps for a long time, so you can keep it in the refrigerator and make many rounds of canelés with the same batch.

Like a cast-iron pan, canelé molds need to be seasoned before their first use, and once you've baked with them, they don't need to be washed. In fact, soap will ruin the coating you've worked so hard to achieve. Simply wipe them out well with a paper towel. Organic beeswax pellets are readily available online. Copper canelé molds are also easy to find online these days. They can be a bit pricey, but they last a lifetime.

1. Combine the milk and butter in a small saucepan. Split the vanilla bean in half lengthwise with a paring knife, scrape out the sticky pulp with the back of the

continues

knife, and add both pulp and pod to the pot. Scald over medium heat until an instant-read thermometer reaches 170°F (82°C).

2. Whisk the eggs and yolks, vanilla, and rum in a mixing bowl to break them up. Add the sugar and whisk to combine. Pour a ladleful of the hot milk mixture into the bowl and whisk to loosen the egg mixture. Add the flour and cornmeal and whisk until smooth. Temper the rest of the egg mixture by adding the remaining hot milk mixture in a slow, steady stream while whisking vigorously. Strain through a fine-mesh sieve into a separate bowl and let cool, then cover and refrigerate overnight, or for up to 2 days.

3. An hour before baking the cornelés, pull the batter from the refrigerator and let it come to room temperature.

4. Place an oven rack in the middle position and preheat the oven to 550°F (288°C). Line a rimmed baking sheet with parchment paper.

5. Put the ghee and beeswax in a heatproof glass container, such as a Pyrex measuring cup. Fill a medium saucepan halfway with water and bring it up to a boil. Turn off the heat and put the container in the pot.

6. When the wax and ghee have melted, coat each canelé mold by filling it with the wax mixture all the way to the top and immediately emptying it back into the container. Invert the mold on the prepared baking sheet to let any excess coating drip onto the parchment paper. You will reuse the wax mixture until all the molds are coated. If the wax begins to harden, dip the container in the hot water once again. (Alternatively, you can melt the wax and ghee in the microwave.) Once all the molds are properly coated, discard the parchment sheet.

7. Arrange the coated molds on the baking sheet, spreading them out over the entire surface—they will bake more evenly this way. Place the sheet on a surface close to the oven so you don't have to walk far. Stir the batter gently with a wooden spoon, fill the molds almost all the way to the top (think seven-eighths of the way), and place in the oven. Bake for 15 minutes. Then reduce the oven temperature to 350°F (175°C), rotate the baking sheet, and bake for 1 hour, until the tops are deep mahogany brown.

8. Working carefully, use a kitchen towel or oven mitt to invert each mold and release the cornelés while they're still warm. Let them cool completely, then enjoy. Cornelés should be eaten the day they are baked.

SPICED VEGAN TEACAKE

MAKES 1 TEACAKE

EQUIPMENT: 8½-by-4½-inch (22 by 11 cm) loaf pan

1¼ cups (155 g) whole-grain hard red wheat flour, such as Turkey Red or Red Fife
1¾ teaspoons baking powder
¼ teaspoon baking soda
¾ teaspoon kosher salt
2 teaspoons ground cinnamon
1 cup (200 g) sugar
¼ cup plus 2 tablespoons (40 g) flax meal
½ cup (90 g) melted coconut oil
¼ cup (60 ml) unsweetened Applesauce (page 31) or store-bought
1½ teaspoons vanilla extract
1 cup (120 ml) boiling water

My favorite vegan bake is this loaf-shaped teacake. When it's time to slice the cake, the Friends & Family crew line up for end pieces, which make a delicious breakfast for hungry early-morning bakers.

Use a big and bold hard red wheat for this teacake. The flavor of the wheat really comes through, so choose a flour you want to highlight. It's made with lots of softening ingredients, like applesauce and melted coconut oil, so it's hard to overwork or turn tough. Flax meal, in addition to boiling water, helps thicken the batter, ensuring the cake won't fall apart or sink in the middle.

1. Place an oven rack in the middle position and preheat the oven to 350°F (175°C).

2. Cut a 12-by-17-inch (30 by 45 cm) rectangle of parchment paper. Lightly coat an 8½-by-4½-inch (22 by 11 cm) loaf pan with nonstick spray, line it with the parchment paper rectangle, and fold the excess paper outward to the sides. This paper sling will make the step of unmolding the teacake much easier.

3. Sift the flour, baking powder, baking soda, salt, cinnamon, and sugar into a mixing bowl. Add the flax meal and whisk to combine. Using your hands, make a well in the center of the dry ingredients. Pour the coconut oil, applesauce, vanilla, and boiling water into the well and whisk slowly from the center out to draw the dry ingredients into the liquids.

4. Transfer the batter to the prepared loaf pan. Bake for 30 minutes. Then rotate the pan and bake for another 15 minutes, until a skewer inserted in the center comes out clean. Let cool in the pan for at least 1 hour. Carefully run an offset spatula or paring knife along the sides of the pan and pull the sling of parchment paper to remove the teacake from the pan. Slice with a serrated knife. Serve at room temperature. Wrap leftovers tightly with plastic and store at room temperature for up to 2 days.

APRICOT CROSTATA

MAKES ONE 9-INCH (23 CM) TART

EQUIPMENT: 9-inch (23 cm) tart pan, plain pastry wheel cutter

1½ cups (190 g) whole-grain all-purpose wheat flour, such as Sonora or Frederick

1½ cups (210 g) all-purpose flour, plus extra for dusting

⅔ cup (130 g) sugar, plus extra for sprinkling

1½ teaspoons baking powder

½ teaspoon kosher salt

1 cup (224 g/2 sticks/8 ounces) cold unsalted butter, cut into ½-inch (1.25 cm) cubes

2 large eggs plus 1 large beaten egg for brushing

½ teaspoon almond extract

170 g (6 ounces) marzipan

1 batch Apricot Jam (page 297) or store-bought

Crostata is a classic Italian-style tart made with pasta frolla—the Italian shortcrust par excellence. It differs from other sweet dough recipes slightly because it contains baking powder, which adds a bit of lift and makes the dough more tender. In this recipe, to highlight the affinity between apricots and aromatic almonds, the dough is perfumed with a touch of almond extract and the bottom of the shell is lined with a thin layer of rolled marzipan, but you can certainly skip both additions and make an equally delightful crostata.

If you are new to lattice tops, this dough is very easy to work with. I also use a trick to ensure the dough is strong yet malleable enough for latticing: Roll all the pasta frolla, even if it seems more than what you need, then cut a circle large enough to cover the bottom of the tart pan. Gather the scraps and roll once again, then cut the strips to form the lattice. It is this roll, gather, and reroll method that helps work the dough so it can withstand the necessary handling. This recipe calls for a soft, all-purpose whole-grain flour like Sonora in combination with refined all-purpose flour, which will make the dough less prone to breaking as you work with it.

1. In the bowl of a stand mixer fitted with the paddle attachment, combine the flours, sugar, baking powder, and salt with the butter. Mix on low speed until the mixture resembles a coarse meal, about 4 minutes. Add the eggs and almond extract and mix until the dough comes together. Turn the dough onto a lightly floured surface and flatten into a disk. Wrap tightly with plastic. Refrigerate for at least 30 minutes and up to 2 days.

2. Place an oven rack in the middle position and preheat the oven to 350°F (175°C).

continues

3. Remove the dough from the refrigerator. With a rolling pin, flatten the dough into a rough 12-inch (30.5 cm) circle that's ¼ inch (6 mm) thick, dusting with flour as necessary to prevent sticking. Using a paring knife, cut a 10-inch (25 cm) dough circle. Pick up the dough circle by rolling it onto the rolling pin, then lay it in a 9-inch (23 cm) tart pan. Gently press the dough up the sides of the pan and let the excess dough hang over the rim. If the dough rips while shaping the tart shell, patch it with a lump of additional dough.

4. Gather the scraps and roll into a rough 10-inch (25.5 cm) circle. Using a pastry wheel cutter, cut the dough into 1-inch (2.5 cm) wide strips. Refrigerate the strips while you roll the marzipan.

5. Knead the marzipan with your hands, flatten it into a disk, and put it between two sheets of parchment paper. Roll it with the rolling pin into a circle that fits the bottom of the pastry-lined tart shell neatly, just under 9 inches (23 cm) in diameter. Transfer the marzipan to the tart pan and center it so it covers the flat bottom from edge to edge. Cover the marzipan layer with the apricot jam.

6. To form the lattice, lay the longest dough strip horizontally in the center of the tart. Lay another long strip vertically in the center of the tart. Lay another strip 1 inch (2.5 cm) to the left of the vertical strip, weaving it under the horizontal strip. Continue in this fashion, laying another strip 1 inch (2.5 cm) to the left of the previous vertical one and weaving every other under the horizontal strip until you reach the edge of the pan. Repeat on the right side. Then rotate the tart pan 90 degrees to continue adding and weaving strips in the opposite direction.

7. Use the rolling pin to press the pastry firmly against the tart pan to sever the excess dough. Brush the lattice strips with the beaten egg and sprinkle them with sugar, avoiding the pockets of jam in between them.

8. Put the tart pan on a rimmed baking sheet and bake for 30 minutes. Then rotate the sheet and bake for another 30 minutes, until the top crust is golden.

9. Remove from the oven and let the crostata cool completely before releasing it from the pan. Slice and serve. Leftovers keep in an airtight container at room temperature for up to 2 days.

APRICOT JAM

MAKES ABOUT 2 CUPS/475 ML

- 2 cups (400 g) sugar
- 1 cup (240 ml) water
- 1 vanilla bean
- 4 heaping cups (800 g/about 8 large) roughly chopped ripe apricots

Put the sugar in a medium saucepan. Add ½ cup (120 ml) of the water to moisten the sugar, but do not stir. Split the vanilla bean lengthwise with a paring knife, scrape out the sticky pulp with the back of the knife, and put both pulp and pod in the pan. Cook over high heat until the mixture comes to a boil. Lower the heat to medium and reduce the mixture to a thick syrup, 3 to 5 minutes. Add the chopped apricots and cook for 8 to 10 minutes while stirring constantly. (Stirring is crucial, because it breaks down the fruit while preventing overcaramelization, which may cause the jam to stick to the bottom of the pan.) To test the jam's readiness, chill a small plate in the freezer, spoon a bit of jam onto it, and run your finger through the jam. If your finger leaves a trace on the plate, the jam is ready. Transfer to a separate bowl to cool completely. Remove the vanilla bean and discard. The jam can be stored in an airtight container in the refrigerator for up to 1 month.

CHOCOLATE CHIFFON CAKE

MAKES 1 BUNDT CAKE

EQUIPMENT: 12-cup Bundt cake pan

½ cup (55 g) Dutch-processed cocoa powder
¾ cup (180 ml) boiling water
1 cup packed (225 g) dark brown sugar
½ cup (120 ml) vegetable oil
2 teaspoons vanilla extract
2 teaspoons baking powder
¼ teaspoon baking soda
½ teaspoon kosher salt
1¾ cups (230 g) whole-grain all-purpose wheat flour, such as Sonora or Frederick, sifted, plus extra for sprinkling
7 large eggs, separated
½ cup plus 2 tablespoons (125 g) granulated sugar

FOR THE CHOCOLATE GLAZE
¾ cup (110 g) bittersweet (65–80%) chocolate chips
¾ cup (180 ml) heavy cream
1 tablespoon whiskey (optional)

Tall, proud chiffon cake gets its airy texture from a meringue-like base of whipped eggs. It's notably moist thanks to a healthy portion of oil, and has a soft, springy texture and a subtly sweet flavor. Chiffon is usually baked in a Bundt or tube pan, giving it impressive stature (not unlike angel food cake), but it can also be divided into multiple pans and assembled like a layer cake. It differs slightly from other sponge cakes because it calls for whole eggs rather than only egg whites—the yolks make it richer.

In this cake, I rely on the heft of whole-grain wheat flour to build a stable structure that can sustain a tall cake. It's important to "bloom," or cook, the cocoa powder prior to folding it into the batter. Dissolving the cocoa powder helps incorporate it into the batter more evenly. It also intensifies the dark chocolate flavor of the cocoa and gets rid of any lumps. You'll also notice that using vegetable oil instead of butter results in a lighter, more delicate cake. Chiffons tend to be served simply with just a dusting of confectioners' sugar, fresh fruits, and whipped cream. This chocolate version is finished with a glaze spiked with a touch of whiskey. This isn't the most decadent chocolate cake, but it still checks all the chocoholic boxes: smooth, crave-worthy, and satisfying.

1. Place an oven rack in the middle position and preheat the oven to 350°F (175°C). Coat a 12-cup Bundt cake pan generously with nonstick spray and sprinkle with additional flour. Tap over the kitchen sink to remove the excess flour.

2. Combine the cocoa powder and boiling water in a mixing bowl. Whisk to work out the lumps, then let it cool completely.

3. Add the brown sugar, oil, vanilla, baking powder, baking soda, and salt to the cooled cocoa mixture and whisk well to combine. Add the flour last and whisk until smooth.

4. In the bowl of a stand mixer fitted with the whisk attachment, beat the egg whites on high speed until frothy. Slowly add the granulated sugar while the mixer is running and continue to mix until the egg whites hold medium peaks. Add the yolks one at a time and mix to combine. The mixture should be very creamy and airy. Add a cupful of the beaten eggs to the cocoa mixture and mix with a silicone spatula to loosen the batter. Then, working gently, fold in the remaining beaten eggs using wide, circular scoop-and-fold strokes. Resist the urge to stir rapidly, but do rotate the bowl as you fold to ensure the batter is evenly lightened.

5. Transfer the batter to the prepared cake pan and bake for 30 minutes. Then rotate the pan and bake for another 10 to 15 minutes, until a skewer inserted in the center comes out clean. Remove the cake from the oven and let it cool completely, then gently invert the pan over a cooling rack to release from the pan.

6. To make the chocolate glaze, put the chocolate chips in a medium heatproof bowl. Fill a medium pot a quarter of the way with water and place over low heat. When the water is barely simmering, fit the bowl on top, making sure the bottom of the bowl doesn't touch the simmering water. Stir occasionally with a silicone spatula until the chocolate is completely melted.

7. Place the cooling rack with the cake on a rimmed baking sheet to catch the excess glaze. Remove the bowl from the heat, stir in the heavy cream and whiskey (if using) with the spatula, and immediately pour over the cake. Let the excess glaze drip. Set the cooling rack with the cake aside briefly to collect the glaze pooling on the baking sheet into a cup. If the glaze thickens, you can melt it over the warm bath until loosened. Put the cooling rack back on the baking sheet and pour the glaze over the cake one more time. Let it sit until the glaze sets completely.

8. Transfer to a cake plate and serve. Leftovers will keep in an airtight container at room temperature for up to 2 days.

COCONUT LAYER CAKE WITH WHITE CHOCOLATE BUTTERCREAM

MAKES ONE 8-INCH (20 CM) LAYER CAKE

EQUIPMENT: two 8-inch (20 cm) cake pans, instant-read thermometer

FOR THE CAKE
1¾ cups (230 g) whole-grain all-purpose wheat flour, such as Sonora or Frederick
1½ teaspoons baking powder
½ teaspoon baking soda
½ teaspoon kosher salt
½ cup (35 g) unsweetened shredded coconut
¾ cup (170 g/1½ sticks/6 ounces) unsalted butter at room temperature
1⅓ cups (265 g) sugar
3 large eggs
¾ cup (175 ml) (400 ml) unsweetened coconut milk
1 tablespoon vanilla extract
Finely grated zest of 1 lime

FOR THE COCONUT PASTRY CREAM
½ cup (35 g) unsweetened shredded coconut
1⅔ cups unsweetened coconut milk
½ cup (100 g) sugar
¼ cup (35 g) all-purpose flour
4 large egg yolks
2 tablespoons unsalted butter
1 teaspoon vanilla extract
Finely grated zest of ½ lime

FOR THE BUTTERCREAM
¾ cup (126 g/4½ ounces) white chocolate chips
1 cup (224 g/2 sticks/8 ounces) unsalted butter at room temperature
½ cup plus 2 tablespoons (150 ml) sweetened condensed milk
1 teaspoon vanilla extract

As a coconut lover and fierce advocate, I wanted to create a coconut cake that would elicit more than "I guess I'll try that." Holding back on the sugar content was key. This included using unsweetened coconut products—specifically shredded coconut and coconut milk—but also throwing a bit of lime zest into the cake batter and the coconut pastry cream to add another layer of flavor. Unsweetened coconut milk is easy to find in well-stocked grocery stores. Look for popular Thai brands such as Mae Ploy, Chaokoh, or Thai Kitchen. (You will need about 1½ [13½ fluid ounce/400 ml] cans to make this cake.) I use soft, all-purpose whole-grain Sonora wheat flour, which makes a fairly creamy cake. Normally, it's recommended to sift the flour, but since the flour is blitzed with the coconut in the food processor, sifting isn't necessary. The cake is frosted with a delicious white chocolate buttercream. And before you claim that you don't really like white chocolate, let me warn you that your mind is about to change. Not only is this frosting delicious and decisively not as sweet as you would think, it's easy to make and a dream to work with. Is there a coconut lover in your life? Save it for their birthday. They'll love you even more.

continues

1. Place an oven rack in the middle position and preheat the oven to 350°F (175°C). Cut two 8-inch (20 cm) circles of parchment paper. Lightly coat the bottoms of two 8-inch (20 cm) cake pans with nonstick spray and line them with the parchment circles.

2. To make the cake, in a food processor, pulse together the flour, baking powder, baking soda, salt, and shredded coconut until the coconut is broken into almost imperceptible pieces.

3. In the bowl of a stand mixer fitted with the paddle attachment, cream the butter and sugar on medium speed until light and creamy. Add the eggs one by one, mixing well to combine. Add the dry ingredients in three additions, alternating with the coconut milk and mixing well after each addition. Stir in the vanilla and lime zest and mix just to incorporate.

4. Divide the batter evenly between the two prepared pans and spread with an offset spatula into an even layer.

5. Bake for 20 minutes. Then rotate the pans and bake for another 10 to 15 minutes, until a skewer inserted in the center comes out clean. Let the cakes cool completely. Do not turn off the oven.

6. To make the coconut pastry cream, scatter the shredded coconut on a rimmed baking sheet. Toast in the oven for 3 to 4 minutes, until lightly toasted.

7. In a small saucepan, combine the coconut milk, sugar, flour, and half the toasted coconut. Cook over medium-high heat while whisking continuously until the mixture comes to a boil. Cook for 2 more minutes, whisking nonstop to prevent the cream from sticking to the bottom of the pan. Turn off the heat. Working quickly, whisk the yolks in a small bowl to break them up. Add a spoonful of the warm cream to the yolks and whisk vigorously. Pour the tempered yolks into the saucepan and cook for 2 minutes over medium heat while whisking vigorously.

8. Strain through a fine-mesh sieve into a bowl. Stir in the butter, vanilla, lime zest, and remaining toasted coconut until the butter is completely melted and fully incorporated. Let the pastry cream cool completely.

9. To make the buttercream, put the chocolate chips in a medium heatproof bowl. Fill a medium pot a quarter of the way with water and place over low heat. When the water is barely simmering, fit the bowl on top, making sure the bottom of the bowl doesn't touch the simmering water. Stir occasionally with a silicone spatula until the chocolate is completely melted. Remove from the heat and let it cool, stirring occasionally with a silicone spatula, until an instant-read thermometer reaches 90°F (32°C).

10. In the bowl of a stand mixer fitted with the paddle attachment, cream the butter on medium speed until fluffy. Add the condensed milk and mix to combine. Working quickly, add the melted chocolate and mix on low speed until fully combined. Add the vanilla and mix to incorporate.

11. Transfer one of the cakes to a serving plate. Spread the coconut pastry cream on top in an even layer. Top with the second cake facing down—the bottom is flatter and easier to frost—and cover the top and sides of the cake decoratively with the buttercream. Refrigerate for 1 hour, until the buttercream is firmer but not completely hard—this will make cutting the cake a lot easier. Slice and serve. The frosted cake will keep in an airtight container in the refrigerator for up to 1 week.

SOUR CREAM PIE DOUGH

MAKES TWO 9-INCH (23 CM) PIECRUSTS OR ENOUGH FOR ONE 9-INCH (23 CM) CUTOUT PIE (OPPOSITE)

- 1½ cups (195 g) whole-grain all-purpose wheat flour, such as Sonora or Frederick
- ¾ cup (105 g) all-purpose flour, plus extra for dusting
- 1 tablespoon sugar
- 1 teaspoon kosher salt
- 1 cup (224 g/2 sticks/8 ounces) cold unsalted butter, cut into ½-inch (1.25 cm) cubes
- ⅔ cup (160 ml) sour cream

Sour cream pie dough is simple, flavorful, and endlessly versatile. Sour cream adds more flavor than the standard water to traditional pie dough. With its lactic acid and higher fat content, sour cream also tenderizes the whole-grain flour in the dough. I recommend using a soft whole-grain flour such as Sonora or Frederick but have found that higher-gluten varieties (such as a hard white) also work well because the rich sour cream coats the protein in the flour efficiently, hydrating it and making it delicate. I combine the whole-grain flour with a portion of refined all-purpose flour to make it more resistant to the juicy pie filling. The dough can be made up to 2 days in advance and kept tightly wrapped in the refrigerator. It also freezes well for up to 1 month.

1. Combine the flours, sugar, and salt in a mixing bowl. Quickly cut the cold butter cubes into the dry ingredients by pinching the butter with your fingertips—imagine you're snapping your fingers—until the mixture resembles a coarse meal with butter pieces the size of cornflakes. Using your hands, make a well in the center of the dry ingredients. Add the sour cream to the well. Mix gently by hand until a raggedy dough forms; don't worry if bits of butter are still visible.

2. Transfer to a lightly floured surface, divide into 2 equal portions, and knead each briefly into a ball. Wrap them tightly with plastic. Refrigerate for at least 30 minutes and up to 2 days.

CHERRY CUTOUT PIE

MAKES ONE 9-INCH (23 CM) PIE

EQUIPMENT: 9-inch (23 cm) pie pan, 1½-inch (3.8 cm) round (or decorative) cookie cutter

5 heaping cups (750 g) cherries, pitted
½ cup (100 g) sugar, plus extra for sprinkling
¼ cup (35 g) cornstarch
½ cup (120 ml) Apricot Jam (page 297) or store-bought
1 tablespoon kirsch (optional)
1 batch Sour Cream Pie Dough (opposite)
1 large egg, beaten

Cherry season in California is a whirlwind. It comes in full force at the end of May and lasts 4 to 6 weeks. The vast majority of the crop consists of sweet varieties like Brooks, Bing, Tulare, and Lapins, which tend to be meaty and juicy, ideal for cherry pie. While this recipe has a few untraditional twists—whole-grain crust, naturally, and apricot jam to help with the filling's viscosity and sweet-tart balance—it exists firmly within the parameters of a classic cherry pie. I finish with a decorative top, made by arranging dough cutouts over the filling. I use a plain round cutter, about 1½ inches (3.8 cm) in diameter, but you could use any cookie cutter with similar dimensions. You could also use two different cutter sizes for a more whimsical look.

To ensure the pie isn't too soggy from the liquid the cherries release while cooking, I suggest partially cooking half the cherries with cornstarch until a thick compote forms. Once they have cooled, combine with the other half and fill the pie. Having these two textures will give you a balance between beefy and jammy morsels. The kirsch is optional, but it really amplifies the cherry flavor and adds subtle almond notes.

1. Combine the cherries, sugar, and cornstarch in a mixing bowl and toss until the fruit is well coated. Macerate for 30 minutes to 1 hour at room temperature.

2. Strain the cherries through a fine-mesh sieve, making sure to save every bit of juice. Return half the drained cherries to the bowl and put the juice in a small saucepan with the remaining cherries. Cook over medium heat, stirring constantly, until the mixture has thickened, about 5 minutes. Transfer to a heatproof bowl and let cool completely. Combine the reserved cherries with the thickened cherry mixture, apricot jam, and kirsch (if using).

3. Preheat the oven to 375°F (190°C) and place an oven rack in the middle position. Coat a 9-inch (23 cm) pie pan lightly with nonstick spray.

continues

4. Remove the pie dough from the refrigerator. With a rolling pin, flatten one of the dough portions into a circle about 11 inches (28 cm) in diameter, dusting with flour as necessary to prevent sticking. Pick up the dough by rolling it onto the rolling pin, then lay it into the prepared pie pan. Gently press the dough into the bottom of the pan and up the sides, leaving a lip of excess dough hanging over the rim of the pie pan. Trim the excess dough, leaving 1 inch (2.5 cm) of dough along the border. Gather the dough to form a border along the edge of the pan. Crimp the border by pinching the dough with your fingertips, forming small triangles along the edge.

5. Fill the piecrust with the cherry filling, using a spatula to even it out.

6. Roll the other dough portion into a rough 11-inch (28 cm) circle. Using a 1½-inch (3.8 cm) round cutter or your preferred cookie cutter, cut out as many pieces as possible. Arrange the dough cutouts in a decorative circular pattern—the cutouts should overlap slightly—atop the cherry filling, making sure the entire surface is covered. Brush the decorated top with the beaten egg and sprinkle with sugar.

7. Put the pie pan on a rimmed baking sheet to catch the drips and bake for 15 minutes. Then rotate the baking sheet and lower the oven temperature to 350°F (175°C). Bake for another 40 to 45 minutes, until the top is golden brown and the filling forms thick bubbles. Let it sit for at least 1 hour before serving. Store leftovers covered in the refrigerator for up to 2 days. Reheat to reheat the pie in a preheated 350°F (175°C) oven for 5 to 8 minutes before enjoying again.

PERFECT QUICHE

MAKES ONE 9-INCH (23 CM) QUICHE

EQUIPMENT: 9-inch (23 cm) pie pan or deep 9-inch (23 cm) cast-iron pan, dried beans or pie weights, instant-read thermometer

FOR THE QUICHE CRUST
- 1 cup plus 2 tablespoons (150 g) whole-grain all-purpose wheat flour, such as Sonora or Frederick, plus extra for dusting
- 1 teaspoon sugar
- ½ teaspoon kosher salt
- ½ cup (112 g/1 stick/4 ounces) cold unsalted butter, cut into ½-inch (1.25 cm) cubes
- ⅓ cup (80 ml) ice water

FOR THE CUSTARD
- ¾ cup (180 ml) whole milk
- ¾ cup (180 ml) heavy cream
- 1 teaspoon kosher salt
- Pinch of freshly ground black pepper
- 1 thyme sprig
- 2 large eggs
- 2 large egg yolks
- ½ cup (30 g) grated Gruyère
- Filling of your choice (see pages 310 to 311)

My favorite recipe for quiche crust is a classic pâte brisée made solely with whole-grain flour. Pâte brisée is a traditional French pastry dough used to make tarts and pies. It includes flour, butter, and salt, all bound together with a little ice water. Brisée translates to "broken," a reference to the crispy, shattery texture of the pastry. While it's relatively easy to make, the process cannot be rushed. To achieve maximum flakiness, the butter needs to be cut into smaller pieces in the dry ingredients while it is still cold. Once the dough comes together, refrigerate it for as little as 30 minutes or as long as 2 days. During this chilling period, the moisture is absorbed by the flour. If you don't plan on using the dough within this time, freeze it for up to 2 weeks. Rolling on a lightly floured surface is key. Shape the crust in a deep pie pan or glass pie dish that can hold enough custard and fillings—a deep cast-iron pan also works. Baking the crust before the filling goes in is known as "blind baking," and it's a crucial step to prevent soggy bottoms. You will need dried beans or pie weights to keep the puffy crust where intended: in the pie pan.

The quiche custard is pretty neutral and can serve as the background for everything under the sun. In this recipe, equal parts milk and heavy cream make a perfectly silky custard that isn't too rich but still leaves you with a creamy mouthfeel. Using whole eggs and additional yolks might seem like overkill, but it doesn't taste overly eggy and ensures the custard sets nicely. In the oven, the custard won't set like a flan. It will puff a little, not unlike a soufflé.

Customize your custard with your choice of additional elements—from traditional bacon to roasted cherry tomatoes—to make it a complete quiche filling. Be sure to peruse the filling suggestions on pages 310–311.

1. To make the crust, combine the flour, sugar, and salt in a mixing bowl. Quickly cut the cold butter cubes into the dry ingredients by pinching the butter with your fingertips—imagine you're snapping your fingers—until the mixture resembles a coarse meal with butter pieces the size of a cornflake. Using your hands, make a well in the center of the mixture. Pour the ice water into the well. Mix gently until a raggedy dough forms; don't worry if bits of butter are still visible.

2. Transfer the dough to a lightly floured surface and knead briefly into a ball. Flatten into a disk and wrap tightly with plastic. Refrigerate for at least 30 minutes and up to 2 days.

3. Roll out the dough on a lightly floured surface, forming a round about 11 inches (28 cm) in diameter. Pick up the round by rolling it onto the rolling pin, then lay it in a 9-inch (23 cm) pie pan or deep 9-inch (23 cm) cast-iron pan. Gently press the dough into the bottom of the pan, leaving a lip on the edge. Trim any excess dough with kitchen scissors, leaving 1 inch (2.5 cm) of dough hanging over the edge of the pan. Gather the dough to form a border along the edge of the pan. Crimp around the edge by pinching the dough with your fingertips, forming triangles along the edge of the pan. Refrigerate the shaped crust for 20 minutes or longer.

4. Place an oven rack in the middle position and preheat the oven to 350°F (175°C).

5. Cut a 12-inch (30 cm) parchment paper circle. Place the pie pan on a rimmed baking sheet. Coat the piecrust lightly with nonstick spray and line with the parchment. Fill it three-quarters of the way with dried beans or pie weights.

6. Bake for 20 minutes. Then rotate the baking sheet and bake for 20 to 25 minutes more. To check if the shell is ready, carefully lift a section of the parchment paper and see if the bottom is golden. Let cool completely before removing the parchment paper and pie weights.

7. Reduce the oven temperature to 325°F (160°C).

8. To make the custard, combine the milk, heavy cream, salt, pepper, and thyme in a small saucepan and scald over medium heat. The mixture should be warm (about 120°F/49°C) but not boiling. In a mixing bowl, whisk the eggs and yolks together. Temper the eggs by slowly adding a ladleful of the warm liquid while whisking the eggs vigorously. Continue adding the liquid to the eggs until you've added all of it. Whisk in the Gruyère. Finish the custard by adding your choice of filling.

9. Pour the finished custard into the baked crust. Bake for 40 to 45 minutes, until the center is golden, slightly puffy (like a soufflé), and firm to the touch. Let it cool for at least 20 minutes before slicing. Serve warm or at room temperature.

QUICHE FILLING IDEAS

Spinach and Scallion Quiche

Melt 2 tablespoons unsalted butter in a medium skillet, add 1 cup (75 g) thinly sliced scallions (white and light green parts), and cook until soft, 3 to 4 minutes. Add 2 cups tightly packed (120 g) baby spinach, cook until wilted, about 2 minutes, and season with kosher salt. Gently stir the cooked spinach and ½ cup (100 g) whole-milk ricotta into the quiche custard.

Bacon and Leek Quiche

Heat 1 tablespoon vegetable oil in a medium skillet over medium-low heat. Add 2 slices (50 g) thick-cut bacon, cut into lardons or ½-inch (1.25 cm) strips, and sauté until just crispy, 3 to 4 minutes. Transfer to a paper towel–lined plate to drain the fat. Add 2 tablespoons vegetable oil to the same skillet. Add 1 thinly sliced medium leek (white and light green parts) and sauté until soft, about 5 minutes. Season with kosher salt. Add the cooked bacon and leeks and ¼ cup (20 g) grated Parmesan to the quiche custard.

Ham and Peas Quiche

Melt 2 tablespoons unsalted butter in a medium skillet over medium-low heat. Add 1 diced onion and sauté until soft, 6 to 7 minutes. Add 1 cup (130 g) frozen peas and cook until soft, about 2 minutes. Stir in 6 slices (60 g) smoked ham, diced, and season with kosher salt. Add the cooked peas and ham and ¼ cup (20 g) grated Parmesan to the quiche custard.

Asparagus Quiche with Pancetta and Gruyère

Heat 1 tablespoon vegetable oil in a medium skillet over medium-low heat. Add ¼ cup (30 g) diced pancetta and sauté until it starts crisping up, 2 to 3 minutes. Transfer to a paper towel–lined plate to drain the fat. Remove the ends from 1 bunch thin asparagus, cut each spear into 2-inch (5 cm) pieces, and blanch in boiling salted water until tender, 2 to 3 minutes. Add the cooked pancetta, asparagus, and ¼ cup (20 g) grated Gruyère to the quiche custard.

Roasted Tomato and Goat Cheese Quiche

Toss 1 pint cherry tomatoes with 1 tablespoon olive oil in a roasting pan and season with kosher salt. Roast the tomatoes in a preheated 400°F (205°C) oven until they start to blister, 4 to 5 minutes. Let them cool completely. Gently stir the roasted tomatoes and ½ cup (100 g) crumbled goat cheese into the quiche custard.

Mushroom and Comté Quiche

Heat 3 tablespoons vegetable oil in a large skillet over medium heat. Add 1 finely diced shallot and 1 minced garlic clove and cook until soft, about 2 minutes. Add 4 cups (580 g) sliced shiitake mushrooms, sauté until soft, 9 to 10 minutes, and season with kosher salt. Add the cooked mushrooms and 1 cup (100 g) grated Comté to the quiche custard.

Smoked Salmon Quiche with Potato and Dill

Fill a medium saucepan with water. Bring to a boil over high heat. Season with 1 teaspoon kosher salt, add 1 cup (100 g) fingerling potatoes, and cook until tender, 10 to 15 minutes. To check if the potatoes are ready, pierce one with a paring knife; if it releases easily, the potatoes are done. If not, cook for a few more minutes. Drain the potatoes and let them cool completely. Cut into ½-inch (1.25 cm) thick rounds. Gently stir the cooked potatoes, 2 slices (75 g/2½ ounces) smoked salmon, cut into ½-inch (1.25 cm) pieces, 1 tablespoon minced fresh dill, and ½ cup (100 g) whole-milk ricotta into the quiche custard.

Long-Cooked Broccoli and Fontina Quiche

Blanch 4 cups (260 g) broccoli florets in boiling salted water until tender, 3 to 4 minutes. Heat 3 tablespoons olive oil in a large saucepan over medium heat. Add 1 diced onion and sauté until soft, 6 to 7 minutes. Add the blanched broccoli and a pinch of chili flakes and cook for 15 minutes while stirring constantly until the broccoli is fall-apart tender. Season with kosher salt. Add the cooked broccoli and 1 cup (115 g) grated fontina to the quiche custard.

MY FAVORITE FLOURS

All-Purpose Whole-Grain Wheat Flour

Wheats in this category are generally mild-tasting and considered "soft" or low in gluten, the protein that gives wheat structure and elasticity. Here on the West Coast, Sonora wheat is a very popular, affordable, go-to variety, and it's the flour I use the most. Sonora is a landrace wheat, meaning it's a heritage variety that has been grown in the region for a long time, is tied to our agricultural history, and has adapted to the local environment. A similar variety is Frederick, which is common in the Midwest. Like Sonora, this soft white winter wheat doesn't contain the strong-tasting phenolic compounds found in red wheats. Equally versatile is Sirvinta, an Estonian heritage wheat that is relatively new to the artisan wheat market but is growing in popularity, especially on the East Coast.

You may notice that many purveyors of freshly milled whole-grain flours don't always include the specific variety in their labels. They may use more generic nomenclature such as "all-purpose whole-grain flour." This might mean that the miller doesn't always use the same wheat variety to produce this flour, or that it may be a blend of a few different varieties. What's important is that the miller, who knows about the makeup and provenance of each batch of flour, has deemed it appropriate for all-purpose baking. Use their flour with confidence.

RECOMMENDED PRODUCTS:
- Cairnspring Mills Sequoia T85 All-Purpose Flour
- Camas Country Mill Sonora Soft White Wheat Flour
- Camas Country Mill All-Purpose Low-Gluten Wheat Flour
- Central Milling Organic Whole Wheat Pastry Flour
- Grist & Toll Sonora Wheat Flour
- Hayden Flour Mills All-Purpose Flour
- Janie's Mill Frederick White Wheat Flour
- Maine Grains Organic Sirvinta Wheat Flour

Barley, Flakes

Barley flakes are very similar to the more common oat flakes. They are made by steaming, rolling, and drying barley berries. With their chewy texture and mild, nutty taste, they can be used in any way that oat flakes are used.

RECOMMENDED PRODUCTS:
- Camas Country Mill Organic Purple Karma Barley Flakes
- Janie's Mill Organic Barley Flakes

Barley, Malt

Barley malt syrup, also known as malt extract, is a byproduct of malting, a process in which grain is soaked and allowed to germinate to develop enzymes that convert the grain's starch into sugar. Barley malt can be found in health food stores or well-stocked grocery stores and has many applications in the kitchen. I like to use it as a sweetener or flavor enhancer in place of honey or molasses in my recipes, as in the Finnish Malt Bread (page 232). It's also a common additive to doughs to encourage yeast performance, improving rise and caramelization, which is why I include it in my Hybrid Croissant Dough (page 145).

RECOMMENDED PRODUCT:
- Eden Foods Organic Barley Malt Syrup

Brown Rice Flour

Brown rice flour is often bone white, despite containing the bran and germ. It's very fine, with a slightly gritty texture and a milky, toasty flavor. It contains no gluten—it is one of the components in Roxana's Whole-Grain Gluten-Free Flour (page 95)—and cannot replace wheat flour on its own. However, it can enhance crispness in cookies or lightness in cakes. It's also used in savory dishes as a coating for fried foods. The flavor of rice flour ranges from clean and creamy to rich and nutty. This is not to be confused with regular refined rice flour, which is cheaper and commonly used in bread baking for flouring bannetons.

RECOMMENDED PRODUCTS:
- Anson Mills Carolina Gold Rice Flour
- Bob's Red Mill Brown Rice Flour

Buckwheat Flour

Outside of wheat, buckwheat is one of the flours I use most. It's widely available and can be found in many grocery stores. It's made by grinding whole groats and is sometimes classified as light or dark depending on how much hull is left in the flour. Interestingly, dark buckwheat flour is far more popular than the refined version. Despite its name, it's completely unrelated to wheat. When combined with moist ingredients, buckwheat flour develops a gluey texture. This rare binding property makes it a popular choice for gluten-free baking. In fact, it is one of the components in Roxana's Whole-Grain Gluten-Free Flour (page 95). When gluten is not a concern, I mix it with all-purpose flour, which adds structure to breads and cakes and helps tame buckwheat's assertive flavor.

RECOMMENDED PRODUCTS:
- Anson Mills Rustic Aromatic Buckwheat Flour
- Bob's Red Mill Organic Buckwheat Flour
- Camas Country Mill Organic Buckwheat Flour
- Central Milling Organic Buckwheat Flour
- Janie's Mill Organic Buckwheat Flour
- Maine Grains Organic Buckwheat Flour

Cornmeal and Polenta

Cornmeal is made by grinding flint corn, a variety that dries into a hard kernel and is grown far and wide across the US. I like to call it a little bit of sunshine. Think of it this way: The sun's energy helps the corn ripen, locking vitamins, minerals, and flavor into each kernel that will eventually be ground into cornmeal. Not only is it nutritious but it adds great texture, restrained sweetness, and earthy flavor to recipes. Cornmeal is as varied as the kernels from which it comes. Although the yellow and white varieties are the most common, cornmeal comes in a plethora of colors, from pink and red to blue and green. You can swap colors freely, but pay attention to the specific grind. Cornmeal is typically labeled fine, medium, or coarse. Fine cornmeal is more compact than coarse cornmeal and therefore different in both weight and volume.

Polenta is a coarse cornmeal. (It's also the name of a common dish in Italy, cooked low and slow in milk, stock, or water, and finished with butter and cheese.) It can be enjoyed as a hot cereal for breakfast. In baking, it can be used in all the ways that you use cornmeal. It adds a pleasant toothy feel and earthy and grounding flavors to cakes and cookies.

RECOMMENDED PRODUCTS:

- Anson Mills Artisan Handmade Fine Yellow Polenta
- Anson Mills Coarse or Fine White Cornmeal
- Anson Mills Coarse or Fine Yellow Cornmeal
- Anson Mills Native Fine Blue Cornmeal
- Bob's Red Mill Medium Grind and Coarse Grind Cornmeal
- Janie's Mill Organic Bloody Butcher or Golden Yellow Cornmeal
- Janie's Mill Organic Golden Yellow Polenta/Grits
- Grist & Toll Blue Cornmeal
- Maine Grains Organic Corn Polenta
- Maine Grains Organic Yellow Flint or Liberation Farms Cornmeal

Durum Flour

Durum is the hardest variety of wheat we know. Its stubborn kernel resists milling, so grinding it into flour is a complex, multistep process in which the grain is milled several times. It's popular among pasta and bread makers for its high protein content. Whole-grain durum flour is not to be confused with semolina, which could have been sifted and, therefore, more refined than durum flour even if milled coarser. Durum is a great addition to baked goods. I find that, like cornmeal, it adds a pleasant gritty texture, golden hue, and warm feel to recipes.

RECOMMENDED PRODUCTS:

- Camas Country Mill Oregon Durum Wheat Flour
- Central Milling Organic Whole Wheat Durum Flour
- Janie's Mill Organic Durum Flour

Einkorn

Native to Armenia, Georgia, and Turkey and domesticated around 7500 BC, einkorn is the oldest wheat variety we know. In fact, almost every wheat variety descends from it. It makes a beautiful cream-colored flour that acts like a soft flour and should never be considered a hard wheat. Though einkorn has one of the highest protein contents in the wheat world, it isn't the type that translates into high gluten. It can be used as an all-purpose flour, but since it tends to be a bit pricier than other wheat flours, I save it for recipes in which I can really taste it, like the Einkorn Carrot Muffins (page 28) or the Pear, Chocolate, and Einkorn Scones (page 65). This versatile flour has an assertive yet familiar flavor ranging from popcorny and nutty to earthy and mushroomy.

RECOMMENDED PRODUCTS:

- Camas Country Mill Einkorn Flour
- Carolina Ground Einkorn Flour
- Central Milling Organic Whole Einkorn Flour
- Grist & Toll Einkorn Flour
- Janie's Mill Organic Einkorn Flour
- Maine Grains Organic Einkorn Flour

Hard Wheat Flour, Red or White

Wheat is categorized according to three criteria: color, protein content, and planting season. Color denotes whether the variety is red or white; protein content indicates if it's low (soft) or high (hard) in gluten, and season of planting tells if it's a spring or winter wheat. Naturally occurring pigments are responsible for the color of the kernel. In general terms, redder wheats tend to have a bolder flavor than white ones. I use this data point to select the most suitable type of hard wheat in a specific recipe.

Hard reds can range from yellowish-orange to dark brown. Red wheats cover a wide range of flavor profiles, from subtle and sweet to harsh and astringent. Grain farmers tend to favor those with the most versatility, so you aren't likely to come across a super challenging variety unless you're seeking it out, but every now and again you might wind up baking something that's rather intense. As with many ancient, heirloom, and modern wheats, the environment in which the grain is grown leads to substantial variations. It's a good reminder of what California-based miller and grain advocate Nan Kohler likes to say: "Wheat is like wine." Seed sources, farming practices, and soil quality affect the outcome of every wheat harvest. Sometimes the flour is mellow and nutty; other times it's high in tannins, which turn things bitter. Popular hard reds include Red Fife, Turkey Red, Rouge de Bordeaux, Glenn, Joaquín Oro, and Yecora Rojo, among many others.

Hard whites can range from bone white to pale yellow and clay gray. Their flavor is noticeably more subdued. Hard whites are planted a lot less at the moment, but I hope higher demand will prompt producers to grow them more. Common varieties are Starr, Edison, and Patwin.

Although the trend hasn't always been upward, the number of popular varieties grown by American wheat producers has increased over the last thirty years. Breeders are also doing the hard work of expanding wheat diversity by experimenting with lesser-known varieties and developing new hybrids, so we can expect to see newer wheats coming to the market in the future.

Throughout the book, I may ask you to use red over white or vice versa, sometimes suggesting a few varieties within the category. Whenever the color doesn't alter the final product in a significant way, the recipe will clearly say so. When purchasing flour, you may notice that many producers don't include the variety in the label. This is a very common practice. Instead, you might find products labeled with a generic "Hard Red" or "Hard White." Use the flour with confidence.

RECOMMENDED HARD RED WHEAT PRODUCTS:
- Cairnspring Mills Organic Whole Grain Expresso Bread Flour
- Camas Country Mill Artisan Hard Red Winter Flour
- Camas Country Mill Hard Red Spring Wheat Flour
- Camas Country Mill Organic Emmer Flour
- Camas Country Mill Red Fife Wheat Flour
- Camas Country Mill Rouge de Bordeaux Hard Red Spring Wheat Flour
- Carolina Ground Whole Wheat Bread Flour
- Grist & Toll Hard Red Wheat Flour
- Hayden Flour Mills Artisan Bread Flour
- Janie's Mill Organic Red Fife Heirloom Flour
- Janie's Mill Organic Turkey Red Flour
- Maine Grains Heritage Øland Wheat Flour
- Maine Grains Heritage Red Fife Wheat Flour

RECOMMENDED HARD WHITE WHEAT PRODUCTS:
- Camas Country Mill Edison Hard White Wheat Flour
- Camas Country Mill Organic Hard White Wheat Flour
- Central Milling Organic Hard White Whole Wheat Flour
- Grist & Toll Hard White Wheat Flour

Kamut/Khorasan Flour

Often sold under the brand name Kamut, this wheat variety originated in the ancient province of Khorasan, located in northern Iran and portions of Afghanistan. Despite arriving in the 1950s, Khorasan didn't catch on in the US until the late '70s, when father-son farming duo Mack and Bob Quinn began growing it in Montana. In 1990, they trademarked it as Kamut. As a condition of the trademark, Kamut can only be grown organically, and farmers can't alter the seed in any way. The kernel is visually striking—large and slender with an amber hue. Khorasan berries are popular and can be used just as you would farro in savory cooking. The flour's flavor is robust yet creamy, reminiscent of cornbread and comforting grits. Its high protein content makes it a favorite of many bread bakers, including the Friends & Family crew, who love it in their Khorasan Baguettes (page 209).

RECOMMENDED PRODUCTS:
- Central Milling Organic Whole Khorasan Flour
- Maine Grains Ancient Kamut Wheat Flour

Masa Harina or Nixtamalized Corn Flour

Masa is the product of a process known as nixtamalization, in which dent corn kernels are soaked or cooked in an alkaline solution like lye or lime water. Once nixtamalized, the whole kernel becomes hominy. Masa harina is hominy that has been milled and dehydrated to make it shelf-stable. Just like cornmeal, masa takes on the kernel's pigmentation. In Mesoamerica, the region that extends from Mexico to Panamá, masa is an abundant and affordable staple, used to prepare traditional recipes like tortillas and tamales. In the US, immigrants from across the region have helped popularize it, and masa-derived products are mass-produced nationwide.

Never try replacing masa with cornmeal, which is coarser and not nixtamalized, so it will behave completely differently in a recipe.

RECOMMENDED PRODUCTS:
- Bob's Red Mill Organic Masa Harina
- Masienda White, Blue, Yellow, or Red Masa Harina

Oat Flour

Ground from whole oat groats, oat flour has a subtle, sweet cereal flavor. Oat flour is well suited for a wide range of recipes. It's naturally gluten-free and one of the components in Roxana's Whole-Grain Gluten-Free Flour (page 95). Its high bran content often translates into tender and moist baked goods. This silky flour makes light-bodied, cottony muffins and cakes with a delicate crumb. Its nutty taste and pillowy feel are similar to those of whole wheat, but with plusher qualities. In preparations that require gluten so they don't fall apart, like the Hearty Pancake Mix for Campers (page 107), oat flour can be combined with wheat flour.

RECOMMENDED PRODUCTS:
- Anson Mills 18th Century Style Rustic Toasted Oat Flour
- Bob's Red Mill Oat Flour
- King Arthur Oat Flour

Old-Fashioned Rolled Oats

Rolled oats are the most common oat product on the market. To make rolled oats, groats are steamed until soft and then pressed between steel rollers. Oats rolled even thinner to reduce cooking time are known as instant or quick oats. Whole rolled oats or old-fashioned rolled oats are thicker and therefore slightly chewier. They're also considered more wholesome and nutritious. I use oats in multiple ways in my baking. Sometimes they play a central role, like in the Berry Oat Muffins (page 30) and Build-Your-Own Granola (page 280). Other times, I'm happy to sprinkle a bit on top of a cake or bread for its rustic look, familiar warm cereal flavor, and desirable texture.

RECOMMENDED PRODUCTS:
- Anson Mills Handmade Toasted Stone Cut Oats
- Camas Country Mill Organic Oat Flakes
- Janie's Mill Organic Oat Flakes

Refined Flour, All-Purpose or Bread

Used in combination with the many whole-grain flours in this book, all-purpose flour allows other grains to shine. Because it's neutral in flavor and higher in gluten, it can provide the perfect canvas for more flavor-forward flours to take center stage. These recipes were developed to use the minimum amount necessary of refined flour, just enough to get the job done without taking anything away from the more interesting whole-grain flours. Mechanically, refined flour's main job in whole-grain baking is to troubleshoot issues that whole grains might present, including lack of elasticity, gritty texture, starchy aftertaste, or bitter flavor.

RECOMMENDED PRODUCTS:
- Central Milling Organic All-Purpose "Beehive" Flour
- King Arthur All-Purpose Flour
- Whole Foods Market 365 All-Purpose Flour

Rye Flakes

Just like oats, rye flakes are made by flattening rye berries through steel rollers. The flakes are as versatile as rolled oats and can be prepared as a hot cereal. They can also be added to cookies, cakes, muffins, and granola. Unlike oats, which are steamed and then rolled, rye berries are roasted and then rolled. The resulting flake is slightly thicker than oat or barley flakes, with a nutty flavor and crispy texture.

RECOMMENDED PRODUCTS:
- Camas Country Mill Organic Dark Northern Rye Flakes
- Janie's Mill Organic Rye Flakes

Rye Flour

I'm happy to report that at the time of this writing, there are more reputable sources for rye flour in the US than ever. Shopping for rye flour can be confusing. Like wheat, rye is often sifted after milling to remove portions of the bran and germ. I recommend avoiding flours labeled "white rye" or "medium rye," which are all forms of refined rye flour. Most producers never use the label "whole-grain rye," instead opting for names like "dark rye" or "pumpernickel," which don't necessarily explain the product. Always read the label to ensure you're buying whole-grain flour. I strongly recommend purchasing whole-grain rye flour from an independent mill. The flour will be fresher and likely ground from a single variety grown on a single farm. Traceability isn't an easy task with a lot of the grains we buy, but I find it's easier to do with rye. Provenance doesn't necessarily dictate the quality of our bakes, but it helps us grasp the enormous effort it takes farmers and millers to bring these flours to us.

RECOMMENDED PRODUCTS:
- Anson Mills Abruzzi Heirloom Rye Flour
- Bob's Red Mill Organic Dark Rye Flour
- Camas Country Mill Organic Dark Northern Rye Flour
- Carolina Ground Whole Wren's Abruzzi Rye Flour
- Central Milling Organic Whole Dark Rye Flour
- Grist & Toll Rye Flour
- Janie's Mill Organic Dark Rye Flour
- Maine Grains Organic Rye Flour

Spelt Flour

Spelt isn't a wheat variety per se, but a close relative that performs like one. It's been grown for seven thousand years and was Europe's favored bread flour for centuries. Though it eventually fell out of vogue, spelt remained a niche crop in Central Europe and parts of Spain and is currently experiencing a vigorous revival in those regions. Propelling its modern resurgence is spelt's reputation as healthful and climate resilient. Spelt's superpowers include being naturally pest resistant, highly adaptable to diverse growing conditions, and not requiring a high fertilizer input.

In *Mother Grains*, I called spelt the best known of all the ancient wheats. I think this still stands. I consider it a gateway for bakers starting to explore whole-grain baking. It behaves similarly to most wheat flours and performs well in many applications, from sourdough and enriched breads to cakes, cookies, and laminated pastries. I consider it an all-purpose flour and often substitute it in a one-to-one ratio for refined all-purpose flour whenever I want to whole-grain-ify a recipe.

RECOMMENDED PRODUCTS:
- Bob's Red Mill Spelt Flour
- Camas Country Mill Organic Spelt Flour
- Carolina Ground Whole Spelt
- Central Milling Organic Whole Spelt Flour
- Grist & Toll Spelt Flour
- Janie's Mill Organic Spelt Flour
- Maine Grains Organic Whole Spelt Flour

Wheat Berries

Whole wheat berries are sold by local grain mills and in the bulk section of well-stocked grocery stores. Many home bakers might even run into them at their local farmers' market. Wheat berries can be milled into flour at home or cooked like barley or farro (which is a wheat berry) and added to salads, grain bowls, soups, stews, and pilafs. At Friends & Family, we sprout wheat berries to add to our Sprouted Grain Loaf (page 266). Sprouting is easy to do at home. I like it because it softens the toothy grain, making it easier to munch on and more digestible.

RECOMMENDED PRODUCTS:
- Camas Country Mill Edison Hard White Wheat Berries
- Camas Country Mill Hard Red Spring Wheat Berries
- Central Milling Whole Hard White or Red Wheat Berries
- Hayden Flour Mills White Sonora Wheat Berries
- Janie's Mill Organic Glenn, Warthog, Turkey Red, or Red Fife Wheat Berries

SOURCES

Anson Mills
AnsonMills.com
South Carolina–based artisan mills. Available online. Ships nationwide.

Barton Springs Mill
BartonSpringsMill.com
Based in Texas. Provider of locally grown heirloom grains. One of my favorite sources for cornmeal. Available online. Ships nationwide.

Bob's Red Mill
BobsRedMill.com
Provider of a comprehensive line of whole-grain products available in grocery stores and online. Ships nationwide.

Burlap & Barrel
BurlapAndBarrel.com
Boutique vendor of a wide variety of single-origin spices from smallholder farmers. Available online. Ships nationwide.

Cairnspring Mills
Cairnspring.com
Based in Washington State. Producer of locally grown flours. Available online. Ships nationwide.

Camas Country Mill
CamasCountryMill.com
Based in Oregon. Popular West Coast mill. Available online. Ships nationwide.

Carolina Ground
CarolinaGround.com
Based in North Carolina. Focuses on regionally grown and milled grains. Available online. Ships nationwide.

Central Milling
CentralMilling.com
Medium- to large-scale mill based in California and Utah. Available online. Ships nationwide.

Challenger Breadware
ChallengerBreadware.com
Popular, high-quality cast-iron baking pan ideal for baking bread at home. Available online. Ships nationwide.

Fat Daddio's
FatDaddios.com
Domestic manufacturer of baking equipment, including nonstick bakeware. Available online. Ships nationwide.

Hayden Flour Mills
HaydenFlourMills.com
Family-owned and -operated mill offering Arizona-grown flours. Available online. Ships nationwide.

If You Care
IfYouCare.com
Environmentally friendly kitchen and household products. Available online. Ships nationwide.

India Tree

IndiaTree.com

Provider of gourmet decorating ingredients such as colored sugars and sprinkles. Available online. Ships nationwide.

In the Raw

InTheRaw.com

Makers of natural sweeteners widely available in grocery stores and online. Excellent brand of turbinado sugar. Ships nationwide.

Janie's Mill

JaniesMill.com

Based in Illinois. Excellent provider of whole-grain flours in the Midwest. Available online. Ships nationwide.

King Arthur Baking Company

KingArthurBaking.com

Based in Vermont. Reputable supplier of flour and other baking ingredients and equipment. Available online. Ships nationwide.

Maine Grains

MaineGrains.com

Based in Maine. Mill and distributor of organic, heritage grains and flours sourced from the Northeast. Available online. Ships nationwide.

Mandelin

Mandelin.com

Based in California. Producer of almond pastes and marzipan. Available online. Ships nationwide.

Masienda

Masienda.com

Provider of artisanal masa harina. Available online. Ships nationwide.

Nordic Ware

NordicWare.com

Notable maker of cake pans based in the Midwest. Famous for their beautiful Bundt pans. Available online. Ships nationwide.

Rack Master

RackMaster.co.uk

Based in the UK. Manufacturer of custom bench knives, baking molds, and pans, offering competitive shipping rates to the US.

TCHO Chocolate

TCHO.com

A young chocolate company based in California. Excellent source of chocolate and natural cocoa powder. Available online. Ships nationwide.

Weck Jars

WeckJars.com

Glass jars of excellent quality available in multiple sizes. Ideal to hold your sourdough starter or to store dry goods at home. Available online. Ships nationwide.

ACKNOWLEDGMENTS

I'm the middle sister in a family of five. When we were kids, I had to wake up at 4:45 a.m. so we'd all have time to shower, get dressed, eat breakfast, and hop on the school bus by 7 a.m. I never missed an alarm. For helping me build the lifelong skill of waking up early—and for a lifetime of unconditional support—I thank my sister María and my brothers Miguel, Bernardo, and Ignacio. Truth be told, I took the first shift only because none of you would . . . and because it took me that long to do my hair.

Thanks to my mom, Rose Marie, for encouraging me to read and write from a very young age—and for insisting I keep at it, even if it was just to write recipes. Can you believe I wrote a second book?

There aren't enough words to thank my husband, Daniel Mattern—Friends & Family's chef, co-founder, mastermind, and chief strategist—for keeping the wheels on the bus at work and at home while I wrote this cookbook. When I got stuck, quiet time at home with Dan and our sweet cat, Gilbert, was just what I needed to refocus and finish. Thanks for trying all my testers (many of which weren't great), for your honest insight, for making sure I ate real dinners, and for never stopping with the who's-gonna-make-the-coffee jokes (which are actually pretty funny).

To my co-writer, Ari Smolin: We jumped into this project four years ago, and you've stood by me through every bout of indecision and procrastination. When I lost my sense of direction halfway through, you stayed steady and determined. When I got my groove back, you said, "Now we're cooking with gas." Thank you for never losing faith. I still don't know how you got everything done with such precision and grace.

Thanks to my literary agent, Nicole Tourtelot, for always having my back and representing me with conviction and resolve.

I was lucky to work once again with editor Melanie Tortoroli and the talented editorial and design teams at W. W. Norton and Company. Thank you for guiding this book's journey with care and exacting attention to detail at every stage. Thanks for hearing me out when I had a change of heart—and for helping me rediscover the true purpose of this book.

To the wildly talented photo team—photographers Kristin Teig and David Kuong, prop stylist Nidia Cueva, and food stylists Carrie Purcell and Daniela Swamp—thank you for the most fun (and delicious) photo week. You worked tirelessly to make sure these images captured the magic of the morning, and you nailed it!

Thanks to David Thorne and Julia Meltzer for welcoming us—again!—to dreamy Elysian LA. You've spoiled me! I can't imagine shooting anywhere else!

To a personal hero of mine, miller and grain advocate Nan Kohler: Thank you for your ever-growing mission to bring whole-grain flour and knowledge to the people. Your flour remains the best I've ever worked with—and I've worked with a lot of flour!

Now, to the bakers—I saved you for last.

To the many bakers who've spent time at the bench at Friends & Family: Thank you for letting me witness each of you uncover that part of yourself that thrives in creativity, routine, and hard work. Watching you find purpose in the morning bake is a joy and a privilege I'll never take for granted.

Thanks to Olivia Leadbetter, who helped me tackle recipe testing when the table of contents felt insurmountable. There will always be a cornelé here for you. To Maja Almskou, who's been at F&F almost as long as I have: You're right. You *do* make the best banana bread. To my pastry chef and true peer, Sarah Hipwell: Thank you for running the shop, making everyone laugh, obsessing over lists and numbers, and still having the time and energy to cheer me on to the finish line.

I'm equally indebted to the rest of the baking crew who worked with us during the production of this book: Yesenia "Yessi" Alvarado, Jenevieve "JenJen" Apolonario, Bertrand "Bert" Ng, Courteney Tobin, Irene Ginakakis, Zarlasht Sahki, Lucas "Luquinhas" Albuquerque, Ana "Banana" Santiago, Shelby Rifkin, David Chernyavsky, Jesse Lossi, Manasa Madishetty, and Hannah Chang.

And finally, to our customers, friends, and neighbors at Friends & Family—many of whom have become *actual* family: Thank you for your years of support and patronage. Just so you know, it's you— and your oper. hearts—I'm thinking about when I come to work every morning.

INDEX

Note: Page references in *italics* indicate photographs.

A

all-purpose flour, 15, 320
almonds. *See also* marzipan
    Pistachio-Almond Croissants, *151*, 155–56
anise seeds
    Dark Rye Rolls, *236*, 237–38
apples
    Apple and Roquefort Grilled Cheese Sandwich, 252, *253*
    Apple Levain, 250–52, *253*
    Applesauce, 31
    Apple Upside-Down Pancakes, 91–92, *93*
    Buckwheat Joy Muffins, *22*, 46–47
applesauce (in recipes)
    Berry Oat Muffins, *22*, 30–31
    Buckwheat Joy Muffins, *22*, 46–47
    Cara Cara Orange Marmalade, 177
    Spiced Vegan Teacake, 294
apricot jam (in recipes)
    Apricot Crostata, 295–96, *297*
    Cherry Cutout Pie, 305–7, *306*
apricots
    Apricot Butterscotch Muffins, *22*, 32–33
    Apricot Jam, *77*, 297
    Asparagus Quiche with Pancetta and Gruyère, 310
    Austrian Soufflé Pancake (Kaiserschmarrn), 101–2, *102*
autolyse technique, 189

B

bacon
    Asparagus Quiche with Pancetta and Gruyère, 310
    Bacon and Leek Quiche, 310
    Bacon and Onion Blossoms, 161–62, *163*
Baguettes, Khorasan, 209–11
baking pans, 278
bananas
    Banana-Date Muffins, *34*, 35–36
    Banana Pancakes, 88
banneton, 191
barley flakes, 314
barley malt syrup
    about, 314
    Finnish Malt Bread, *186*, 232–33
basil
    Basil Pesto, 173
    Friends & Family Famous Hippie Sandwich, *270*, 271–72
batter scoop, 25
beeswax pellets
    Cornelés, 291–92, *293*
bench knife, 190
berries. *See also specific berries*
    Berries 'n' Cream Puffs, 166–67, *168*
    Berry Oat Muffins, *22*, 30–31
biscuits
    baking from frozen dough, 66
    Buttermilk Whole-Grain Biscuits, 53–54, *55*
    compared with scones, 52
    Parmesan-Rosemary Biscuits, *55*, 56–57
    preparing, tips for, 50–51
    preparing dough for freezer, 66
    storing, 51
blackberries
    Blackberry Jam with a Touch of Lime, 76, *77*
    Blackberry Swirls, *178*, 179

black pepper
    Dill, Chive, and Black Pepper Loaf, *186*, 260–62
    Herby Cottage Cheese Scones, *69* 67–68
blueberries
    Berries 'n' Cream Puffs, 166–67, *168*
    Berry Oat Muffins, *22*, 30–31
    Blueberry Pancakes, 86–87, *87*
    Fried Blueberry Hand Pies, 135–37, *134*
Boule, Caramelized Onion, Comté, and Nigella, *186*, 263–65
bran, in whole-grain flour, 15
bread flour, 15, 320
breads. *See also* flatbreads; French toast; sourdough breads; yeasted breads
    autolyse technique, 189
    bread-making tools, 190–91
    cleaning as you go, 191
    folding and stretching dough technique, 189
    how to read bread dough, 196
    no-knead method, 188
    salt in, 243
brioche
    Brioche à la Crème, *226*, 227–28
    Brioche Jam Buns, 223–24, *225*
    Cinnamon-Raisin Brioche, *220*, 221–22
    Milk and Honey Brioche, *216*, 217–19
    preparing, tips for, 219
Broccoli, Long-Cooked, and Fontina Quiche, 311

brown rice
    1970s Multigrain Pancakes, 106
brown rice flour
    about, 314
    Roxana's Whole-Grain Gluten-Free Flour, 95
buckwheat flour
    about, 315
    Apple Upside-Down Pancakes, 91–92, *93*
    Buckwheat Joy Muffins, *22*, 46–47
    Roxana's Whole-Grain Gluten-Free Flour, 95
Build-Your-Own Granola, *279*, 280–82, *282*
buns
    Brioche Jam Buns, 223–24, *225*
    Potato Nigella Buns, 230–31
buttermilk
    Buttermilk Whole-Grain Biscuits, 53–54, *55*
    nondairy, how to make, 80
Butterscotch Apricot Muffins, *22*, 32–33

C

cakes
    Chocolate Chiffon Cake, 298–99
    Coconut Layer Cake with White Chocolate Buttercream, *300*, 301–3
    Spiced Vegan Teacake, 294
Caramelized Onions, 162
cardamom
    Dark Rye Rolls, *236*, 237–38
    Honey French Toast with a Touch of Cardamom and Orange, 114, *115*
    Morning Buns, *174*, 175–76
carrots
    Einkorn Carrot Muffins with Cream Cheese Glaze, *22*, 28–29
    Open-Face Carrot Sandwich, 257–58, *259*
cheddar
    Cheddar and Jalapeño Cornmeal Scones, *60*, 61–62
    Fried Onion Hand Pies, 137
    Stuffed Ham, Cheddar, and Scallion French Toast, 113
cheese. *See also* cream cheese
    Apple and Roquefort Grilled Cheese Sandwich, 252, *253*
    Asparagus Quiche with Pancetta and Gruyère, 310
    Bacon and Leek Quiche, 310
    Brunch Red Pepper and Goat Cheese Scones, *70*, 71–72
    Caramelized Onion, Comté, and Nigella Boule, *186*, 263–65
    Cheddar and Jalapeño Cornmeal Scones, *60*, 61–62
    Cherry Tomato Crests, *163*, 172–73
    Clark Street Bakery's Nordic Breakfast Plate, 234, *235*
    Fried Onion Hand Pies, 137
    Friends & Family Famous Hippie Sandwich, *270*, 271–72
    Ham and Peas Quiche, 310
    Herby Cottage Cheese Scones, *69* 67–68
    Long-Cooked Broccoli and Fontina Quiche, 311
    Mushroom and Comté Quiche, 311
    Open-Face Carrot Sandwich, 257–58, *259*
    Parmesan-Rosemary Biscuits, *55*, 56–57
    Perfect Quiche, 308–11
    Prosciutto en Croûte, *163*, 164–65
    Roasted Tomato and Goat Cheese Quiche, 310
    Smoked Ham and Gruyère Croissants, 159–60, *163*
    Smoked Salmon Quiche with Potato and Dill, 311
    Spinach and Scallion Quiche, 310
    Stuffed Ham, Cheddar, and Scallion French Toast, 113
    Swiss Chard, Feta, and Egg Pide, 197–98, *199*
    Tortillas Aliñadas, *204*, 205–6
cherries
    Cherry Cutout Pie, 305–7, *306*
    Chocolate-Cherry Pan Loaf, *186*, 273–75
    Cherry Tomato Crests, *163*, 172–73
chia seeds
    Hearty Pancake Mix for Campers, 107
    New-School Whole-Grain Muffins, *22*, 26–27
Chiffon Cake, Chocolate, 298–99
chives
    Dill, Chive, and Black Pepper Loaf, *186*, 260–62
    Friends & Family Famous Hippie Sandwich, *270*, 271–72
    Herby Cottage Cheese Scones, *69* 67–68
chocolate
    Build-Your-Own Granola, *279*, 280–82, *282*
    Chocolate-Cherry Pan Loaf, *186*, 273–75
    Chocolate Chiffon Cake, 298–99
    Chocolate Earl Grey Pains au Chocolat, 158
    Chocolate Glaze, *124*, 126
    Chocolate Morning Muffins, 43–44, *45*
    Chocolate Raspberry Pains au Chocolat, 158
    Cocoa Nib Pains au Chocolat, 158
    Coconut Layer Cake with White Chocolate Buttercream, *300*, 301–3
    Espresso Pains au Chocolat, 157–58
    Midnight Cookies, 283–84
    Pear, Chocolate, and Einkorn Scones, *48*, 65–66
Ciabatta, Durum, *186*, 214–15
cinnamon
    Cinnamon-Raisin Brioche, *220*, 221–22
    Crunchy Bites, 184

Glazed or Sugared Doughnuts, *120*, 121–23
Morning Buns, *174*, 175–76
Pumpkin Pancakes, 89
Clark Street Bakery's Nordic Breakfast Plate, 234, *235*
Cocktail Scones, 68
Cocoa Nib Pains au Chocolat, 158
coconut
  Coconut Layer Cake with White Chocolate Buttercream, *300*, 301–3
  New-School Whole-Grain Muffins, *22*, 26–27
Comté
  Caramelized Onion, Comté, and Nigella Boule, *186*, 263–65
  Mushroom and Comté Quiche, 311
cookies
  Fig-Strawberry Pillows, 289–90
  Midnight Cookies, 283–84
cookie scoop, 25
Cornelés, 291–92, *293*
cornmeal
  about, 315–16
  Blueberry Pancakes, 86–87, *87*
  Cheddar and Jalapeño Cornmeal Scones, *60*, 61–62
  Cornelés, 291–92, *293*
  Herby Cottage Cheese Scones, *69* 67–68
  New-School Whole-Grain Muffins, *22*, 26–27
cotija
  Tortillas Aliñadas, *204*, 205–6
Cottage Cheese Scones, Herby, *69* 67–68
Crackers, Multigrain, 193–94
cream
  Cream Glaze, 121–23, *124*
  Cream Scones with Lemon Curd, *48*, 58–59
cream cheese
  Berries 'n' Cream Puffs, 166–67, *168*
  Cream Cheese Filling, 167

Einkorn Carrot Muffins with Cream Cheese Glaze, *22*, 28–29
Fried Blueberry Hand Pies, 135–37, *134*
Fried Onion Hand Pies, 137
Fried Peach Hand Pies, 137
Strawberry Poppies, *168*, 180
crème fraîche
  Potato Dillies, 170–71
croissants
  Bacon and Onion Blossoms, 161–62, *163*
  Berries 'n' Cream Puffs, 166–67, *168*
  Blackberry Swirls, *178*, 179
  Cherry Tomato Crests, *163*, 172–73
  Chocolate Earl Grey Pains au Chocolat, 158
  Chocolate Raspberry Pains au Chocolat, 158
  Cocoa Nib Pains au Chocolat, 158
  Crunchy Bites, 184
  cutting guide, 148–49
  equipment for, 141
  Espresso Pains au Chocolat, 157–58
  Hybrid Croissant Dough, 145–47
  leftover, uses for, 141
  Morning Buns, *174*, 175–76
  Pineapple Suns, 181–82, *183*
  Pistachio-Almond Croissants, *151*, 155–56
  Potato Dillies, 170–71
  preparing, tips for, 140–41, 142–44
  Prosciutto en Croûte, *163*, 164–65
  Raspberry Fairies, *168*, 169
  rectangles, cutting, 148
  Salted Honey Croissants, 152–53, *153*
  shelf life, 141
  Smoked Ham and Gruyère Croissants, 159–60, *163*
  squares, cutting, 148–49
  Strawberry Poppies, *168*, 180

strips, cutting, 149
triangles, cutting, 148
Whole-Grain Croissant Dough, 147
Crostata, Apricot, 295–96, *297*
Crunchy Bites, 184
cucumbers
  Clark Street Bakery's Nordic Breakfast Plate, 234, *235*
  Friends & Family Famous Hippie Sandwich, *270*, 271–72
cumin
  Pumpkin Spelt Bread, *186*, 254–56
Curd, Lemon, 59
currants
  Cream Scones with Lemon Curd, *48*, 58–59

D

Date-Banana Muffins, *34*, 35–36
deep-frying, 119
digital scale, 16, 190
dill
  Dill, Chive, and Black Pepper Loaf, *186*, 260–62
  Friends & Family Famous Hippie Sandwich, *270*, 271–72
  Herby Cottage Cheese Scones, 67–68, *69*
  Potato Dillies, 170–71
  Smoked Salmon Quiche with Potato and Dill, 311
dipping measuring method, 17
doughnut cutters, 119
doughnuts
  cake, about, 118
  deep-frying, 119
  equipment for, 119
  Glazed or Sugared Doughnuts, *120*, 121–23
  Jelly Doughnuts, *128*, 129
  preparing, tips for, 118–19
  raised, about, 118
  shelf life, 119
  Sour Cream Cake Doughnuts, 132–33
dough scraper, 191
durum wheat flour
  about, 316

durum wheat flour (continued)
Durum Ciabatta, *186*, 214–15
Glazed Lemon, Poppy Seed, and Olive Oil Muffins, *22*, 41–42
Parmesan-Rosemary Biscuits, *55*, 56–57
Dutch Baby, 108, *109*
Dutch oven, 190

E
Earl Grey Chocolate Pains au Chocolat, 158
eggs
Clark Street Bakery's Nordic Breakfast Plate, 234, *235*
Swiss Chard, Feta, and Egg Pide, 197–98, *199*
einkorn flour
about, 316–17
Einkorn Carrot Muffins with Cream Cheese Glaze, *22*, 28–29
Pear, Chocolate, and Einkorn Scones, *48*, 65–66
Espresso Pains au Chocolat, 157–58

F
fennel seeds
Dark Rye Rolls, *236*, 237–38
feta
Friends & Family Famous Hippie Sandwich, *270*, 271–72
Open-Face Carrot Sandwich, 257–58, *259*
Swiss Chard, Feta, and Egg Pide, 197–98, *199*
Fig-Strawberry Pillows, 289–90
fine sea salt, 16
Finnish Malt Bread, *186*, 232–33
flatbreads
about, 192
Heirloom Masa Tortillas, 200–201
Hybrid Tortillas, 202–3
Multigrain Crackers, 193–94
Swiss Chard, Feta, and Egg Pide, 197–98, *199*
Tortillas Aliñadas, *204*, 205–6

Za'atar Flatbreads, 195–96
flax meal or seeds
Crispy Flax Seed Waffles, 110–11
New-School Whole-Grain Muffins, *22*, 26–27
1970s Multigrain Pancakes, 106
Spiced Vegan Teacake, 294
Sprouted Grain Loaf, 266–69, *270*
flours. *See also specific flour types*
all-purpose, about, 15, 320
bread, about, 15, 320
dipping measuring method, 17
favorite, 313
refined, about, 15, 320
Roxana's Whole-Grain Gluten-Free Flour, 95
spooning measuring method, 17
types of, 14–15
used in recipe testing, 17
whole-grain, baking with, 14–15, 313
fontina
Long-Cooked Broccoli and Fontina Quiche, 311
Prosciutto en Croûte, *163*, 164–65
French toast
Honey French Toast with a Touch of Cardamom and Orange, 114, *115*
preparing, tips for, 112
Stuffed Ham, Cheddar, and Scallion French Toast, 113
Friends & Family Famous Hippie Sandwich, *270*, 271–72
fritters
Pineapple Fritters, 130–31
shelf life, 119
fruits. *See also specific fruits*
Build-Your-Own Granola, *279*, 280–82, *282*
New-School Whole-Grain Muffins, *22*, 26–27

G
ginger
Rhuberry Roly Poly, 73–74, *75*
glass jar, 191

glazes
Chocolate Glaze, *124*, 126
Cream Glaze, 121–23, *124*
Maple–Brown Butter Glaze, *124*, 127
Peanut Butter Glaze, *125*, 126
Pink Glaze, *125*, 127
gluten-free flour
Gluten-Free Pancakes, 94
Roxana's Whole-Grain Gluten-Free Flour, 95
goat cheese
Brunch Red Pepper and Goat Cheese Scones, *70*, 71–72
Roasted Tomato and Goat Cheese Quiche, 310
grains. *See whole-grain flour; specific grain types*
granola
Build-Your-Own Granola, *279*, 280–82, *282*
winning combinations, 282
Gruyère
Asparagus Quiche with Pancetta and Gruyère, 310
Perfect Quiche, 308–11
Smoked Ham and Gruyère Croissants, 159–60, *163*

H
ham
Clark Street Bakery's Nordic Breakfast Plate, 234, *235*
Ham and Peas Quiche, 310
Prosciutto en Croûte, *163*, 164–65
Smoked Ham and Gruyère Croissants, 159–60, *163*
Stuffed Ham, Cheddar, and Scallion French Toast, 113
hand pies
Fried Blueberry Hand Pies, 135–37, *134*
Fried Onion Hand Pies, 137
Fried Peach Hand Pies, 137
hard wheat flours, about, 317–18
Havarti
Clark Street Bakery's Nordic Breakfast Plate, 234, *235*
Heart Tarts, *286*, 287–88

herbs. *See also specific herbs*
    Herby Cottage Cheese Scones, *69* 67–68
honey
    Buckwheat Joy Muffins, *22*, 46–47
    Honey French Toast with a Touch of Cardamom and Orange, 114, *115*
    Milk and Honey Brioche, *216*, 217–19
    Salted Honey Croissants, 152–53, *153*
Hybrid Croissant Dough, 145–47
Hybrid Tortillas, 202–3

I
Individual Prosciuttos en Croûte, 165
instant-read thermometer, 191

J
jam
    Apricot Jam, *77*, 297
    Blackberry Jam with a Touch of Lime, 76, *77*
    fig-strawberry jam, 289
    Raspberry Jam, 76
    Rhuberry Jam, 76, *77*
    Strawberry-Rhubarb Jam, 76, *77*
jam (in recipes)
    Apricot Crostata, 295–96, *297*
    Blackberry Swirls, *178*, 179
    Brioche Jam Buns, 223–24, *225*
    Cherry Cutout Pie, 305–7, *306*
    Heart Tarts, *286*, 287–88
    Jelly Doughnuts, *128*, 129
    Raspberry Fairies, *168*, 169
    Rhuberry Roly Poly, 73–74, *75*
    Strawberry Poppies, *168*, 180
Jelly Doughnuts, *128*, 129

K
Kaiserschmarrn (Austrian Soufflé Pancake), 101–2, *102*
Kamut, about, 318–19
Khorasan flour
    about, 318–19
    Khorasan Baguettes, 209–11
kosher salt, 16

kumquats
    Brioche à la Crème, *226*, 227–28
    Candied Kumquats, 229

L
lame, 191
Leek and Bacon Quiche, 310
lemon
    Glazed Lemon, Poppy Seed, and Olive Oil Muffins, *22*, 41–42
    Lemon Curd, 59
lidded glass jar, 191
lime
    Blackberry Jam with a Touch of Lime, 76, *77*
    Coconut Layer Cake with White Chocolate Buttercream, *300*, 301–3
liquid measuring cup, 16
loaf pan, 191

M
Maple–Brown Butter Glaze, *124*, 127
marmalade
    Brioche Jam Buns, 223–24, *225*
    Cara Cara Orange Marmalade, 177
    Morning Buns, *174*, 175–76
marzipan
    Apricot Crostata, 295–96, *297*
    Pistachio-Almond Croissants, *151*, 155–56
masa harina
    about, 203, 319
    Heirloom Masa Tortillas, 200–201
    Hybrid Tortillas, 202–3
    Tortillas Aliñadas, *204*, 205–6
measuring spoons, 16
metric weights, 16
Midnight Cookies, 283–84
Milk and Honey Brioche, *216*, 217–19
Morning Buns, *174*, 175–76
mozzarella
    Tortillas Aliñadas, *204*, 205–6
muffins
    Apricot Butterscotch Muffins, *22*, 32–33
    Banana-Date Muffins, *34*, 35–36
    Berry Oat Muffins, *22*, 30–31

    Buckwheat Joy Muffins, *22*, 46–47
    Chocolate Morning Muffins, 43–44, *45*
    Einkorn Carrot Muffins with Cream Cheese Glaze, *22*, 28–29
    freezing, 25
    Glazed Lemon, Poppy Seed, and Olive Oil Muffins, *22*, 41–42
    New-School Whole-Grain Muffins, *22*, 26–27
    preparing, tips for, 24–25
    Sweet Potato Muffins with Pecan Streusel, 37–38, *39*
    warming up, 25
muffin tins, 25
Multigrain Crackers, 193–94
Mushroom and Comté Quiche, 311

N
New-School Whole-Grain Muffins, *22*, 26–27
nigella seeds
    Caramelized Onion, Comté, and Nigella Boule, *186*, 263–65
    Potato Nigella Buns, 230–31
1970s Multigrain Pancakes, 106
nixtamalized corn flour, 319
nixtamalized foods, 203
nonstick pans, 278
Nordic Breakfast Plate, Clark Street Bakery's, 234, *235*
nuts
    Banana-Date Muffins, *34*, 35–36
    Build-Your-Own Granola, *279*, 280–82, *282*
    Einkorn Carrot Muffins with Cream Cheese Glaze, *22*, 28–29
    Pistachio-Almond Croissants, *151*, 155–56
    Sweet Potato Muffins with Pecan Streusel, 37–38, *39*

O
oat flour
    about, 319
    Hearty Pancake Mix for Campers, 107

oat flour (continued)
  Roxana's Whole-Grain Gluten-Free Flour, 95
oats
  about, 320
  Berry Oat Muffins, *22*, 30–31
  Build-Your-Own Granola, *279*, 280–82, *282*
  Finnish Malt Bread, *186*, 232–33
  New-School Whole-Grain Muffins, *22*, 26–27
  1970s Multigrain Pancakes, 106
Olive Oil, Lemon, and Poppy Seed Muffins, Glazed, *22*, 41–42
onions
  Bacon and Onion Blossoms, 161–62, *163*
  Caramelized Onion, Comté, and Nigella Boule, *186*, 263–65
  Caramelized Onions, 162
  Fried Onion Hand Pies, 137
oranges
  Cara Cara Orange Marmalade, 177
  Dark Rye Rolls, *236*, 237–38
  Honey French Toast with a Touch of Cardamom and Orange, 114, *115*
oven
  creating steam in, 211
  temperature, 25

P

pains au chocolat
  Chocolate Earl Grey Pains au Chocolat, 158
  Chocolate Raspberry Pains au Chocolat, 158
  Cocoa Nib Pains au Chocolat, 158
  Espresso Pains au Chocolat, 157–58
pancakes
  Apple Upside-Down Pancakes, 91–92, *93*
  artificially leavened, about, 82
  Banana Pancakes, 88
  Blueberry Pancakes, 86–87, *87*
  Don't Wait Sourdough Discard Pancakes, 100
  Dutch Baby, 108, *109*
  Gluten-Free Pancakes, 94
  Hearty Pancake Mix for Campers, 107
  Kaiserschmarrn (Austrian Soufflé Pancake), 101–2, *102*
  keeping warm, 81
  naturally leavened, about, 82
  1970s Multigrain Pancakes, 106
  Overnight Sourdough Pancakes, 99
  Pancakes for Purists, 84–85
  pan-fried *versus* baked, 83
  preparing, tips for, 80–81
  Pumpkin Pancakes, 89
  sourdough, two ways to make, 98
  Swedish Pancakes, 103–4, *105*
  thin *versus* thick, 83
  yeasted, about, 82
  Yeasted Pancakes, 96–97
Pancetta and Gruyère, Asparagus Quiche with, 310
Parmesan
  Bacon and Leek Quiche, 310
  Cherry Tomato Crests, *163*, 172–73
  Ham and Peas Quiche, 310
  Parmesan-Rosemary Biscuits, *55*, 56–57
parsley
  Friends & Family Famous Hippie Sandwich, *270*, 271–72
  Open-Face Carrot Sandwich, 257–58, *259*
pastry case, setting up the, 19–21
Pastry Cream, 182
pastry dough
  pasta frolla, 295
  pâte brisée, 308
  Rye Shortcrust, 285
  Sour Cream Pie Dough, 304
pastry wheel cutter, 141
Peach Hand Pies, Fried, 137
Peanut Butter Glaze, *125*, 126
Pear, Chocolate, and Einkorn Scones, *48*, 65–66
peas
  Friends & Family Famous Hippie Sandwich, *270*, 271–72
  Ham and Peas Quiche, 310
  Pecan Streusel, Sweet Potato Muffins with, 37–38, *39*
peppers
  Brunch Red Pepper and Goat Cheese Scones, *70*, 71–72
  Cheddar and Jalapeño Cornmeal Scones, *60*, 61–62
Pesto, Basil, 173
Pide, Swiss Chard, Feta, and Egg, 197–98, *199*
Pie Dough, Sour Cream, 304
pies. *See also* hand pies
  Cherry Cutout Pie, 305–7, *306*
pineapple
  Pineapple Fritters, 130–31
  Pineapple Suns, 181–82, *183*
Pink Glaze, *125*, 127
pistachios
  Einkorn Carrot Muffins with Cream Cheese Glaze, *22*, 28–29
  Pistachio-Almond Croissants, *151*, 155–56
plastic dough scraper, 191
polenta, about, 315–16
poppy seeds
  Glazed Lemon, Poppy Seed, and Olive Oil Muffins, *22*, 41–42
  Seeded Benched Sourdough Rolls, 249, *249*
potatoes
  Potato Dillies, 170–71
  Potato Nigella Buns, 230–31
  Smoked Salmon Quiche with Potato and Dill, 311
  Sweet Potato Muffins with Pecan Streusel, 37–38, *39*
Prosciutto en Croûte, *163*, 164–65
pumpkin
  Pumpkin Pancakes, 89
  Pumpkin Puree, 90
  Pumpkin Spelt Bread, *186*, 254–56
pumpkin seeds
  Open-Face Carrot Sandwich, 257–58, *259*
  Pumpkin Spelt Bread, *186*, 254–56

Seeded Benched Sourdough Rolls, 249, *249*
Sprouted Grain Loaf, 266–69, *270*

Q

quiche
Asparagus Quiche with Pancetta and Gruyère, 310
Bacon and Leek Quiche, 310
Ham and Peas Quiche, 310
Long-Cooked Broccoli and Fontina Quiche, 311
Mushroom and Comté Quiche, 311
Perfect Quiche, 308–11
Roasted Tomato and Goat Cheese Quiche, 310
Smoked Salmon Quiche with Potato and Dill, 311
Spinach and Scallion Quiche, 310

R

raisins
Cinnamon-Raisin Brioche, *220*, 221–22
Sweet Potato Muffins with Pecan Streusel, 37–38, *39*
raspberries
Chocolate Raspberry Pains au Chocolat, 158
Pink Glaze, *125*, 127
Raspberry Fairies, *168*, 169
Raspberry Jam, 76
Rhuberry Jam, 76, *77*
Rhuberry Roly Poly, 73–74, *75*
raspberry jam (in recipes)
Heart Tarts, *286*, 287–88
Raspberry Fairies, *168*, 169
recipe testing, notes on, 17
rhubarb
Rhuberry Jam, 76, *77*
Rhuberry Roly Poly, 73–74, *75*
Strawberry-Rhubarb Jam, 76, *77*
ricotta
Smoked Salmon Quiche with Potato and Dill, 311
Spinach and Scallion Quiche, 310

rolling pins, 119, 141
rolls
Benched Sourdough Rolls, 248–49
Dark Rye Rolls, *236*, 237–38
Seeded Benched Sourdough Rolls, 249, *249*
Roly Poly, Rhuberry, 73–74, *75*
Roquefort and Apple Grilled Cheese Sandwich, 252, *253*
rosemary
Parmesan-Rosemary Biscuits, *55*, 56–57
Rosemary Sandwich Loaf, 212–13
rose water
Pistachio-Almond Croissants, *151*, 155–56
rum
Cornelés, 291–92, *293*
Kaiserschmarrn (Austrian Soufflé Pancake), 101–2, *102*
rye flakes, 321
rye flour
about, 321
Chocolate-Cherry Pan Loaf, *186*, 273–75
Chocolate Morning Muffins, 43–44, *45*
Dark Rye Rolls, *236*, 237–38
Finnish Malt Bread, *186*, 232–33
Midnight Cookies, 283–84
Multigrain Crackers, 193–94
Rye Shortcrust, 285
Swedish Pancakes, 103–4, *105*

S

salt, 16, 243
Salted Butter Brown Scones, *48*, 63–64
Salted Honey Croissants, 152–53, *153*
sandwiches
Apple and Roquefort Grilled Cheese Sandwich, 252, *253*
Friends & Family Famous Hippie Sandwich, *270*, 271–72

Open-Face Carrot Sandwich, 257–58, *259*
scallions
Herby Cottage Cheese Scones, *69* 67–68
Spinach and Scallion Quiche, 310
Stuffed Ham, Cheddar, and Scallion French Toast, 113
scones
baking from frozen dough, 66
Brunch Red Pepper and Goat Cheese Scones, *70*, 71–72
Cheddar and Jalapeño Cornmeal Scones, *60*, 61–62
Cocktail Scones, 68
compared with biscuits, 52
Cream Scones with Lemon Curd, *48*, 58–59
Herby Cottage Cheese Scones, *69* 67–68
Pear, Chocolate, and Einkorn Scones, *48*, 65–66
preparing, tips for, 50–51
preparing dough for freezer, 66
Rhuberry Roly Poly, 73–74, *75*
Salted Butter Brown Scones, *48*, 63–64
storing, 51
seeds. *See also specific seeds*
Build-Your-Own Granola, *279*, 280–82, *282*
Seeded Benched Sourdough Rolls, 249, *249*
sesame seeds
1970s Multigrain Pancakes, 106
Seeded Benched Sourdough Rolls, 249, *249*
Shortcrust, Rye, 285
Smoked Salmon Quiche with Potato and Dill, 311
Soufflé Pancake, Austrian (Kaiserschmarrn), 101–2, *102*
sour cream
Brioche à la Crème, *226*, 227–28
Kaiserschmarrn (Austrian Soufflé Pancake), 101–2, *102*
Potato Dillies, 170–71

sour cream (continued)
    Sour Cream Cake Doughnuts, 132–33
    Sour Cream Pie Dough, 304
    Tortillas Aliñadas, *204*, 205–6

sourdough breads
    about, 239
    Apple and Roquefort Grilled Cheese Sandwich, 252, *253*
    Apple Levain, 250–52, *253*
    Basic Sourdough Bread, 244–46, *247*
    Benched Sourdough Rolls, 248–49
    Caramelized Onion, Comté, and Nigella Boule, *186*, 263–65
    Chocolate-Cherry Pan Loaf, *186*, 273–75
    Dill, Chive, and Black Pepper Loaf, *186*, 260–62
    Friends & Family Famous Hippie Sandwich, *270*, 271–72
    Open-Face Carrot Sandwich, 257–58, *259*
    Pumpkin Spelt Bread, *186*, 254–56
    Seeded Benched Sourdough Rolls, 249, *249*
    Sprouted Grain Loaf, 266–69, *270*

sourdough pancakes
    Don't Wait Sourdough Discard Pancakes, 100
    Overnight Sourdough Pancakes, 99
    two ways to make, 98

sourdough starter
    feeding schedule, 242
    Make Your Own Sourdough Starter, 240–41
    retarding activity of, 242–43
    signs of mold on, 243
    troubleshooting, 242–43

spelt flour
    about, 322
    Apricot Butterscotch Muffins, *22*, 32–33
    Brunch Red Pepper and Goat Cheese Scones, *70*, 71–72
    Hybrid Croissant Dough, 145–47
    Multigrain Crackers, 193–94
    Pumpkin Spelt Bread, *186*, 254–56
    Whole-Grain Croissant Dough, 147

Spinach and Scallion Quiche, 310
spooning measuring method, 17
Sprouted Grain Loaf, 266–69, *270*

squash
    Pumpkin Pancakes, 89
    Pumpkin Puree, 90
    Pumpkin Spelt Bread, *186*, 254–56

stand mixer, 119
steam, in oven, 211

strawberries
    Fig-Strawberry Pillows, 289–90
    Kaiserschmarrn (Austrian Soufflé Pancake), 101–2, *102*
    Pink Glaze, *125*, 127
    Strawberry Poppies, *168*, 180
    Strawberry-Rhubarb Jam, 76, *77*

streusel, about, 224

sunflower seeds
    1970s Multigrain Pancakes, 106
    Seeded Benched Sourdough Rolls, 249, *249*
    Sprouted Grain Loaf, 266–69, *270*

Swedish Pancakes, 103–4, *105*
Sweet Potato Muffins with Pecan Streusel, 37–38, *39*
Swiss Chard, Feta, and Egg Pide, 197–98, *199*

T

tarts
    Apricot Crostata, 295–96, *297*
    Brioche à la Crème, *226*, 227–28
    Heart Tarts, *286*, 287–88

Teacake, Spiced Vegan, 294
thermometer, 191

tomatoes
    Cherry Tomato Crests, *163*, 172–73
    Roasted Tomato and Goat Cheese Quiche, 310

tortillas
    Heirloom Masa Tortillas, 200–201
    Hybrid Tortillas, 202–3
    Tortillas Aliñadas, *204*, 205–6

V

Vegan Teacake, Spiced, 294
volume measurements, 16, 17

W

Waffles, Crispy Flax Seed, 110–11

walnuts
    Banana-Date Muffins, *34*, 35–36

weight measurements, 16, 17

wheat berries
    about, 322–23
    Sprouted Grain Loaf, 266–69, *270*

White Chocolate Buttercream, Coconut Layer Cake with, *300*, 301–3
Whole-Grain Croissant Dough, 147

whole-grain flour. *See also specific types*
    baking with, 14–15
    compared with refined flours, 15
    favorites, 313
    Roxana's Whole-Grain Gluten-Free Flour, 95

Y

yeasted breads
    about, 207

Brioche à la Crème, *226*, 227–28
Brioche Jam Buns, 223–24, *225*
Cinnamon-Raisin Brioche, *220*, 221–22
Clark Street Bakery's Nordic Breakfast Plate, 234, *235*
Dark Rye Rolls, *236*, 237–38
Durum Ciabatta, *186*, 214–15

Finnish Malt Bread, *186*, 232–33
Khorasan Baguettes, 209–11
Milk and Honey Brioche, *216*, 217–19
Potato Nigella Buns, 230–31
Rosemary Sandwich Loaf, 212–13

yogurt
    Chocolate Morning Muffins, 43–44, *45*
    Swiss Chard, Feta, and Egg Pide, 197–98, *199*
    Za'atar Flatbreads, 195–96

Z

Za'atar Flatbreads, 195–96

Copyright © 2026 by Roxana Jullapat
Photographs © 2026 by Kristin Teig

All rights reserved
Printed in China
First Edition

For information about permission to reproduce selections from this book, write to Permissions, W. W. Norton & Company, Inc., 500 Fifth Avenue, New York, NY 10110

For information about special discounts for bulk purchases, please contact W. W. Norton Special Sales at specialsales@wwnorton.com or 800-233-4830

Manufacturing by Toppan Leefung
Book design by Allison Chi
Production manager: Lauren Abbate

Library of Congress Cataloging-in-Publication Data is available.

ISBN 978-1-324-05135-0

W. W. Norton & Company, Inc., 500 Fifth Avenue, New York, NY 10110
www.wwnorton.com

W. W. Norton & Company Ltd., 15 Carlisle Street, London W1D 3BS

Authorized EU representative: EAS, Mustamäe tee 50, 10621 Tallinn, Estonia

1 2 3 4 5 6 7 8 9 0